AF654246

Women in Dharmaśāstras

Women in Dharmaśāstras

A Phenomenological and Critical Analysis

Edited by

Chandrakala Padia

RAWAT PUBLICATIONS

Jaipur • New Delhi • Bangalore • Guwahati • Kolkata

ISBN 978-81-316-0241-6

© Contributors, 2009

No part of this book may be reproduced or transmitted in any form or by any means, electronic or mechanical, including photocopying, recording or by any information storage and retrieval system, without permission in writing from the publisher.

Published by
Prem Rawat for **Rawat Publications**
Satyam Apts, Sector 3, Jawahar Nagar, Jaipur 302 004 (India)
Phones: 0141 265 1748 / 265 7006
E-mail: info@rawatbooks.com
Website: www.rawatbooks.com

New Delhi Office
4858/24, Ansari Road, Daryaganj, New Delhi 110 002
Phone: 011 2326 3290

Also at *Bangalore, Guwahati* and *Kolkata*

Typeset by Rawat Computers, Jaipur
Printed and bound in India

Contents

Acknowledgement

This book is the result of a seminar on 'Women and Dharmaśāstras: A Phenomenological and Critical Analysis' organized under the auspices of Centre for Women's Studies and Development, Banaras Hindu University. My deepest appreciation and thanks go to all those researchers who shared their perception about the status of women in *Dharmaśāstras*. In addition, I wish to acknowledge the contribution of the many friends, colleagues and research students who shared their wisdom with me over the years. Among them I would especially like to thank Prof. Kireet Joshi and Prof. S.K. Saxena for their unfladdging love, encouragement and support. The person who deserver my special thanks and gratitude is my own research student Ms. Preeti Singh, without whose unfailing support, the book would not have seen the light of the day. Special thanks go to Dr. Ramesh Chandra Singh, Dr. Meenakshi Jha and Dr. Binda Paranjape for assisting me in various ways.

For their enthusiastic interest, support, patience and individual specialness, I shall always be indebted to my children Dr. Abhishek and Dr. Abhinav and to my daughter-in-law Ms. Vinita and to my grandson Parth whose tinkering eyes and baffling smile did not let me feel tired.

I must gratefully acknowledge my sense of gratitude to my father and to my mother in whose company I have lived the continuity of tradition and innovation which go to make an enlightened Indian household a literal paradise on earth.

I would like to thank Indian Council of Philosophical Research for providing the necessary financial support to the seminar.

I appreciate the efforts my daughter in law Ms Vinita Chandra and also of Sri Vijay Kabraji for meticulously checking all diacritical marks and to Sri Pranit Rawat of Rawat Publications for showing interest in the publication of this book.

Introduction

Chandrakala Padia

In spite of the fact that there is unaccounted lapse of centuries between the age of the *Vedas* and *Upaniṣads* and that of the *Dharmaśāstras* (a gap of 1,300-1,600 years), the *Dharmaśāstras* which mainly consist of *Sūtras*, *Smṛtis*, *Arthaśāstra* of Kauṭilya, epics, *Purāṇas* and commentaries and digests constitute an integral part of India's intellectual tradition. The *Vedas* and *Upaniṣads* present conceptual formulation whereas the *Dharmaśāstras* are concerned with the do's and don'ts, the detailed codes of conduct in the daily life of the community. The impersonal absorption in abstruse idea is replaced by the practical concerns of the custodian of social propriety and the urgency behind the formulation of edicts required to ensure the stability of the social structure. Again, centuries intervene between the composition of *Dharmaśāstras* and their compilation. Take the example of *Manusmṛti*. Most of the scholars believe that *Manusmṛti* was composed between 200 BC and 200 AD, whereas the earliest commentator, Medhātithi of Kashmir, lived and worked in the ninth century AD. The gap here is of about 1,300 years. During the intervening time the *sūktas* were all preserved predominantly in oral tradition (*Smṛti*) by those who preached and practised. Their voice, reflecting the social priorities of their own time, might have found its way into the text, even as the compiler, on his arrival at a still later point of time, might have added a touch or two, keeping in mind the special needs in his own content.

However, the predominant tone in the social philosophy of the *Dharmaśāstras* has been of a woman who is different but equal other half of man. It repeatedly emphasizes the complementarity of the relationship between man and woman. In a proper social order they would not be competing but cooperating. But some of the Western feminist thinkers present an altogether different picture of it. They allege that in the *Dharmaśāstras* women occupy a subjugated/inferior status.

The Western feminist discourse often seeks to promote the image of woman after the image of man. The slogans of abstract equality and freedom have been raised, so that women might be able to compete with men in fair measure. Unfortunately, the contemporary feminist discourse in India has been more or less dominated by the Western feminist viewpoint overlooking India's own tradition and culture. There has never been a serious effort either to develop an indigeneous methodology or to study the Indian socio-philosophical texts as Western thought holds the field today in almost every region of intellectual activity, and quite a few of our scholars today find it convenient to fit the Indian social reality into the borrowed frameworks of thought. In this process, they have unquestionably accepted all Western assumptions and constructs. This is hardly proper, for Indian very way of looking at life and the world differs from that of the West. The underlying idea that resonates most clearly in Indian basic philosophical tradition is that a person is not only an individual among other individuals but is in principle knit indissolubly with a family, a community, and ultimately with the whole human race. Though different roles are assigned to different persons in accordance with their individual nature and aptitudes yet such arrangement is not oppressive as the social philosophy of *Dharmaśāstras* has recognized different functions as reciprocal and not as superior or inferior. Generally, the emphasis is on doing one's duty (*dharma*), as against the egoistic play of individual tastes and wishes, that is, on the inner cultivation of the right sense of values than on merely formal propriety. The whole social philosophy rests on the need to cooperate with, and to understand each other, and also to appreciate individual differences and abilities.

Further, the concept of identity in *Dharmaśāstras* is not based on annihilation of the identity of smaller wholes but cohere in their richness and variety and attains to its fuller realization by permitting them a realization of their own. The social philosophy of *Dharmaśāstras* postulates that the individual as a whole exists within a complex of other interlocking wholes, a complex in which each whole has a relative autonomy and yet is related to other wholes for self-development. The autonomy must be compatible with and complementary to determination of the autonomy of other wholes and ultimately to community itself which has its own specificity, its own moral values and kinds and levels of development. By providing such all encompassing concept of identity these applied philosophical texts have transcended the dichotomy between individual and society and have made it clear that there is no place for individualistic, calculative, and contractarian values in their philosophy as they believe in collective, communicative and spiritual values.

In such a social set-up, it is obvious, women could never be regarded as inferior to men. *Dharmaśāstras,* in fact, accorded her a very high position in society. Moreover, *Dharmaśāstras* have invested women with multiple identities as mother, daughter, sister and so on. This multiple identity has a deeply useful psycho-ethical effect of curbing one's ego, of taking the focus away from his or her own self, and enabling one to seek satisfaction by doing things for others. Moreover, they were invested with very high position in all such roles. To illustrate:

(1) *Ślokas* 225-32 in Chapter II of *Manusmṛti* mention the three figures to be held in highest esteem in life and these are the Preceptor, the Father and the Mother. The Preceptor represents *Brāhman,* Father represents *Brahmā,* the Creator, and Mother represents the Earth. Mother shares the same floor as the other two.

(2) *Ślokas 179-80* in Chapter IV of it advise relations of respect and affection with the preceptor, the performer of *yajñas,* the priest, the father, mother, sister, daughter-in-law, son, wife, daughters and brothers. No gender discrimination here.

(3) *Śloka* 55-59 in Chapter III of the same text enjoin respectful treatment of women in the family and pronounce the relatively familiar dictum that a house in which women are held in respect (are worshipped) delight the gods and it prospers. A family in which women languish in neglect is sure to be ruined.

(4) Particular attention may be drawn to a cluster of *Ślokas* (238-40, Ch II) of this text which offers the advice that a woman like a gem could be taken from the lower strata. The *Ślokas*, however, do not belong exclusively to the context of women. The group of *Ślokas* tells us what is acceptable from whom, and we are told that learning or knowledge is to be respectfully received even from lower castes, valuable religious advice is to be accepted from a *Cāṇḍāla* – social outcast though he be, an excellent woman is to be accepted even from a base family, good counsel should be accepted even from a little boy, *amṛta* is to be collected even from a mixture with poison. Woman, gems, knowledge, religious values, purity, good counsel- and the numerous fine arts all these, we are assured, anyone may accept from anyone. Taken in its true context, the *Ślokas* yield a positive perception regarding women.

Like *Manusmṛti,* other *Dharmaśāstra* texts too reflect in flashes a positive perception of the female phenomenon. Rights of women are ungrudgingly recognized in certain spheres. Desertion of a blameless wife is a sin–all the *Śāstras* agree; and even in case of the desertion of a wife living with another man, or turned alcoholic, subsistence allowance has to be arranged. The system of male domination leaves pockets of liberal consideration: (1) Following Manu, other *Śāstrakāras* too mention the rights of a *'putrikā'*. (2) *Yājñavalkya Smṛti* assigns to the mother share of the father's property equal with the sons *(Vyavahāra,* 115, 123). (3) Daughters have a claim to part of the father's property. (4) Sons of unmarried daughters, known as *'Kāneenaputra',* too have property rights *(Vyavahāra,* 124, 129).

Further texts on man-woman relationship occasionally reflect remarkable understanding and wisdom. A few instances may be cited from the *Yājñavalkya Smṛti.*

(1) The section on marriage, *Vivāha Prakaraṇam,* enumerates features of an ideal bride as well as of an ideal groom, and the *Ślokas* reflect open-eyed recognition of ground realities, not excluding sexual potency in the case of the groom (55 and the Mitākśarā Commentary).

(2) In a situation where no male guardians are available formally to give away the bride in marriage, the bride herself, the sage assures, can marry the chosen person (*Ācāra Adhyāya*, 63-64).

(3) Formulating rules to be observed in order to maintain good marital relation Yājñavalkya says that physical union of the husband and wife is best when desired by the wife; a good husband should respect and protect the wife in every way (81). This, in a starling flash, forbids what is mentioned as 'rape in wedlock' in Feminist parlance of our time.

(4) These ancient texts formulate a principle of '*strīdhana'*, wealth' to which women have an exclusive right. The husband cannot use it except in cases of big crises like famines etc. Sons do not inherit it. The line of inheritance extends to daughters and grand-daughter.

We may glance over some of the *Pārāśara Vacanas* on the issue of women.

(1) He defines situations, five in number, in which a woman can remarry: if the husband is lost, i.e., untraced, if the husband is dead, if he has taken *Sannyāsa* and left home, if he is impotent, if he is condemned, or convicted, for misdeeds, the women should take a second husband.

(2) Interesting to note that next couple of *Ślokas (Prāyaścitta Kāṇḍa,* IV,-29-30) reiterate the earlier view that the wife who practises *Brahmacarya* after the death of her husband is sure to attain bliss.

(3) Yet the very next sloka (31) startles us with the use of an unusual analogy. We are told that just as a snake-charmer forcibly drags a snake out of its hole, a virtuous woman too elevates her husband by virtue of her own goodness and competently leads him to heaven. The initiative, the authority and the lead, unambiguously shifts from the husband to the wife.

(4) Murder of an innocent wife is equated with *Brahmahatyā,* the most serious and the most heinous sin (*Pr.K.*XII, 33). A good warning to husband and in-laws in present times of bride burning, dowry death and other forms of violence against women.

(5) *Śloka* 22 in Chapter 10*(Pr.K.)* assures us that no hard penance need ever be prescribed for women; the purity of women, like the purity of the earth, is inviolable.

(6) In the next Śloka Pārāśara declares that the victim of rape, a woman forcibly subjected to sexual intercourse, bears no blame.

Thus, while analyzing the question of position of woman in *Dharmaśāstras* above positive verses must not be ignored. One must keep it in mind that the man in *Dharmaśāstras* is not a hedonistic, econocentric or a heroistic being who finds his self fulfillment in using others for his narrow interests but is a value seeking being who finds his self enhancement in transforming himself into an authentic being and this authenticity he acquires by serving the society to best of his ability. Thus, by assigning duties towards society to the individuals, *Dharmaśāstras* attempt to transform the bio-rational being into an authentic being and thus the duties assigned to woman by *Dharmaśāstras* should not be looked as oppressive but as emancipatory.

But it is a matter of deep concern that the so called modernists have misinterpreted these rich socio-philosophical texts in order to demonstrate the adequacy of Western theory. The chief case in point is, of course the distorted interpretation of a mantra of *Ṛgveda*. When in September 1987, one eighteen-year-old woman Roop Kanwar immolated herself in the name of *Satī*, many modern Indian writers claimed that this *Satī prathā* had the sanction of the *Vedas*. In support of this claim, they cited a hymn from the *Ṛgveda* which, they say, requires the widow to sit within the fire that burns her dead husband's body.

इमा नारीरविधवाः सुपत्नीराञ्जनेन सर्पिषा सं विशन्तु।
अनश्रवोऽनमीवाः सुरत्ना आ रोहन्तु जनयो योनिमग्रे।।

Ṛgveda, X. 18.7

This verse has been misread as "may these very good and holy women who are devoted to their husbands enter fire together with the body of the husband". But Vedic scholars later proved that this reading of the hymn is based on an orthographic mistake. The significant word is *agre* (in front), not *agne* (O, *Agni*). Even if we accept the reading *agne,* it would not mean 'into the fire' for the word would still be in the vocative case and signify that '*agni*' was being addressed. The sense of 'into the fire' would be yielded only if the word were in the dative case, which would be *agnaye*. P.V. Kane claims that the verse has been presented in the corrupt form because the interpreter probably read the last quarter of *Ṛgveda* X. 18.7 as *'arohantu jalayonim-agne'* (let them ascend the watery seat or origin, O, fire!) meaning "may fire be to them as cool as water". All other verses make it clear that either the hymn directs the widow to sit facing her dead husband; or that this *mantra* was not addressed to widows at all, but to ladies of the diseased man's household whose husbands were living. Such a view has been availed of in the *gṛhyasūtra* of *Āśvalāyana-śrauta-sūtra.*

However, the point that the disputed *Ṛgvedic* verse can never be interpreted as requiring the widow to die with her husband becomes all the more clear when one reads the very next verse. Here, the wife is being directed to quietly accept her loving husband's death, to arise from her husband's side, and to resume her place in the world:

उदीर्ष्व नार्यभि जीवलोकं गतासुमेतमुप शेष एहि।
हस्तग्राभस्य दिधिषोस्तवेदं पत्युर्जनित्वमभि सं बभूथ।।

Ṛgveda, X. 18.8

Thus, these texts are studied by some of the scholars on the basis of 'selective quotation' to make us look at it 'with an excited horror'. Evidences to contrary are generally withheld. For example, the critiques very frequently quote Manu on dependence of women [see Ch. V. Verse 148-49] but ignore the duties Manu has imposed on husbands [see Ch. IX. Verse 74].

Such partial and biased interpretation has contributed to the distortion of the rich Indian tradition. Thus what is required is to recover the lost Indian tradition in the construction of feminist theory. There is a need to reemphasize and reinterpret the Indian ideals of *Ardhanāriśwar*, *Dharmapatnī*, and *Sahadharmiṇi*. It would further help in deconstructing the myth of the so-called superior 'public' (male) and inferior 'private' (female) in the Western philosophical tradition as the *Dharmaśāstras'* ideal is self-realization equally both for men and women. Each finds a distinct place in the domestic and social scheme; never entering into conflict with each other, rather supplementing the qualities of each other and thus ever making life's way smoother for each other. Thus, in the scheme of *Dharmaśāstras* an egoistic, competitive equality of man and woman is not contemplated. Their ideal for the whole human race is that of identity, not equality. In *Dharmaśāstras,* we find no narrow parochialism, no provincialism, not even nationalism, but only humanism, the organization, into one joint family, of all the types, all the families, races and sub-races, of the whole human race or even still more, that wider same-sightedness which sees all the kingdoms of Nature ever indissolubly linked into one continuous chain of world order and world process. If *Dharmaśāstras'* ideal is such for all the Human Race with all its widely divergent forms and types and colours and capacities, if it regard all of them as organs of the same identical organism how much more must their ideal be such for man and woman, husband and wife, within the same house. The two are regarded as supplementary halves of one whole. And, for the time difference of sex lasts, the vocations of the two are accepted as different in the same way as the functions of the two halves of one organ. Each half is as a sort of assistant, supplement, reserve of force for the other.

In this background, it would not be an exaggeration to say that by studing the rich Indian socio-philosophical tradition it its proper context, a more balanced feminist theory can be evolved that would not be reactionary but action-oriented; would not believe in 'freedom from' but in 'freedom to' and would not define itself in reference to 'other' for 'the other' would neither be a threat to it's identity nor be a source of confirmation of its uniqueness.

This book contains the papers presented in the seminar organized by the Centre for Women's Studies and Development in 2006. An effort was made to invite eminent scholars who tried to analyze the rich Indian socio-philosophical tradition and to bring Indian perspectives into the mainstream thinking in the realm of feminist thinking. The present book with the following objectives is a modest attempt in the direction of evolving such a feminist theory:

- To present a critique to the critiques of women's position in the social philosophy of *Dharmaśāstras* coming from both the East and the West.
- To challenge the authoritative status of the Western philosophical interpretation, its fabrication of the orient in terms of founding essences invulnerable to historical changes and its incestuous relationship with the Western exercise of power over the countries of Third World.
- To evolve and reinforce Indian conceptual categories in place of intellectual dominance of the West and thus save Indians from historical amnesia and political schizophrenia.

- To provide an alternative to West centred paradigms of women's empowerment.
- To initiate a critical and constant dialogue with our own as well as other tradition.
- To bring Indian perspectives into the mainstream thinking in sphere of feminist theory.

However, the book is not aimed at eulogizing the *Dharmaśāstras* but at making a candid analysis of women's position in *Dharmaśāstras*. As we can neither merely acquiesce in all that, these socio-philosophical texts say, or are supposed to say about women, nor reject it impatiently in toto. We have to discover and seize the basic human values in them and to reject what is offensive to common sense and disrespectful to human dignity.

I may now set out to say something about the essays that make this volume.

Pranati Ghoshal's article on "Women's Education in Vedic India" provides a comprehensive account of scholarly success reached by women in the Vedic age. Their scholarship is proved in the composition of *Ṛgvedic* hymns by them. It is remarkable that in the context of daily *Ṛṣi Tarpaṇ,* the *Āśavalāyan Gṛhyasūtra* has mentioned a host of women teachers, viz., Gārgī Vācaknavi, Vādavā Parthitheyi, Sulbhā Maitreyī to whom water libations were offered. Besides, women had also acquired expertise in the field of vocal music, dancing and military training etc. But, unfortunately, this exalted position of women came to an end with the increasing foreign invasions in the later age. In an attempt to check this social deterioration, and to maintain the purity of heritage and family traditions, orthodox school imposed several restrictions on women. One of the restrictions having far reaching implications was the ban on women's right to education, which led to their perpetual dependence on menfolk.

Chandrakala Padia's article, "Women in India's Intellectual Tradition" puts emphasis on three things. First, it seeks to show that ontologically, or as human beings, women have all along been given an equal status in the Indian intellectual tradition; second, that in respect of character and contribution to cohesion and welfare of society, they have even been regarded superior to men; and thirdly, that it is unwarranted to hold the view that the intellectual traditions of India have never thought highly of woman.

She gives several references in support of the argument. The *Nāsadīya Sūkta* of *Ṛgveda* (X-129) clearly speaks of a process through which one Will manifested itself in many forms, including the male and the female. This thought of a common origin is supported by *Kaṭhopaniṣad* (II, ii, 15) which clearly says that before creation began there was only one primal will – crystallizing itself as the golden cosmic egg, which split itself and gave birth to all kinds of diverse beings. Manu repeats the same when he proclaims that the one split itself into two halves and assumed the male form with the one half and the female form with the other (M.I. 32). The implication here obviously is that at the ontological level there was gender differentiation but no gender discrimination. Even in the post-*Saṁhitā* period, woman was regarded as '*ardhāṅgini*', that is, one half of the very being of men. She is also '*sahadharmiṇi*', that is, a co-participator in discharging the obligations of life and fully capable of taking her own decisions. Further, there are many illustrious examples of women's ability to exercise their own judgement, e.g., Maitreyī, Ṛṣkā Ghoṣā, Dakṣiṇā, Romśā, Lopamudrā, Vāgabhṛṇi etc. Women are being regarded as Kulapālaka (family nurturer), Dhruvā (steadfast), Śivā and Kalyāṇi (the source of welfare and prosperity). Then the author quotes several verses from the *Ṛgveda* (V.61.61), the *Śatapatha Brāhmaṇa,* the *Vasiṣṭha Dharmasūtra, Pārāśarasmṛti, Āpastamba Dharmasūtra,* where women are being regarded as superior to men.

In the third section of the paper, she presents a critique of those authors who have criticized *Dharmaśāstra* literature for giving a lower status to women. She gives several instances which prove that women were given rights to divorce and remarriage; there were people who really wished birth of a daughter and performed certain rituals to this effect; and women did have the right to education. *Brahmavādinīs* were allowed to remain life-long students of theology and philosophy. The author concludes by saying that quite a few criticisms leveled against the place of women in India's intellectual tradition arise from a clear misinterpretation of our Indian texts.

Kapil Kapoor's paper "Woman and the *Dharmaśāstras*" emphasizes upon the need for a careful reading and a theory-bound interpretation of the *Dharmśāstras.* These texts are not prescriptive texts but are a record of widely divergent practices and also describe what ought to be. The *Dharmaśāstras* discuss both the actual and desirable aspects of man's life. Moreover, the *Dharmaśāstras* by providing different injunctions on several matters attest the evolving nature of Indian sociological thinking and the non-normative approach of Indian sociology. The verses retaled to women (either in commendement of women or in their condemnation) can only be understood in their proper context. For example, the condemnatory passages, according to the *Mīmāṁsā* rules of interpretation, are understood as praise of the opposite. Further there is a need to historicize these texts and to put them in the context of the times. The following passage of the article is worth quoting as it depicts the whole scenario in a succinct way:

> The conceptualization of women in fact takes place from three points of view: ontological, as individual and as social. As an individual, a woman is seen as fragile and delicate psysically in a certain sense but emotionally and spiritually stronger than man. As a social being, she is central to the whole social structure in her bio-social role as mother. It is the profound ontological conceptualization of women which is uniquely Indian. Ontologically, woman is a primal force, the *śakti-tattva,* the energy principle. This needs to be reconciled to the *sāṁkhya puruṣa-prakṛti* structure in which *prakṛti* is erroneously understood by modern commentators as the female principle. In fact, *prakṛti* is 'matter' and *puruṣa* is 'energy' – the word *puruṣa* in *sāṁkhya* etymologically means that which inhabits the body, that is *ātmā* which is a spark of the universal creative energy, the *'param-ātmā'* or *Brāhman* (of *Vedānta*). It may be noted parenthetically that the word *ātmā* grammatically is feminine gender. So *ātmātattva* is *śaktitattva. Strītattva* is a *dharma* of the physical body. Woman therefore in the Hindu *Śāstra* apart from being the source of life and happiness is recognized as a spiritual force as well – it is said that man is *yajñapradhāna,* action-oriented but woman is *tapapradhāna,* devotion oriented.

Pushpa Tiwari, in her article, "Social Dimensions of the Discourse on Women and Sex as Reflected in *Manusmṛti* – the Earliest Known Indian Code of Life", attempts to correlate the textual tradition of *Dharmaśāstra* particularly of *Manusmṛti* with that of the archaeological evidences reflecting on the sociocultural milieu during the period between c. 200 BC to c. 200 AD – the time frame generally accepted for *Manusmṛti.* The paper proposes to investigate, scrutinize and isolate the discourse of *Manusmṛti* on women and sex, which is blended with the discourse on *Dharma* in general. The Essaysist insists that the *Dharmaśāstra* of Manu and its views concerning sex and women cannot be understood without having an idea of the contemporary socio – cultural realities.

It is in the backdrop of the historical context that Manu seems to have composed his text. Manu has taken care of every unforeseen situation relating to sexual behaviour by laying down specific laws and code of conduct as a system of checks and balances to ensure the sanctity of well defined social relations be they familial or institutional. Except a few verses (2.213), most of the other verses are there to regulate male sexuality and desires. Manu has laid down several rules for males entering into *gurukul*. He categorically states that the king should punish a person indulging into sexual relationship with a female other than his wife through severe punishments (8.352). Manu has laid down several rules and punishment for persons indulging into adultery (8.352-388). All these references prove that Manu has provided effective and adequate injunctions and laws to ensure the practice of socially and morally sanctioned behaviour in sexual sphere both by men and women. He does not seem liberal to either of them, although in some cases he provides harsher punishment to the male offender for the same kind of offence.

In view of the above discussion, the author concludes that "*Manusmṛti* ought to be situated in its proper historical context, and archaeologically revealed historical facts should be taken in account, in the interpretation of this significant code of law. An archaeo-historical approach unravels the anxieties of the traditional society and provides a concrete archaeo-religious backdrop against which Manu was codifying customary laws. He was neither anti-female nor pro-male; he was a great scholar dealing with the problems of his society which were breaking and endamaging the fabric of traditional society."

The paper "Women and the Notion of *Kāma* in the *Dharmaśāstrīya* Discourse" by Shalini Shah sets out to discuss the notion of *kāma* or sexual desire. According to the author, the *Dharmaśāstrīya* laws were concerned with the procreative aspect of sex and not with the pleasure associated with it. Hence in the man-woman sexual relationship, it was the procreative and not erotic angle that was focused upon. In fact, the erotic was subordinated to the procreative. She concludes on a note that in spite of the *Dharmaśāstras* essentially presenting a picture of a patriarchal society one can discover space or niches within these *Śāstric* traditions where either patriarchy was not functional at all or was greatly diluted. We find eight forms of marriage listed in the *Dharmaśāstras*. Even though the more acceptable forms of marriage (*brahma, daiva, ārṣa, and prajāpatya*) were the ones where men's (father's/husband's) *svāmya* or authority over women was established. The other four forms (*rākśasa, asura, paiśāca and gandharva*) were not excluded by the lawmakers and these were relatively non patriarchal forms of marriage, where property rights and consent agency all point towards greater if not absolute control by women and their kin. The *Śāstras* also note the presence of a variety of sons. Thus, the *Dharmaśāstras* refer to *kānīna* (son of maiden), *sahoḍha* (son of a twice-married woman), who were all accepted as part of family (*bāndhava*). The very manner of the birth of these sons allows a more lenient view of female sexuality within patriarchal society.

Preeti Singh's paper, "Re-reading *Dharmaśāstras* through Indian Eyes: A Feminist Perspective" attempts to analyze whether the distinction between public and private which is deeply rooted in the western philosophical discourse also exists in the *Dharmaśāstrīya* discourse. Revealing the deep roots of public-private dichotomy in the dominant Western philosophy, she writes that Western philosophical thought suffers from dualism on several dimensions. Separating public from private, particular from universal, human from divine, family from state, and male from female realms of experience and action form a crucial aspect of Western philosophical tradition. With the disjunction of public and private, male and female, the family (i.e., private) becomes inherently naturalized, depoliticized, and dehistoricized. Private is always regarded inferior to the public. According to the Greek view of life, the private person or *idiot* was a being of lower purpose, goodness, rationality and worth than the *polites* or public citizens who belonged to and participated in the city. The author argues that in fact the domestication of women or confinement of women in private sphere is not discrimination but to perceive private as valueless is real discrimination. In the second part of the article, the author attempts to show that though the *Dharmaśāstras* recommend division of labour between the two sexes for smooth functioning of the society, they do not perceive male and female realm of life as superior and inferior respectively. *Dharmaśāstras* have not the least idea of any inherent superiority of one in relation to other while assigning different types of work to man and woman. It is only a kind of division of labour, that men and women are required to do different jobs suited to their respective physical and mental capacities. Thus, public and private is regarded as complementary to each other. To quote her:

> One thing which must be pointed out here is that the logic of Western scholars behind confining women to private realm of life was that as the private realm of life is based on narrow interests so women are suitable for it as they can never think in the broader interest of whole humanity. But none of the *Dharmaśāstras* has perceived the private realm of life as an institution based on narrow interests. Moreover, in the philosophy of *Dharmaśāstras* private realm of life is regarded as a place where all the public responsibilities get fulfilled. Unlike Plato who in his communism regarded family as an impediment in the attainment of ideal state wherein individual would be free from any kind of parochialism, *Dharmaśāstrakāras* perceive it (the order of the householder) as the institution where one learns the practice of self-control and self-sacrifice.

On the basis of this comparative study (between Western and *Dharmaśāstrīya* discourse), she reaches to the conclusion that there is an urgent need to study the *Dharmaśāstras* holistically in their particular socio-cultural context. What is required is to evolve an indigenous methodology to study these texts and to analyse the position of women in it.

Devopriya Roy, in her paper, "My Hours with Manu and Some Unlikely Answers" suggests that the key to unlocking the *Manusmṛti* lies in understanding the metaphysical precepts of the text, and that indeed through the prism of these one might seek to reread the social practices, and correct them where faulty. She further argues that while the *Manusmṛti* is quite clearly concerned with the day to day aspects of marriage and sexuality (for instance it seems to privilege reproductive sex over unproductive, pleasure-oriented sex), there are verses within it which deal with the philosophical aspects of sexuality. In the realm of sexuality, the idea of one body divided into two, and ever desirous to be one again forms the central concept.

And indeed both man and woman are regarded as equal partners in the ideal sexual union, which is the physical manifestation of a metaphysical yearning. There is a wide pervasion of these concepts in texts like Vātsyāyan's *Kāmasūtra*, Jayadeva's *Gītagovindam* and the later *Vaiṣṇav Padas*. Significantly, these throw new light on the position of women within the metaphysical framework of the tradition. However the author accepts that in spite of the essential equality between man and woman in creation, various contradictory notions exist about the position of women in society. She opines there would be no hesitation in us to completely reject that which common sense and indeed, the egalitarian philosophy underlying the text itself find unfair, cruel or irrelevant to our times. Emphasizing the dynamic nature of the tradition of *Dharmaśāstras,* the author writes in her conclusion:

> According to the *Nāradasmṛti*, Manu had written one lakh *Ślokas*, divided into twenty-four chapters in the original *Dharmaśāstras*. Reading this text Nārada felt that its length was definitely a deterrent, and he edited it accordingly bringing it down to 12,000 verses. It was subsequently given to Mārkaṇḍeya who revised it into 8,000 ślokas, and finally it was Bhṛgu who gave it the present form of around 4,000 verses. Indeed, this exemplifies the fact that the tradition of *Dharmaśāstras* in particular, and of Hinduism in general, is not static but is rather subject to the needs and requirements of its age. Thus we see that even the 'much maligned' *Manusmṛti* contains the basic egalitarian and deeply philosophical precepts that must be evoked in order to evolve a vibrant, Indic model of feminism where woman, where deprived would be readily restored to a position of equality.

Kavita A. Sharma's paper "*Mahābhārata* through the Eyes of Women" is an attempt to portray that though the society of *Mahābhārata* was patriarchal in nature and structure, women created a remarkable space for themselves within the limits set for them. The author refers to several such women who played a decisive role in the *Mahābhārata*. Women were divided into two classes: the utterly destructive because of their unbridled sexuality and the chaste wives and mothers. Within this polarity lay the ambiguities of *niyoga* or polyandry and a woman's freedom to take the initiative in approaching a man. There are instances which tend to indicate that women were enjoying greater sexual freedom in the then society. Women too could approach men on their own and it was imperative upon the men so approached to gratify their wishes. For example, Gaṅgā approached Pratipa, Śāntanu's father in the form of a beautiful woman when she sat on his right thigh. Arjuna was punished for not responding to the advances of Uravaśī and had to spend his time as a eunuch in the court of Virāṭa surrounded by women. Hiḍimbā too approached Bhīma when the Pāṇḍavas were in exile. As a result Ghatotkacha was born who rendered great service during the *Mahābhārata* war.

Mahābhārata is full of such verses wherein very esteemed position has been accorded to the chaste wife. The position of a chaste wife was of primary importance as stability of family rested on her. She was vital for bringing forth the much needed sons and for making a home. The duties of a chaste wife are expounded over and over again in *Mahābhārata*. However, all the obligations are not on the wife alone. Some space has been created for a wife's rights within this framework. When a chaste wife deviates the fault is that of the husband. The conclusion to which the author reaches is worth quoting here:

> "Thus, the world of *Mahābhārata* when seen from the point of view of women is one of power structures, both in the private and public spheres, totally controlled by men. They can attain a voice in this world through their status as wives and mothers acting through their husbands and sons. Independent women are branded as unchaste because their unbridled sexuality, can so easily destroy this carefully constructed power structure. As wives and mothers, the sexuality of women is subjugated and regulated to fulfilling the societal demands of producing as many sons as possible. However, women manage to create space for themselves within those limitations and become powerful figures capable of changing the course of events. Hence, they become a force to be reckoned with through their own intelligence, acumen and endeavour. It is more often the men rather than the women who appear at crucial moments to be indecisive, lacking in sagacity and in need of support to move them to action."

Vinita Chandra's paper "Women in *Manusmṛti*" aims at an objective analysis of *Manusmṛti*. She argues that in fact *Manusmṛti* was a response or reaction to the then prevailing social, economic, political and religious conditions. Therefore the laws and indictments laid down by Manu need to be studied in the context of social, political and economic development of the times. The period of the text which is circa 2nd century BC to circa 2nd century AD was a period of different political events. It started with Maurya period with its centralized monarchy followed by disintegration of larger kingdoms into small kingdoms and tribal republics. Mauryan rule was replaced by Sungas around 185 BC followed by the Kaṇvas and then the Andhras. Petty kings ruled the region after the withdrawl of the Andhras. In the south this period was marked with frequent conflicts between Ceras, Cholas and Pāṇḍyas. In some respects the period witnessed the great activities of Church and marked the heyday of the faith. The period is also marked with brisk economic activity and a fabulous expansion in trade and industry. It was both, the political chaos and flourishing trade, which brought the foreigners in India. This explain the continuous reiteration in the *Manusmṛti* of the inherent superiority of the *Brāhmaṇas* as compared to the other classes. Thus, an analysis of the social condition of the time presents that the society was in transition and there was a constant threat for the disintergration of the existent social order. The threads of the initial social fabric were loosened and the social reality was far removed from the normative model set by the Brahmanical texts. The author emphasizes that all that Manu laid down for women needs to be analyzed in the backdrop of these conditions. To quote her: "What seems to be an attempt to control women perhaps was an attempt rather to preserve the older order where the threads of the older fabric were getting loosened." An anxiousness to marry girls at an early age might have resulted because of the fact that there was an influx of foreigners, which could have made the girls vulnerable or even if not that, at least susceptible to having married in the foreign population. Similarly independence of women might have been feared because of their moving out of the Brāhmaṇical order. Women were to be protected from the incoming foreigners. Perhaps the idea of keeping women guarded originated out of a fear of admixture of castes, which becomes pronounced in the seventh verse of Chapter IX of *Manusmṛti* when it is said that he who carefully guards his wife, preserves the purity of his offspring, virtuous conduct, his family, himself and his means of acquiring merits. Adultery was condemned for the same reason in verse 353 of Chapter VIII of *Manusmṛti*.

She further concludes that even the epigraphs belonging to that period serve as indirect evidences regarding the position of women in that period. She refers to many such epigraphic evidences such as: Bedsa Cave Inscription of Mahādevī Sāmadinikā, Kanheri Cave Inscription of Māhārathini Nāgamūlanikā and Nasik Cave Eulogy of Queen Gautami Balaśri.

Anjali Chatterji's paper entitled "Social Status of Women in *Dharmaśāstras*" argues that the controversial verses of *Dharmaśāstras* concerning women's protection tend to prove that woman was regarded as very precious social unit and so she must be guarded with great care during all the stages of her life. She further argues that woman's status in the *Dharmaśāstras* was co-related with different stages of her life. The status of women as depicted in the *Dharmaśāstras* clearly shows that a woman as a girl child, as a married woman and as a widow had to observe a set of prescribed duties and sacraments in their lives. Actually in the ideology of Manu and other *Smṛti* writers the home and the family constitute the bedrock of society and woman is that figure on whom the stability and sanctity of the home and household life depend. The lawgivers had a conception of woman according to which they did not like woman to be exposed to the rough and an unprotected independent life, and it is in this spirit that Manu says "Woman shall always be taken care of by some one. She is not fit for freedom". The lawgivers tried to prescribe whatever suited in a particular environment. She opines that strictures on women in Manu and other *Smṛtis* should not prejudice us as the real intention of all the *Śāstrakāras* is to praise the greatness of chastity i.e. '*pātivratya*'. In fact, Manu and other *Smṛti* writers adopted two stand points, first conceding to some extent as a result of the vogue and the second stating their personal or ideal opinion.

V.C. Srivastava's article "Gender Perspective of Law in Classical India" propounds that by and large the attitude of Indians in the *Vedic* period was egalitarian in the sense that women were equal partners in offering sacrifices; participated independently in public life; and were equally educated. He has discussed at length property rights of women and concluded that 500 AD onwards the daughter's right to inheritance was well established. The Kolahapur inscription (E.I.III, p. 215) and the Mysore epigraphs of 1168 AD provide examples of it. The denial of a share in the patrimony to a daughter was tried to be compensated by the rule that the brother should spend in his sisters' marriage an amount equal to one-fourth of his own share (Yāj. II. 124). This rule shows that the classical laws were concerned with the welfare of daughter. Since the property was generally landed, a share to a daughter married to someone in distant village may not have been very practical. Even a brother was to spend out of his self-acquired property for the sister's marriage. The author, however, feels that many of the modernists do not understand the motive behind not giving a share to the daughter in the landed property and argue that this rule of no share in inheritance was dishonest and unethical on the part of patriarchal and male-dominated ancient Indian society. The fact according to author is that women occupied somewhat an egalitarian position and the classical law gave the women the right to full control over the *strīdhana*.

Sati Chatterji, in her paper on "The Economic Position of Women: As the Ancient *Dharmaśāstras* Define", analyzes at length the economic position of women in the *Dharmaśāstras*. She bases her study on the law of inheritance as enunciated in the *Smṛti Śāstra* which according to her can be studied in three major clusters: inheritance laws in general; special laws of succession; and separate laws governing the case of '*strīdhana*'. According to her, though there is no doubt that in formulating general laws of inheritance, priority was assigned to the eldest born male child, women enjoyed exclusive ownership of wealth falling into the category of *strīdhana*. *Manusmṛti* has categorically defined six forms of *strīdhana*. Besides this, women were claimants to maintenance. Maintenance would come from the father in childhood, from husband in the prime of life, from the son(s) in old age. Even when the husband deserts a wife and takes another, the earlier wedded woman must be given economic protection (Yāj. I. 74). When desertion is for no fault of wife, the husband would have to assign one-third of his possession to her (Yāj. I. 76). In case the husband lacks resources he must make subsistence provision for the wife he deserts. Women who have no sons must be provided maintenance by the family. However, the author feels that in spite of all protection and maintenance, women somehow have formed a secondary group in the *Dharmaśāstras*. What is assuring, is the fact that in the absence of son, there is unqualified reliance on the *Putrikā*.

Annupurna Chattopodhyay, in her paper "Studying the Economic Position of Women on the Basis of *Dharmaśāstras*:

Perspectives in Occupation, *Strīdhana,* Property and Inheritance" tries to emphasize that the socio-economic status of women should be judged in the background of that period only. It would be unfair to discuss the socio-economic status of women of *Smṛti* period in comparison with their status in the 20th century or 21st century. If we look into the *Smṛti* period, we discover that there were no uniform rules pertaining to the privileges of sexes. Surprisingly, the status of women belonging to upper classes was much lower than that of the lower sections where women enjoyed higher status and greater legal privileges.

She also described how the society though patriarchal in structure during the early Vedic period, women took an active part in economic production. There are references to such women *Vagitri/ Siri* (female weaver) *Pesakāri* (female embroider) *Bidalakāri* (female splitter of bamboos), *Ragyitṛ* (female dyer), *Upalapraksini* (women corn grinder) etc. The teaching profession was followed by women from the Vedic down to the Sūtra period. The reference to Vispālā who lost a leg in battle makes it evident that women could take part in wars. The Buddhist and Jain texts refer to several women of the *Brahmavādini* class who remained unmarried to carry on their studies. Moreover, women were also employed as bodyguards as our present day security guards in the Maurya period. The female bodyguards of the king are mentioned in Kauṭilya's *Arthaśāstra* which informs us that the king getting up from his bed shall be received by the troops of women armed with bows. Besides, women were also appointed as spies of the king. The Bhārhut scultputures portray a woman riding a fully caparisoned horse and carrying a standerd.

This paper is full of such evidences from both, the *śāstras* and inscriptions. On the basis of these epigraphic and *śāstric* evidences the authoress has come to the conclusion that it is evident that women were engaged in different types of jobs as mentioned in the *RigVeda, Arthaśāstra, Kāmaśāstra, Dharmaśāstra* and in epigraphic records. A woman would also own property which she has received as gifts from her relatives at the time of marriage or inherited from her mother. Women were also entitled to own and bequeath their special property or *strīdhana*. There are several examples where queens and princes made donations. Sometimes it seems that women's right to inheritance is categorically denied in the *Dharmaśāstra*. But from the 2nd century BC onwards there seems to have been a reversal in the unfavourable attitude of the

Brahmanical lawgivers for women's right to property. This is evident from the contemporary Pāli texts and epigraphic records which mention a large number of women as donors.

Anita Singh's article "Property Rights of Daughter in Ancient India" with special reference to Dharmaśāstras attempts to analyse economic status of daughter as per the provisions laid down by the *Dharmaśāstras*. The paper focuses on three types of property rights of daughters viz. right to inheritance, right at partition and right over *strīdhana*. The authoress discusses different types of daughters viz. brotherless daughters (*Putrikā*) and daughters with brothers and their property rights at length. Apart from enumerating *Dharmaśāstric* provisions concerning daughter's right to inheritance, the paper also discusses the socio-economic factors that led to such provisions. The concluding remark of the essayist is worth quoting here:

> In an agricultural society where the joint family was the unit, the threat of segmenting the cultivable land by the family was very genuine. The motive of patriarchal family system was to keep the immovable property intact and in such a patriarchal society where marriage was obligatory, and the daughter was to leave the father's family and as she was not allowed to offer funeral oblations to his father, the *Dharmaśāstrakāras* make as best legal provision as was possible in such a social backdrop.

Binda Paranjape's article, "Revisiting *Dharmaśāstras* during the Colonial Period" is an attempt towards highlighting the political dimension of the reform movement related to women resulting into passing of certain legislations for the first time in India. The British rule brought about significant changes in the lives of the Indians. Britishers introduced new administrative system where the whole of India was treated by and large as a single entity. While establishing the constitution of the personal law, they used the Islamic and Brāhmaṇical scriptures as the law books of the Indians. The author argues that the fact that the scriptures, at least the Hindu scriptures, were rarely used as the sources of law during the pre-British period was not paid enough attention.

Manu was declared as "the parent of Hindu jurisprudence". Thus, during the colonial period the scriptures, more than any other period of Indian history, became the sources of law. She is of the opinion that giving legitimacy to the *Dharmaśāstras* was not the compulsion of the Britishers only, it was also required for strengthening the political position of the nationalist leaders of both the revolutionary and moderate streams. This is clearly visible in case of the legislations passed as regards to the Hindu women. The nationalist leaders, who were against British interference in the customs and practices of the Hindus, started revisiting the Hindu *Dharmaśāstras* to extract support for their arguments. Be it the issue of the education of girls or the age of consent the *Dharmaśāstras* were brought forth as the testimony of the ancient law of the Hindus. It is significant to note that the *Dharmaśāstras* had been used by both the reformist groups as well as the nationalists during this period, either for supporting the reforms or for opposing them.

Priyamvada's paper "The Nineteenth Century Construct of *Dharmaśāstras*: A Historiographical Enquiry" is a brief study of various historiographical schools of thought and the different interpretations rendered to the ancient scripture during nineteenth century. The essayist intends to speculate on the possible motives behind the undertaking of such studies. She raises several questions: was it a colonial attempt to 'recast' women as scholars like Kumkum Sangari, Uma Chakravarti, Lata Mani, Susie Tharu, Sumant Banerji would have us believe? Or was there a 'hidden agenda' of using women as currency in the complex set of exchanges that the struggle for hegemony between the Indian western-educated pro-British and the paternalistic civilizing British bureaucracy presumed? The conclusion given by the essayist answers many of the above questions raised by her in the beginning:

> The fact that becomes clearly evident after this brief survey of sources is that women became critical matter for public discourse in the nineteenth century. The genuineness or even the presence of any form of concern for women is highly dubitable in the notion of women and scripture as repositories of tradition was common among the reforms and even those against reform movement. The core issue here was more of a concern to confront and negotiate moral challenge of colonial rule. Women were either viewed as weak creature that had to be protected through legislation and education, or the valiant keeper of tradition who must be protected.

I

Persona of Women in India's Intellectual Tradition

1

Women's Education in Vedic India

Pranati Ghoshal

The *Dharmaśāstras* generally prescribe the norms for post-Vedic Indian society, when the position of women had somewhat a descending graph. This continued in the later and medieval India, when lots of restrictions were imposed on women for different reasons and particularly for the repeated attacks by foreigners. The situation in the Vedic India is, however, different and by large a better picture emerges in the texts of that period. Hence, discussion on "Women's Education in Vedic India" requires a survey of the entire background. At first, we are to confess here that there is hardly any direct evidence of imparting lessons to the girls. This absence of direct reference and assemblage of some factors prevalent during the age of *Dharmaśāstras,* e.g. (1) girls' marriage at early age, (2) Manu's famous dictum against women's liberty (*na strí svātantryam arhati* – 5.148) and (3) Sāyaṇa's bold rejection of girls' right to the Vedic studies (*strī śudrayostu satyāmapi jñānāpekṅāyām ...vede' dhikāraḥ pratiśiddhaḥ* – Sā on RV Intro.) – made the situation more confusing. But a careful and thorough study in the Vedic passages reveals the fact that the situation was not disappointing.

While discussing on the women's position in the field of education, A.S. Altekar[1] has observed a strange phenomenon of our country: "The history of the most of the known civilization shows that further back we go to the antiquity, the more unsatisfactory is found to be the general position of women. In this respect, Indian civilization is unique because here we find a surprising exception to the general rule. The further back we go, the more satisfactory is found to be the position of women in more spheres than one; and the field of education is most noteworthy among them. We can, however, understand this strange phenomenon when we remember that for long time education in ancient India meant Vedic education and that it had to be necessarily imparted to all who were expected to take part in Vedic sacrifices, irrespective of their sex."

It is true, that there is no explicit mention about the arrangement of girls' education, but from the references (scattered throughout Vedic texts) to women seers[2], teachers[3], their active participation in Vedic sacrifices[4], their investiture of holy thread[5], their involvement in music and dance[6], war-field[7], as well as in different vocations[8], we can decipher that in spite of the absence of institution-based training system, girls in Vedic India were not deprived of education.

Women as Scholars/Savants

P.V. Kane[9] in his *History of Dharmaśāstras* says: "It appears that in very ancient times, status of women as to their education was much higher than in medieval and modern times in India." Even the orthodox tradition (family books) admits that Ṛgvedic collection contains hymns composed by poetesses who were known as *ṛṣikā* or *brahmavādinī*. At least twenty such names of poetesses have been traced in the *Ṛgveda*. They were Romaśā (ṚV 1.126.7), Lopāmudrā (ṚV 1.179.1-6), Apālā (8.91.1-7), Kadrȳ (2.6.8), Viśvavārā (5.28.3), Ghoṣā (X.39), Juhū (X.109), Yami (X.10), Saramā (X.108), Āmbhṛṇī Vāk (X.125), Paulomi (X.159), Jaritā (X.142), Śraddhā-Kāmāyani (X.151), Urvaśī (X.95), Rātrī (X.127), Indramātar (X.153), Sūryā (X.85), Indrāṇi (X.145), Sarparājī (X.189), Devajāmī (X.108), etc.

The names of Nodhā (*Sāmaveda*, Pūrvārcika 13.1), Sikatānivāvari (SV, Uttarārcika 1.4), Gaupāyanā (SV, Uttarārcika XXII.4), Ākṛṣṭabhāṣā, etc. have been recorded in the *Sāmaveda* as immortal singers. Romaśā, the daughter of Bṛhaspati has been described as *brahmavādinī*[10]. In the AB[11], we have come across a maiden obsessed by a *gandharva* who could instruct people (regarding performance of rituals) in cases of doubt. The BU[12] record names of Gārgī and Maitreyī who also had the epithet *brahmavādinī* before their names. The *Bṛhad-devatā* has enumerated a long list of twenty-seven women seers. From this long queue of female scholars/savants, we can rightly infer that they underwent some sort of training under the able guidance of teachers who might have been their fathers, brothers or husbands because parents had desire for learned daughters also. In this connection, we may mention here the custom of performing an interesting ritual with a desire to have a daughter who would be a learned lady.[13]

Participation in Sacrifice

Not only they were scholars and composers of hymns, but they were also regular participants in the sacrifices of their husbands.[14] The ŚB[15] has declared wife as the integral part of sacrifice. According to Pāṇini[16], the word *patnī* denotes her special connection with her husband's sacrifice. Her presence is so much important that the person became eligible for sacrifice only when he had his wife by his side.[17] The TB[18] has expressed unwillingness of gods to accept offerings from an unmarried person. Both the husband and wife had to undergo a special type of initiation and take equal part in the entire procedure.[19] In the context of Horse Sacrifice, the ŚB[20] along with the king has assigned different duties to the four queens also. Not only they participated in sacrifice physically, but they uttered Vedic hymns also.[21] At the time of marriage, bride also had to utter some *mantrās*. Gobhila[22] prescribes that when the bride pushes forward with her foot on a mat, the bridegroom should make her utter the hymns: "May the way, which my husband goes by, be also assigned to me". In the *Kāṭhaka Gṛhyasūtra*[23], it is said that the *anuvāka* beginning with *"sarasvaté predamate"*, etc. should be recited by both the husband and wife. In the *srastarārohaṇa* ritual of *Āgrayaṇeṣṭī*[24], both the husband and wife had to utter Vedic *mantras*; and harvest sacrifices could be performed by women alone.[25] As regards daily domestic rites, Gobhila[26] instructs the wife to offer the evening *bali*.

Investiture of Holy-thread *(Upanayana)*

Now, the question is whether *upanayana* was ever performed for women? AV's reference to girls' marriage only after the completion of their *brahmacarya*[27], their eligibility and active participation in sacrifices indicate that system of girls' investiture of sacred thread was prevalent since Vedic period. However, *Smṛtikāras* opine differently on this point. Most orthodox Manu[28], was in favour of girls' *upanayana* just for the sanctification of their body, without uttering any *mantra*. But regarding performance of other rituals of *upanayana* (e.g. tending of fire, celibacy, begging of alms, etc.) he opined differently.[29] However, *Yamasaṁhitā* and *Hārītasaṁhitā* quoted in the *Saṁskāraprakāśa* and *Smṛticandrikā*[30] gave a verdict that just like boys, *upanayana* was obligatory for girls. By the term *purākalpa*, most probably *Smṛtikāra* wanted to mean Vedic age. Yama said that girls were entitled for thread ceremony, they studied *Vedas* and uttered *gāyatrī*.

Hārīta[31] observed two types of girl students of that period: (1) *brahmavādinī* (the student of sacred lore) and (2) *sadyovadhū* (girls direct given to marriage). The former were entitled for *upanayana*. They studied *Vedas,* tended fire and begged alms within their house. Girdle of *muñjā*-grass was prescribed for them. But system of wearing matted hair or deerskin was not applicable for them. Normally, they were taught by their fathers, uncles or brothers.[32] In this connection (as an exception), here we may mention Bhavabhūti's description of society where nun Kāmandakī learnt at the feet of teacher[33] with other male students. Normally, these *brahmavādinīs* did not marry; therefore, could be compared with *naiṣṭhika brahmacārī* (lifelong celibate). As an exception to this general rule, Maitreyī's name may be cited here, who in spite of being married was considered as *brahmavādinī*. The latter group was *sadyovadhū*, who were given to marriage after performing a brisk ceremony of *upanayana*[34]; and they might be compared to *upakurvāña brahmacārīs*, who after the completion of their studies, rendered some token honorarium to the teacher and accordingly left *gurukula* for entering next stage of life. The education of *sadyovadhūs* comprised the study of important Vedic hymns necessary for usual prayers and sacrifices. Music and dance also were taught to them.

It is surprising to note that Hārīta has indirectly indicated the age of their *upanayana* also. According to Hārīta's injunction quoted in *Saṁskāraprakāśa*[35], girls' education, convocation, everything was to be completed before the approach of their puberty, which indicates that *brahmavādinī* women had their *upanayana* performed in the 8th year from conception. Then they studied Vedic lore and finished studenthood at the age of puberty. It is interesting to note that in the context of convocation *(samāvartana)*, the ĀGS[36] has mentioned the process of girls' anointment also.

This system of girls' *upanayana* was prevalent up to Sūtra period. Gobhila[37], the renowned author, has stated that the bridegroom catches hold of bride's hands, who has been invested with holy thread and utter the hymn *'somo dadāt gandharvāya'*. The Mbh[38] also has referred to a brahmin who invested Kuntī with holy thread and taught her *Atharvaśiras mantra* of Veda. Even in the 7th century, Bāṇa[39] has referred to Mahāśvetā whose body was sanctified with *brahmasūtra*.

Though nowadays this system has become obsolete in the Indo-Aryan branch of Aryan family but it is prevalent in the Iranian branch of Aryans. Even today in the Zoroastrian families, maidens undergo *upanayana* ceremony termed as *'navzot'*, which has been explained as new birth in the *Avesta*.

Attainments of the Women Savants / Teachers

It is interesting to note that girls' career was not confined in their studenthood only. Names of women savants, e.g., Gārgī, Maitreyī have been recorded in the *Upaniṣads* who were renowned dialecticians. In later texts also we find some names who themselves were teachers. In the context of daily *ṛṣitarpaṇa*, the ĀGS[40] has mentioned a host of women teachers (e.g. Gārgī Vācaknavī, Vaḍavā Prātitheyī, Sulabhā Maitreyī) to whom water libations were offered.

The terms *Vahvṛcī, Kaṭhī, Kalāpī* meant the scholars who were well-versed in *Vedas* of *Vahvṛca, Kaṭha* or *Kalāpa* tradition. The *Mahābhāṣya*[41] teaches formation of *ācāryā* and *upādhyāyā* to mean lady teachers and not merely the wife of teacher *(upādhyāyānī)*. Further, *Mahābhāṣya*[42] has stated how and why a Brahmin woman was called Āpiṣālā (the lady teacher proficient in the grammar of Āpiṣāli), which indicates that women were proficient grammarians also. In course of time, a new horizon, i.e. *Mīmāṁsā* was open to them. Though it was a difficult subject and drier than mathematics, lady students took keen interest in it and in course of time, they became renowned with the appellations like *'Kāśakṛtsnā brāhmaṇī'* (lady who was proficient in the *Mīmāṁsā* text belonging to Kāṣakṛtsna School) or *Audamedhā*[43] (the student of Audamedhī who herself was *Mīmāṁsā* teacher). With the advancement of days, they took interest in the study of other branches of philosophy. Such was the case of Yājñavalkya's wife Maitreyī, who could ignore all the worldly assets just to get comprehensive knowledge of Ultimate Truth/ Immortality from her husband.[44] In this connection, we may refer to another competent philosopher Gārgī Vācaknavī, who by joining philosophical tournament held at Janaka's court put forth a series of questions to Yājñavalkya[45]. Her questions were so subtle and esoteric in character that Yājñavalkya refused to discuss it and stopped her by saying *"mā' ti prākñṣīḥ gārgī mā te mūrdhā vyapatat"*.

Vocational Training

Apart from lessons on Vedic studies, grammar and philosophical problems, some vocational training also were given to women. Existence of some female vocations (mentioned in the VS and TB[46] in the context of Puruṣamedha) proves the validity of the fact. For example, names of *vidalakārī* (basket-maker), *kaṇṭakīkārī* (thorn-worker), *koṣakārī* (scabbard-maker), *āñjanakārī* (ointment-maker), *peṣaskārī* (female embroiderer), *vāsaḥpalpūlī* (landeress), *sirī* (weaver), *rajayitrī* (dyer), *upalaprakṣiṇī* (grinder of corns) can be mentioned. Existence and development of so many small-group cottage-industries must have required some sort of methodical training, existence of which can only be supposed in the absence of direct evidence from *Vedas*. Further, from the ŚB *"tad vā etat strīṇām karma yad ūrṇāsūtram karma"* (12.7.2.11) it appears that cultivation of crafts like sewing, knitting, etc. was mainly fixed for women.

Cultivation of Fine Arts

Besides, fine arts like vocal music, dancing, etc. were mainly cultivated by ladies. *Brāhmaṇa*[47] texts frequently mention that singing and dancing were womanly pastime, their partiality to these arts has been distinctly expressed in the ŚB[48]. They can be easily won over by one who can sing and dance. It seems that women, i.e. wives of *Sāmavedic* priests were formerly entrusted with the singing of Sāma chants in sacrifices. Later on, they were replaced by their husbands. The ŚB[49] states: the Udgātṛs actually perform the duties of their wives (in singing Sāma chants).

Military Training

Apart from these, it is striking to note that the adventurous steps of Vedic women led them to martial field also. References to the female soldiers[50], women's involvement in war[51], their heroic feats makes us suppose that they were provided some military training also. Not only they were able to protect themselves, but in times of emergency, they faced enemy soldiers also. The statement of a puzzled Aryan soldier *"striyo hi dāsa āyudhāni cakre"* (ṚV 5.30.9) indicates that in the Army, there was female squad also. In this connection, we may mention the name of Mudgalānī[52] who drove the chariot of her husband and helped him to encounter with enemy. The ṚV[53] describes her courageous heroic feats in the battlefield where she defeated thousands of soldiers. Viṣpalā, the queen of king Khela, is another example who was severely wounded in the battle and undergone a surgery in her leg.[54] Thus, heroic feats of confident ladies and their competence in warfare have been traced since the time of *Ṛgveda*. Later on, Patañjali.[55] has mentioned *ṣāktikīs* (ladies proficient in throwing lances) in his *Mahābhāṣya*. Lady security guards of Mauryan king Candragupta's palace have been referred to in the travel accounts of Megasthenes.

Conclusion

In spite of this high-class enlightenment and elevation, gradually position of women became worse and worse. As a consequent result of repeated foreign attacks, various types of social detriments were being noticed. In order to check this social deterioration and to maintain the purity of their own heritage and family traditions, orthodox schools started imposing series of restrictions on women. As a result, in the *Dharmasūtras* (especially in *Manusaṁhitā* and *Yājñavalkyasaṁhitā*) women were assigned a position of dependence. Even women of higher class came to be looked upon as equal to *śūdras* so far as Vedic studies and several other matters were concerned. Most probably, Sāyaṇa's rejection of girls' right to the Vedic studies is also a reflection of the same thing.

Notes

1. Altekar, A.S., *Education in Ancient India*, IX, p. 207.
2. ṚV 1.126.7; 1.179.1-6; 2.6.8; 5.28.3; 8.91.1-7; etc.
3. *Kāṣikā* on Pāṇini 3.21; 4.1.59; *Mahābhāṣya* on Pāṇini 4.1.14; ĀGS 3.4; etc.
4. ṚV 1.122.2; 1.131.3; 3.53.4-6; 5.43.15; 8.31.5; 10.86.10; etc.
5. AV 11.6.18; Manu 2.66; *Yama-Saṁhitā* quoted in *Smṛticandrikā I*, p. 24; ĀGS 3.8.11.
6. ŚB 2.4.6; 14.3.1.35.
7. ṚV 1.116.15; 5.80.6; 8.33.19; 10.102.2; etc.
8. VS 30th Ch. and TB 3.12.
9. P.V. Kane, *History of Dharmaśāstras*, Vol.II, p. 365.
10. *Bṛhaspatiputrī romaṣā brahmavādinī* – ṚV 1.126.7.
11. *Etadu hovāca kumarī gandharvagṛhītā vaktāsmo vā idam pitṛbhyo yad vaitad agnihotram ubhayedyur āhūyatānyedyur vāva tad etarhi hūyata iti* – AB 5.29.
12. *Tayor ha maitreyī brahmavādinī babhūva* – BU 4.5.1.
13. *atha ya icched duhitā me paṇṁitā jāyeta sarvam āyuriyāditi tilaudanam pācayitvā sarpiṣmantam aṣnīyātām īṣvarau janayitavai* – BU 6.4.17.
14. ṚV 1.122.2; 1.131.3; 3.53.4-6; 5.43.15; etc.
15. *Jaghanārdho ha vā eṣa yajñasya yat patnī* – ŚB 5.2.1.8.
16. *Patyur no yajña samyoge* – Pā4.1.33.
17. *Ayajñyo vā eṣo yo'patnīkaḥ* – ŚB 5.1.6.10.

18. *na vai apatnīkasya hastāddevā balim gṛhṇanti* – TB 3.8.2.4.
19. TB 3.8.3.
20. ŚB 13.5.2.1-8.
21. GGS 2.3.9.
22. *Paṣcād agneḥ samveṣṭitam kaṭam evamjātīyamvānyatpadā pravartayantī vācayet pra me patiyānaḥ panthāḥ kalpatām* – GGS 2.1.19-20.
23. *Tato gāthām vācayati sarasvati predamatetyanuvākam* – Kāṭh GS 25.23.
24. PGS 3.2.6-16.
25. *striyaṣcopayajeran nācaritatvāt* – PGS 2.17.18.
26. *strī ha vā sāyam prātar pumān iti* – GGS 1.4.19.
27. *brahmacaryeṇa kanyā yuvānam vindate patim* – AV 11.5.18.
28. *amantrikā tu kāryeyam strīṇām āvṛdaṣeṣataḥ* /.
    samskārārtham ṣarīrasya yathākālam yathākramam // Manu 2.66.
29. Manusaṁhitā 2.67.
30. *Yamopi*
    purākalpe kumārīṇām mauñjībandhanam iṣyate /
    adhyāpanam ca vedānāṁ sāvitrī vācanam tathā //
    Yamasaṁhitā quoted in *Saṁskāraprakāśa*, p. 402.
31. *"dvividhā vai striyaḥ, brahmavādinyaḥ sadyovadhvaṣca / tatra brahmavādinīnām upanayanam agnyādhānam vedānām adhyanaṁsvagṛhe bhaikṣacaryā ca"* – *Harītasaṁhitā* quoted in *Smṛticandrikā I*, p. 24.
32. *pitā pitṛvyo bhrātā vā nainām adhyāpayet paraḥ* /
    svagṛhe caiva kanyāyā bhaikṣacaryām vidhīyate /
    varjayed ajinaṁ cīraṁ jaṭādhāraṇam eva ca / *Yamasaṁhitā* quoted in *Saṁskāraprakāśa*, p. 403.
33. *ayi! kiṁ na vetsi yadekatra no vidyā parigrahāya nānādigantavāsinaṁ sāhacaryam āsīt* – *Mālatīmādhava*, Act I.
34. *sadyovadhūnāṁ tūpasthite vivāhe yathākathañcit kṛtvā upanayanaî kāryaî* – *Harītasaṁhita* quoted in *Smṛticandrikā I*, p. 24.
35. *prāgrajasaḥ samāvartanam* – *Ibid.* I, p. 25.
36. *anulepanena pāṇī pralipya mukham agre brāhmaṇo'nulimpet / bāhūrājanyaḥ / udaraṁ vaiṣyaḥ / upasthaṁ strī /* – ĀGS 3.8.11.
37. *prāvṛtāṁ yajñopavitinam abhyudānayan japet somo dadadgandharvāya* – *Saṁskāraprakāśa*, p. 896.
38. *tatastām anavadyāṅgīṁ grāhyāmāsa sa dvijaḥ* /
    mantragrāmaṁ tadārājannatharvaṣirasi ṣrutam // MBh 3.305.20.
39. *brahmasūtreṇa pavitrḥkṛtāyām* – *Kādambari*, Para 133.
40. *sumantu-jaimini-vaiṣampāyana-paila-sūtra-bhāṣya-bhārata-mahābhārata dharmācāryā jānanti ...... gārgi vācaknavḥ vaṁavā prātitheyḥ sulabhā maitreyī ...... ye cānye ācāryāste sarve tṛpyantviti* – ĀGS 3.4.4.
41. *upetyādhḥyate asyā upādhyāyi, upādhyāyā* – *Mahābhāṣya* on Pā 3.3.21, Cf. *Kāṣikā, loc. cit.*

42. *āpiṣalam adhite brāhmaṇi āpiṣālā brāhmaṇi* – Mabh 4.1.14.

43. (i) *kāṣakṛtsninā proktā mimāṁsā kāṣakṛtsni / kāṣakṛtsnim adhḥte kāṣakṛtsnā brāhmaṇi* – Mabh 4.1.14.

    (ii) *audamedhyāyāṣchātrā audamedhāḥ* – Mabh on Pā 4.1.78.

44. *Sā hovāca maitreyi – yenāhaṁ nāmṛtāsyāṁ kimahaṁ tena kuryām / yadeva bhagavān Veda tadeva me brḷhiti* – BU 2.4.3.

45. BU 3.6.1.

46. VS 30.8-14; TB 3.4.5.1 – 3.4.10.1.

47. *nṛttaṁ gitaṁ strīṇāṁ karma* – ṉB 3.2.4.6.

48. *moghasaṁhitā vai striyaḥ* – *Ibid., loc. cit.*

49. *patnī karmaiva ete atra udgātāraḥ kurvanti yat sāmāni gāyanti* – ÍB 14.3.1.35.

50. ṚV 5.30.9; 5.61.5-8; 5.80.6; 7.78.5; 8.33.19; etc.

51. ṚV 1.116.15; 10.102.1-9; etc.

52. *ut sma vāto vahati vāso asyā adhirathaṁ yadajayat sahasram /*

    rathīrabhūn mudgalānī gaviṣṭau bhare kṛtaṁ vyacedindrasenā // – ṚV 10.102.2.

53. ṚV 10.102.1-12.

54. *caritraṁ hi verivācchedi parṇamājā khelasya paritakmyāyām /*

    sadyo jaghām āyasīṁ viṣpalāyai dhane hite sartave pratyadhattam // – ṚV 1.116.15.

55. *Mahābhāṣya* on Pā. 4.4.59.

2

Women in India's Intellectual Tradition

Chandrakala Padia

This paper has three sections. First, it seeks to show that ontologically, or as human beings, women have all along been given an equal status in the Indian intellectual tradition; second, that in respect of character and contribution to cohesion and welfare of society, they have even been regarded superior to man; and thirdly, that it is unwarranted to hold the opposite view (of some critics) that the intellectual traditions of India have never thought highly of woman. Be it noted that, as demanded by the precise phrasing of the subject, my concern will be with *tradition* all along, *and not with things as they are at present;* and further that I will be focussing on intellectual tradition, that is, how women have been *thought of and written about* in the past, not on what their actual state of living and experience was in that period of time.

I

Now, to begin with woman's equality in respect of ontological status as visualized in our ancient texts, I may straight away refer to the *Ṛgveda* commonly regarded as the earliest available text of Indian thought. This *Veda* speaks of a common source from which the diversity of life has emerged. The *Nāsadiya Sūkta (Mandal 10, Ṛg129)*[1] visualizes the state before creation – even before the emergence of light, shade or form; and speaks of a process through which the One will manifest itself in many forms, including the male and the female ones. Now, this very thought of a *common* origin recalcitrates the idea of *inequal* importance of the forms that emerge into existence. It is, in this context, relevant to point out that quite a few saints in India have also argued for the equality of all human beings on the ground that they are all alike the product of the five elements (*pañch-bhūtas).* The *Kaṭhopaniṣad* (II, ii, 15) sounds a similar note where it says that before creation began, there was nothing, neither light nor darkness, neither day nor night, no sky, no stars, no earth – nothing; only when the primal Will – crystallizing itself as the golden cosmic egg, *hiraṇyagarbham* – split itself, that all this diversity of forms came into being; and that, as in respect of its emergence, so in dissolution too, this diversity will lapse back into the one and common Essence, or Being.[2] So all that prevails on the earth is of equal significance, and also alike in impermanence.

It is noteworthy that such a non-discriminatory view of origin and dissolution continued to be held upto the times of *Dharmaśāstras*. Thus, *Manusmṛti,* which is widely acknowledged as the earliest *Dharmaśāstra* text, more or less repeats the view in question (Manu I, 13-39) adding that the process of self-division of the one included gender differentiation as well. The One, we are told, split itself into two halves, and assumed the male form with one half and the female form with the other (I, 32). The implication here obviously is that though at the ontological level gender – *differentiation* there certainly is, it is surely not the same thing as gender *discrimination.*

The *Upniṣads* too speak of human beings generally, not of man as opposed to woman. They formulate problems of life and offer thoughtful solutions for the whole of humanity. What is more, the solutions are based on the faith that an overriding principle is at work in all alike – the faith that all living beings are evolving towards *Mukti,* or spiritual liberation. The evolutionary process is described as a passage from the physical to the spiritual, and, collaterally, from the mundane to the divine, all along making for the realization that, more than a mind-body complex, the individual is the spiritual principle. This supreme objective (of self-realization) is held to be accessible to man and woman alike. Nor is such a view merely a thing of the past. Swami Vivekananda has spoken for it vigorously. Our psychology too insists that both men and women are basically spiritual; that body and mind are but helpful instruments; and that it is the *ātman* (the Self), which is the *tattva* (or Essence), and also the real *Kartā* (or/agent) which is seeking *mokśa.* The *Kaṭhopaniṣad* visualizes the selfsame thought in the form of a beautiful image. The body (it says) is the chariot, the mind is the reins; and the *ātman* is the driver which directs the chariot and keeps it running – in the direction of *mokśa.*[3]

Even in the post-*Saṁhitā* period, we may note, woman was regarded as *ardhāṅgini,* that is, one half of the very being of man and in no way subordinate to him. Another significant term that is used for her is: *sahadharmiṇi,* that is, a co-participator in discharging the obligations of life and fully capable of taking her own decisions. Of all the different women mentioned in *Vedic Saṁhitā* texts, Maitreyī is perhaps the most illustrious example of a woman's ability to exercise her own judgement in respect of a question of values. The relevant situation is, in brief, as follows. *Maharṣi* Yājñavalkya wishes to embrace *sannyāsa* (renunciation, the fourth stage of life). He duly seeks his wives' permission for the change, adding that he was quite willing to divide his property between his two wives. Thereupon, exercising both her individual sense of values and freedom to disagree, Maitreyī emphatically refuses to share the property and pleads instead for being granted the imperishable treasure of self-knowledge or *ātman-jñāna.*[4] This case clearly shows that women in the *Vedic* age were educated and free enough to exercise their own judgment on vital matters. Nor is Maitreyī a solitary example of capable womanhood. There were the following other ladies of substance as well, namely, Ṛṣikā Ghoṣā who had earned this name just because she was fond of emphasizing the value of the *Vedas* everywhere; Dakśiṇā, so called because she would never tire of stressing the significance of *dāna* (gift, offering, endowment); Romśā, Lopāmudrā, Vāgabhṛṇi, all of whom excelled in giving accounts of the process of creation, and Juhu who became known for her sharp intellect. All these women of the *Saṁhitā* period enriched the *Vedic* lore; and, in the process, added to the intellectual status of women in general.

The *Saṁhitā* literature speaks of women as *Kulpālak* (family nurturer), *Dhruva* (steadfast), anchor of the whole society, the guiding agent of life, *Śivā* and *Kalyāṇī* that is the source of welfare and prosperity in general.

I turn now to show how in the Indian intellectual tradition woman has even been regarded as superior to man in many a way. Thus, see the following from *Ṛgveda* (V-61-6):

> ... Many a woman is more steadfast and better than the man who turns away from God ... and [does not offer] prayers.[5]

The *Śatapath Brāhmaṇ* argues for the pre-eminence of women by saying that, as mothers, they are the best and the foremost preceptors of children.

The *Vasiṣṭḥa Dharmasūtra* heightens the emphasis even more by observing that woman is hundred times superior to man in instructing and elevating a child (XIII-48). *Pārāśarsmṛti* declares that wife is the refuge of her husband in times of trouble, and that, therefore, she should not be made the victim of exploitation and oppression by him. It adds (Ch. IV.33) that as a snake-catcher can pull out a snake from its hole, similarly a pious woman can redeem her husband from moral turpitude. Another law-giver of ancient India, Āpastamba has a different, yet commonly acceptable way of arguing for the superiority of woman. He argues that in so far as a mother serves her son in numberless ways and quite selflessly, he should not desert her even if, for some reason, she happens to take to devious ways. He is quite emphatic in honouring the fair sex where he says that all must make way for a woman when she is treading a path (*Āpastamba Dharmasūtra* II-5-11-7).

Manu, who is regarded as the highest authority on social matters, unequivocally assigns to women the status of presiding deities in the home. According to him, there is no difference whatsoever, (Manu, IX-26) between wives who are destined to bear children and who provide the blessings of love and caring, and those idols that are put in the houses of men for worship, as symbols of good fortune and holiness.[6] He adds that where the female relatives are unhappy, the family soon perishes. He lays even greater emphasis on the need to honour women by declaring, in one of his very well-known verses, that the gods are pleased with those who honour women; and that where they are not honoured, even sacred rites do not yield the desired result.

The same sentiments have been variously expressed by other writers of *Dharmaśāstras.* Yājñavalkya, for instance, extols women so much as to call them earthly embodiments of all divine virtues. The typical qualities of women, we are told, are god-given gifts to them. The god *Soma* is supposed to have bestowed purity on women, *Gandharvas,* sweetness of speech; and *Agni,* all his warmth that quickens life. A more or less similar laudatory attitude to women is to be found in our epics. Our most impressive epic, *Mahābhārata,* looks on woman as the light and the very life of a home, and as the pre-eminent source of family happiness.

She has even been regarded as the presiding deity of prosperity and happiness, an embodiment of virtues like patience and forbearance, and therefore as the very diadem of a family. What is more, the *Mahābhārata* looks on women as the anchor not only of family life, but of the social organism. The very future of a country is said to depend on women, essentially because it is they who beget, and nurture children and impart the right *saṁskāras* (or value-based dispositions) to them. However, the most emphatic and comprehensive exaltation of the value of woman comes from the sage Viśvāmitra, who says categorically that ideally (or in principle) a wife is eminently helpful in enabling her husband to strive successfully after all the four principle objectives of life, namely, righteous living, securing material resources, gratification of desires, and spiritual emancipation. Here are some other relevant utterances from our sacred texts:

"Wives can elevate men from the mundane world" (*Durgā Saptaśati, Argalā Strotram*, 24).[7] "One *ācārya* surpasses ten ordinary teachers; one father surpasses one hundred *ācārya;* and above all, mother surpasses a thousand fathers" in respect of imparting a right sense of values to children (*Manu,* II, 145).[8] The *Mahābhārata* sounds a note which is easier to follow when it says, "Sweet-tongued wives are their husbands' friends on the occasion of joy; fathers, on occasions of religious observances; and mothers in hours of illness and woe" (*Mahābhārata, Ādiparva. 74/43).*[9]

Indeed, in the domestic life, women used to reign supreme. In regulating activities at home, her word would be final. Immediately after her marriage, she had to go to the house to be a mistress there *(Ṛgveda, X-85-26)*[10] and to exercise full loving sway over her husband's father, mother, brothers and sisters (Ibid., X-85-46).[11] In *Atharva Veda* she is repeatedly addressed as the queen of the house, who rules over all the members of the family as an ocean rules over ... the rivers ... by embracing them, so to say, open-heartedly (*Atharva, XIV, 1/43).*[12]

In Vedic India, indeed, woman occupied a very proud position in the household. She was the very axis on which the wheel of household life turned. It may here be added, in passing, that the words *Pati* and *Patnī* as used in *Ṛgveda* simply mean *master* and *mistress* respectively, and that this implies only a *difference* of sex, and does not at all hint as to which of the two is *superior* to the other. And if there is any talk of such superiority, the reference is not to man but to woman, as in the following from *Mahābhārata*: "Women, O King, should always be adored and treated with honour. [In a way,] there the very gods are said to be propitiated, where women are treated with respect" (*Mahābhārata, Anuśāsan Parva,* XVI-5). Here is something more in the same vein, from *Mahābhārata* again:

> Those houses which are cursed by women meet with destruction and ruin, as if scorched by some Atharvan rites. Such houses lose their splendour. Their growth and prosperity cease. (*Mahābhārata, Anuśāsan Parva,* XVI-6)

I may here add that scholars like Macdonell and Keith support the view that in ancient India women in homes were indeed treated with honour and due consideration. Incidentally, there were two main reasons for the importance attached to women in domestic life. First, it was believed that man was born with three principal debts, namely, to the *ṛṣis* or sages (*Ṛṣi ṛṇa*), to the deities (*Deva ṛṇa*) and to the ancestors *(Pitṛ ṛṇa);* and that these debts could be repaid in three ways, respectively; by studying the *Vedas*, offering sacrifices, and by begetting children (*Mbh.* XII-28-55). The last of these clearly highlights the value of women. Secondly, only a man with a family could provide proper hospitality to guests and holy men. This is why the *gṛhastha āśrama* was regarded as almost a mother in respect of giving shelter to all. As the sea received all rivers, so a good housewife welcomed everyone (*Mbh.* XII-269-6). It was believed that in the family life alone one could perform great penance, that is by serving the needy in society.

It is important to note that in ancient India society's attitude even towards a fallen woman – say, a prostitute – was quite different from what it is today. She was even considered auspicious enough to be invited to ceremonial occasions, the reason being that such a woman was regarded as the preserver of some of the sixty-fourt arts, specially music and dance. This indeed is what made her welcome at republican assemblies and royal courts.

With a fall in the status of women, the country also began to lose in character. So says *the Mahābhārata.* "In a house where women are honoured, there Gods are pleased. But where they are not honoured and are insulted, nothing done in that house yields good results."[12a]

Here we find a clear agreement of views between Manu and *Mahābhārata*. What is most striking is the fact that even Lord Śiva is said to become a *Śiva* (dead body) without '*Śakti*' because it is a woman's caring attitude which quickens one in difficult times (Saundarya Lahiri, Verse 1).[12b]

II

However, quite a few Western and Indian scholars have alleged that women occupied a very insignificant place in India's intellectual tradition (Susan Wadley, 'Women and the Hindu Tradition' in Rehana Ghadially ed., *Women in Indian Society,* New Delhi, Sage Publications, 1988, p. 30). Here are the main points which they focus on:

(a) The birth of a girl was always regarded as an unwelcome event.

(b) Women were not given proper education; so they were less qualified than men. There was no co-education.

(c) Women had no right in matters of divorce and remarriage.

My answer, here, is as follows:

Our Vedic literature indicates that there were people in ancient times who really wished the birth of a daughter; and so in one of the early *Upniṣads*, a certain ritual has been recommended to a householder for ensuring the birth of a scholarly daughter (*Bṛhadāraṇyaka Upaniṣad,* IV, 4-18).[13]

Cultured parents were often as anxious to get daughters as sons. Some thinkers have even pointed out that a talented and well behaved daughter could prove to be better than a son (*Samyutta Nikāya,* IIIc). Such a daughter was regarded as the pride of the family (*Kumārasaṁbhava, VI, 63).*[14]

The *Vanparva* of *Mahābhārata* (293, 17) contains the following assurance: "with the grace of lord Brahmā a powerful daughter (rstfLouh) will be born to you".[15] In a particular verse of *Yajurveda* the gods are blessing a bride by wishing her birth of both a son and a *daughter.*[16]

These citations indicate that the unfair view that the daughter is less desirable than the son was surely not accepted by all Indian social thinkers. There were quite a few people who realized that the view in question could inflict great harm on society and felt strongly that it had to be counteracted. They therefore championed the daughter's cause partly on the quite valid ground that patricides had always been a monopoly of the male sex, and that no father was ever known to have been killed by a daughter. There are cases on record where daughters like Kuntī and Lopāmudrā are said to have saved their parents from dire calamities. In the *Kathāsaritsāgara* by Somadeva it is said that one has no right to be, elated at the birth of a son and depressed at the birth of a daughter.

Now, turning to the criticism that less importance was given to the education of daughter, I may counter it as follows:

We have instances of lady poets in pre-Vedic period who were thesmelves composing hymns, some of which were even included in the *Vedic Saṁhitās.* According to the orthodox tradition itself, as recorded in *Sarvāṇukramaṇikā* there are as many as twenty women among the 'seers' or authors of *Ṛgveda.* Some of these may well have been mere mythical figures, but internal evidence shows that Lopāmudrā, Visvavārā, Sikatā, Nivavari and Ghoṣā, the authors of the *Ṛgveda* 1.79, V.28, VIII.90, IX. 81. 11-20, and X.39 and 40 respectively, were women in flesh and blood, who once actually lived in Hindu Society. The authors of X. 145 and 159 are undoubtedly ladies, though it may be doubted whether their real names were Indrāṇi and Śachi, as recorded by tradition. Among the authors and scholars to whose memory a daily prayer of respect is enjoined, a few ladies also figure such as Sulabhā, Maitreyī, Vādavā Pratithyī, and Gārgī-Vācaknavī (*Āśvalāyana Gṛhyasūtra,* III, 4, 3).[17]

Women students were divided into two classes *Brahmvādinis* and *Sadyovadhūs.* The former were lifelong students of theology and philosophy; the latter used to prosecute their studies only till their marriage at the age of 15 or 16. *Brahmvādinis* used to aim at a very high excellence in scholarship. Besides studying the *Vedas*, many of them used to specialise in *Pūrva Mīmāṁsā,* which discusses the diverse problems connected with *Vedic* sacrifices. *Mahābhāṣya* speaks of a theologian named *Kāśakṛtsna* who composed a work on *Mīmāṁsā* called *Kāśakritsni;* and lady scholars who used to specialize in it, were designated as *Kāśakṛtisnas.*

In a congregation of philosophical debate held under the auspices of king Janaka, the most subtle philosophical questions were initiated for discussion by the lady philosopher Gārgī. She launched her attack on Yājñavalkya with admirable coolness and confidence. The topics of her inquiry were so abstruse and esoteric in character, that Yājñvalkya declined to discuss them in public. The searching cross-examination of Yājñavalkya by Gārgī shows that she was a dialectician *par excellence* (Br. Up. III, 6 and 8). Of a few distinguished poetesses who appear to have composed poetry of a really high order, Silabhattārikā, we learn, was famous for her easy and graceful style. Vijayankā's fame was second only to that of Kālidāsa. She seems to have attained a really high position among Sanskrit writers, for a distinguished critic and poet like Rājaśekhara likens her to goddess Saraswatī herself.

The third charge can be easily refuted by pointing out that women have been granted the right to divorce and remarriage in a number of our *Dharmaśāstras.* Even Manu, who has been the most frequent target of glib criticism, has declared that a wife is not to be censured where she abandons her husband if he is impotent or suffering from an incurable or contagious disease (IX, 79), and that she may well remarry if her previous marriage has not consummated (IX, 175-176). Again, in his *Arthaśāstra,* Kauṭilya says that the childless wife of a husband who has gone abroad, without making any provision for her proper maintenance, and who does not return even after eight years, should be allowed to remarry (*Arthaśāstra*). Similarly, Pārāśara has expressed the view that if the husband has been away for long and remains untraced, is dead, or has taken to *sannyāsa* (that is, the life of renunciation) and so has gone away for good; or if he has been convicted for some misdeed, the wife may well remarry (Pārāśara IV.30). Kauṭilya has ruled that a husband cannot divorce his wife without her consent, and that divorce is permissible if both husband *and wife* have ill will for each other. In respect of a widow, the intellectual tradition has allowed three options: first, to remain unmarried and practice celibacy; second, to have a child through *niyoga;* and third, to remarry. Several heroes whose account appears in the *Mahābhārata* and *Purāṇas* were born out of *niyoga,* though Manu does not allow this option to a widow who already has a son to support her. Further, though it was surely not imposed on them, celibacy was surely recommended as an ideal for widows. (*Pārāśara, iv 31*). At the same time, due attention was also paid to provision of proper economic relief for widows. (*Mahābhārata, Śāntiparva,* 24; 86). Gautam proposed that a widow may be regarded as a co-heir of her husband's property along with other close relatives (*Sapiṇḍas).* Viṣṇu goes to the extent of saying that if her sons desert her, the whole estate should go to the widow (XVII, 43). It was, however, Bṛhaspati who championed the right of widow to inherit the property most strongly. He pointed out that the *Vedas,* the *Smṛtis,* and sages of antiquity have unanimously declared that husband and wife are the joint owners of family property and that they together constitute one legal personality.

It is, therefore, quite wrong to say, as has been contended by Kumkum Roy (*Women's Studies in India: Contours of Change,* pp. 98, 99) that women in ancient India had no right of inheritance. Indeed, if we consider the socio-cultural context of that time, we would be led to believe that with some limitations, women enjoyed equal property rights with men.

They were debarred from getting the property of their fathers only if their own brothers were alive. At the same time, in the event of her mother's death, she was regarded as the sole inheritor of the latter's property. Most of the *Smṛtikāras* have categorically asserted that the transfer of *strīdhana* should be towards the women inheritors only, and that where a man has no son, the entire property must go to the women inheritors. This has been openly asserted by Manu and others at several places. This clearly proves that our ancient system of inheritance had more of a horizontal than a vertical structure.

Let me also cite those two verses of *Yājñavalkya* where he has clearly suggested that wives and daughters should be given preference in case where a man has no sons (*Yājñavalkya,* II. 135-136).[18] His view, which is very significant, may be put thus : The lawfully wedded wife; the daughter and (the daughter's son); the parents; the brothers, their sons, cognatic relatives,—all have to be regarded as rightful claimants to a man's property *in this order of succession* in case he does not leave any male issue behind him (P.V. Kane, *History of Dharmaśāstras,* Vol. III, 1946 edition, p. 701).[19] *Yājñavalkya* and Viṣṇu among *Smṛti* writers were probably the first to clearly enunciate the rule that the wife was the foremost heir of a man if he died without leaving a male issue. Bṛhaspati makes the wife the first heir of a sonless man and supports his opinion with reasons. He says:

> In the *Vedas* and in the doctrines of the *Smṛtis,* as also in popular usage, the wife is regarded as one-half of a husband's being, and equal in sharing the consequences of his good and evil acts. How then can anybody except his widow be regarded as a lawful heir of his property?

Again, a text attributed to Vṛddha Manu says:

> The wife alone, if she has no son and no illicit sexual relations with anyone and leads a life of religious observances, may offer *piṇḍa* to her deceased husband *and take his entire estate.* (Vṛddha Manu quoted by Mitākśarā on Yājñavalkya. II, 135, *Dāyabhāga* XI. 1.7, *Vivādaratnākara,* p. 589)[20]

Even Manu asks, suggestively, how can another person except the daughter (along with son) take the wealth of the deceased when she, who is the very self of the deceased, lives (Manu, Chapter IX, Verse 30. English version taken from P.V. Kane's *History of Dharmaśāstras).*[21] The most emphatic assertion comes from Prajāpati where he says that the king should punish as thieves those relatives who try to prevent a widow from getting her husband's estate (Prajāpati quoted by *Smṛti Candrikā. II.* p.

294, *Vivādacintāmaṇi,* p. 151. English version from P.V. Kane's, *History of Dharmaśāstras,* Vol. III, 1946 edition, p. 712).

I may point out, in passing, that quite a few criticisms levelled against the place of women in India's intellectual tradition arise from a clear misinterpretation of our ancient texts. Of the several examples that I can give in support of what I here say, let me draw readers' attention to just one (*Manusmṛti* Ch. IX Verse 33):[22]

> Woman may be taken as a field, and man as a seed. All living beings arise from the union of the field and seed.

Focussing on verse 33 of Chapter IX of *Manusmṛti,* Kumkum Roy interprets it as follows :

> Here, the womb is equated with the field, in which men sow *seed,* [the precise] offspring being determined by the nature of *the latter,* with the former conceived as a [merely] passive, supportive receptacle. The field, moreover, is ideally owned by a man, and, by extension, the produce of the field is his.

Hence, the critic concludes, man may well be regarded as superior to woman (Kumkum Roy's essay in *Women and the Hindu Right,* ed. Tanika Sarkar and Urvashi Butalia, Kali For Women, New Delhi, 1995, p. 18).

Now, to my mind, even a casual look at the verse in question shows that here there is not the slightest hint of the categorical view that, by virtue of being a mere 'field', woman is inferior to man. How, indeed, can we decide as to which of the two is of greater value—the seed or the field? The seed remains merely itself until it impregnates the field, so to say; and the field is a mere stretch or receptacle until it is fertilized by the seed. What is more, the very next verse (34) of *Manusmṛti* makes it clear that, according to Manu, the seed or the male person is more important in some contexts; *and the field (or woman) in quite a few others* (Chap. IX, Verse 34). Here we also have the additional suggestion that where the seed and the field *alike* contribute to the act of begetting or production, the maternity involved is commendable. I may, in the end, cite the following powerful words of P.V. Kane:

> Hindu law does not favour the distribution of a deceased man's estate among the several relatives, as some other systems do. It is greatly to the credit of the ancient Hindu law that it boldly gave all the separate property of a deceased male to women, viz., to the

widow and after her to the daughter, in preference to the man's own father or brother or nephew. (P.V. Kane, *History of Dharmaśāstras*, Vol. III, 1946, p. 711)

Notes

1. नासदासीन्नोसदासीत्तदानीं नासीद्रजो नो व्योमा परोयत्।
   किमावरीवः कुह कस्यशर्मन्नम्भः किमासीद्गहनं गभीरम्।। ऋ. X/२२९–१।।

   न मृत्युरासीदमृतं न तर्हि न रात्र्या अह्न आसीत प्रकेतः।
   आनीदवातं स्वधया तदेकं तस्माद्धान्यन्न पुरः किं चनास। ऋ. X/१२९/२

2. न तत्र सूर्यो भाति न चन्द्रतारकं, नेमा विद्युतो भान्ति कुतोऽयमग्निः
   तमेव भान्तमनुभाति सर्वं, तस्य भासा सर्वमिदं विभाति।। (कठोपरिषद, II, ii, 15)

3. आत्मानं रथिनं विद्धि शरीरं रथमेव तु
   बुद्धिं तु सारथि विद्धि मनः प्रग्रहमेव च।। (कठोपनिषद, I, iii, 3-4)

   इन्द्रियाणि हयानाहुर्विषयान् तेषु गोचरान्।
   आत्मेन्द्रियमनोयुक्तं भात्तेत्याहु र्मनीषिणः

4. See, Bṛhdāraṇyak Upaniṣad/IV/V

5. उतत्वा स्त्री शशीयंसी पुंसो भवति वस्यसी।
   अदेवत्रादराधसः।। Ṛgveda V/61.6

6. प्रजनार्थ महाभागाः पूजार्हा ग्रहदीप्तयः
   स्त्रियः श्रियश्च गेहेषु न विशेषोऽस्ति कश्चन।

7. पत्नीं मनोरमां देहि मनोवृत्तानुसारिणीम्।
   तारिणीं दुर्गसंसार सागरस्य कुलोद्भवाम्।। (दुर्गा सप्तशती, अर्गला स्तोत्रम्, २४)

8. उपाध्यायान्दशाचार्य आचार्याणां शतं पिता।
   सहस्त्रं तु पितृन्माता गौरवेणतिरिच्यते।। मनुस्मृति, अध्याय II, 145

9. सा भार्या या गृहे दक्षा सा भार्या या प्रजावती।
   साभार्या या पतिप्राणा सा भार्या या पतिव्रता।।
   अर्ध भार्या मनुष्यस्य भार्या श्रेष्ठतमः सखा।
   भार्या मूलं त्रिवर्गस्य भार्या मूलं तरिष्यतः।।
   भार्यावन्तः क्रियावन्तः सभार्या गृहमेधिनः।

भार्यावन्तः प्रमोदन्ते भार्यावन्तः श्रियान्विताः।।
सखायः प्रविविक्तेषु भवन्त्येताः प्रियंवदाः। आदिपर्व ७४१–४०–४३

10. पूषा त्वेतो नयतु हस्तगृह्याश्विना त्वा प्र वहतां रथेन।
गृहान् गच्छ गृहपत्नी यथासो वशिनी त्वं विदथमा वदासि।। Ṛgveda X/85/26

11. सम्राज्ञी श्वशुरे भव सम्राज्ञी श्वश्र्वाः भवि।
ननान्दरि सम्राज्ञी भव सम्राज्ञी अधि देवृषु।। Ṛgveda X/85/46

12. यथा सिन्धुर्नदीनां साम्राज्यं सुषुवे वृषा।
एवा त्वं सम्राज्ञ्येधि पत्युरस्तं परेत्य।। अथर्ववेद XIV/1/43

सम्राज्ञ्येधि श्वशुरेषु सम्राज्ञ्युत देवृषु।
ननान्दुः सम्राज्ञ्येधि सम्राज्ञ्युत श्वश्र्वाः।। अथर्व. XIV/1/44

12a. स्त्रियाँ यत्र च पूज्यन्ते रमन्ते तत्र देवताः।।
अपूजिताश्च यत्रैताः सर्वास्तत्राफलाः क्रियाः।।

12b. शिवःशक्त्या युक्तो यदि भवतिशक्तः प्रभवितुम्।
न चेदेवं देवो न खलु कुशलः स्पन्दितुमपि।।

13. अथ य इच्छेद् दुहिता में पंडिता जायेत,
सर्वमायुरियादिति तिलौदनं पाचयित्वा सर्पिष्मन्तमश्नीयातामीश्वरौ जनयितवै।।
बृहदारण्यक उपनिषद 4-4-17

14. एतेवयममी दाराः कन्येयं कुलजीवितम्।
ब्रूत येनात्र वः कार्यमनास्था बाह्यवस्तुषु।। कुमार VI/63

15. प्रसादाच्चैव तस्मात् ते स्वूयम्भु विहिताद् भुवि।
कन्या तेजस्विनी सौम्य क्षिप्रमेव भविष्यति।। Vanparva: 293.17

16. ह्वदे त्वा मनसे त्वा दिवे त्वा सूर्याय त्वा।
उर्ध्वमिममध्वरं दिवि देवेषु होत्रा यच्छ।। (यजुर्वेद ६/२५)

17. सुयन्तुजैमिनिवैशम्पायन पैलसूत्रभाष्यभारतमहाभारतधर्माचार्या–
जानन्तिवाहविगार्ग्य गौतमशाकल्यवाभ्रव्यमाण्डव्यमाण्डूकेया
गार्गीवाचक्नवी वडवाप्रातीथेसीयसुलभामैत्रेयी–आश्वलायनगृह्यसूत्रम् २ अध्याय, खण्ड ४, सूत्र–३

18. याज्ञवल्क्य स्मृति, व्यवहाराध्याय,श्लोक ११५

19. पत्नी दुहितरश्चैव पितरौ भ्रातरस्तथा।

तत्सुता गोत्रजा बन्धु शिष्यसब्रह्मचारिणः।।
याज्ञवल्क्यस्मृति व्यवहाराध्याय १३५

एषामभावे पूर्वस्य धनभागुत्तरोत्तरः।
स्वर्यातस्य ह्यपुत्रस्य सर्ववर्णेष्वयं विधिः।। १३६

20. वृद्धमनुरपि पत्न्याः समग्रधन संबंध वक्ति–

'अपुत्राशयनं भर्तुः पालयन्ती व्रते स्थिता।
पत्न्येव दद्यात् तत्पिण्डं कृत्स्नमंशं लभेत च'।।
मिताक्षरा याज्ञवल्क्य II-135

21. यथैवात्मा तथा पुत्रः पुत्रेण दुहिता समा।
तस्यामात्मनि जीवन्त्यां कथमन्यो हरेद्धनम्।। विवादरत्नाकर 84/1070

22. क्षेत्रभूता स्मृता नारी बीजभूतः स्मृतः पुमान–
सेना बीज समायोगात्संम्भवः सर्वदेहिनाम्।।

II

Women in *Dharmaśāstras*: Search for a Perspective

3

Women and the *Dharmaśāstras*

Kapil Kapoor

I

Hindu young women today are the most vital segment of the Indian society. They have entered all the fields and have excelled everywhere, including sports. They are the backbone of medicine and education and IT and civil services,[1] are piloting civil aircraft and even flying fighters for the Indian Air Force. This of course is no surprise to the Hindus as the Hindu traditions celebrate both intellectual women such as the mathematician Lilavati and warrior women such as Rani Durgawati and able rulers such as Ahalyabai Holkar as they also celebrate great mothers such as Gautami and Jijabai.[2]

The contextually necessary restrictions imposed on Hindu women during the vandalizing Muslim period have made us forgetful about the true place and role that women have always had in Hindu society. Indian women, Hindu women, are once again very vital today. They have tremendous problems, challenges. All around these challenges abound and women accept them and try their best to come to terms with them. They suffer from no legal disabilities.[3] They are governed by the very modern Hindu law[4] and its practice.[5] They are privileged to belong to a society that is amenable to reform by law and has always been reflecting on social and moral issues and evolving in the light of new knowledge.

II

Hindu law has an ancient pedigree rooted as it is rooted in the world's earliest attested continuous and cumulative body of sociological literature, *Sūtra, Śāstra* and *Nibandha.* All these three kinds of treatises fall in the general rubric of *Dharmaśāstra* and in the typology of discourse are designated as *Smṛti* next in the validity of knowledge only to *Śruti. Dharmaśāstras* deal with *dharma* in the sense, among its many senses, of duty or righteousness. It is the meta-assumption of Indian sociological thought that performance of one's enjoined duty in a righteous manner ensures *mokśa*, freedom from suffering here and now.[6] The period of *Dharmasūtras*[7] extends from approximately 800 BC to 5/300 BC. The period of the *Dharmaśāstras*[8] extends roughly from 3rd century BC to 7th century AD. From 700 AD to 1794 is the period of *Nibandha*[9] literature.

III

The *Dharmasūtras* are classed as *Kalpa*, one of the six *Vedāṅgas*, sciences auxiliary to the study of *Vedas* and fall into three groups according to the subject matter – *Śrauta* (performance of Vedic ritual), *Gṛhya* (ceremonies of domestic life such as marriage, first pregnancy, oblations to the ancestors) and *Dharma* (right, religion, law, duty, custom and usage with reference to the individual).Their subject matter ranges over time-honoured practices, duties of *varṇa, āśrama*, king's duties and governance, rules about food, duties of women, their property, customary practice, popular behaviour, rectifying wrongs done intentionally or unintentionally or from folly. They treat actual practices and underline those that are popularly considered as ideal conduct and atonement.

The *Dharmaśāstras* came to be composed later to meet new challenges and make new provisions in matters of *dharma*. As is the wont in the Indian intellectual tradition, these treatises superseded the earlier *Sūtras*. The major ones are those by Manu, Nārada, Yājñavalkya, Pārāśara, Bṛhaspati and Kātyāyana. Just as these treatises attest the evolving nature of Indian sociological thinking, their different injunctions on several matters show the non-normative approach of Indian sociology. Thirdly, they acknowledge the primacy of usage and practice demonstrating that they are empirical, not abstract theoretical, texts.

The *Dharmaśāstras* thus are not prescriptive texts – they are primarily records of wide, varied, even divergent, practices and customs. So they differ from each other on crucial matters.[10] Thus, for example,

Baudhāyana differs from Āpastamba on several points. He approves, unlike Āpastamba, of *niyoga*, having a child by a man other than the husband and recognizes eight forms of marriage[11] . *Hārītadharmasūtra* recognizes eight forms of marriage but replaces third and fourth by *Kṣātra* and *Mānuṣa*. Hārīta also distinguishes two kinds of women: (i) *brahmavādinī*, and (ii) *sadyovadhū*. *Brahmavādinī* is devoted to knowledge and has *upanayana,* studies the *Vedas* and earns her living by begging alms. Vasiṣṭha allows remarriage of virgin widows and allows *niyoga* to married women. Śankha and Likhita allow Brahmins to marry all the four castes[12] and allow *niyoga* even when the husband is dead. *Viṣṇudharmasūtra* allows inter-caste marriage and accepts *niyoga*[13]. Kauṭilya is the most radical – he allows widow remarriage, remarriage of women the whereabouts of whose husbands are not known, allows desertion of the husband by the wife if the husband is of bad character, is a traitor, an outcaste or an impotent. He also allows divorce on grounds of mutual hatred. *Kātyāyanasmṛti* is especially devoted to the rights of women, including property rights –*strīdhana.* Thus variation is not only noted – it is recognized as valid.

IV

How do the *Śāstras* handle conflicting practices or theoretical doubt about what is right and what is wrong – a situation that is quite common in the vast social reality that was and is Hindu India? In a remarkable exercise at systematization, the *Śāstras* lay down a cline of valid acceptability strategies to handle situations of *dharma saṅkaṭa* :

(i) reconcile the variation/opposites if possible

(ii) prefer one in accordance with *nyāya*, principles of judgement, and *tarka*, logic

(iii) reject obsolete practices that are no longer acceptable to people

(iv) reject rules not applicable to changed times

(v) reject rules intolerable to people

(vi) reconstruct intention and implication and give a new form to the doubtful practice

(vii) prefer a fact of life to text, practice to theory, and

In all cases *ācāra*, actual conduct of the *Śiṣtas*, the cultured[14] , prevails. A general order of authority is also laid down to help the individual to decide for himself in such situations:

Śruti (Vedic texts/injunctions)=> *Smṛti*(*Śāstrās*)=> *Śila*(the moral framework) =>*Ācāra* (customary practice)=> *Śiṣta vyavahāra* (conduct of the cultured) =>, failing all, *ātmā*, one's own conscience.

V

Crucial to the whole science of Indian social thought is the construct of *dharma*.

What is *dharma*?

It is a modelling principle for the individual, the family and the society and also lays down preferred forms of conduct, interpersonal relationships and duty.

Pārāśara makes the distinction between *sthūla dharma*, gross, self-evident duty or apparent rightness of something and *sūkśma dharma*, subtle notion of duty and of what is right, a notion that may violate and transcend the apparent duty or rightness. Thus, one may transgress gross *dharma* by telling a lie to avoid causing avoidable suffering to someone. Kṛṣṇa's advice to Arjuna to resort to stratagems to get rid of the enemies violates the precepts of *dharma yuddha*, righteous war, but serves the higher *dharma* of getting rid of evil forces not amenable to reason and thereby ensuring wider peace. On the other hand, gross *dharma* may permit a course of action but from the point of view of subtle *dharma*, refraining from such a course may be more meritorious.

Dharma thus cannot be absolutely defined. *Dharma* has in fact been defined variously in the tradition. Manu defines it as "what is followed by those learned in the *Vedas*" and also as "what is approved by the conscience of the virtuous who are free of hatred and inordinate affection". Medhātithi defines it simply as enjoined duty. *Nyāya* defines it in three different ways: 'that which brings welfare of all/others'; 'enjoined duty', and 'natural characteristics and propensities as to what a man should do'. Manu says that that there is hardly any activity of man which is not prompted by desire (*kāma*)but to act solely on desire is not praiseworthy and therefore to enable man to act properly, guided by *Samyagavṛtti*, a total view, *dharma* is promulgated (II.2-5). There is in other words, a marked ethical inflection on the concept of *dharma* and values such as non-violence, forgiveness, truth, purity and control of sense are almost universally accepted as necessary correlates of *dharma*. The *Mahābhārata* says categorically: "*Dharma* has been postulated only for the welfare and development of living beings; so, that which achieves this is *dharma*. Such is the definition laid down by the learned" (XII. 109.10).

The *Dharmaśāstras* discuss both the actual and the desirable aspects of man's life. And these are discussed and described under the rubric of *dharma*. In these texts, *dharma*, as part of *trivarga*, the three ends of life, emerges as the super-ordinate principle, the ultimate touchstone of what should be done, of what is right and of what is wrong.[15] The concept is not easy to define but it is clearly a social concept. The word is derived from the root *dhṛ*[16] which means 'to support' or 'to sustain'. Its meaning ranges from the qualities and characteristic of things to the highest virtue, natural characteristics and tendencies of human beings as also what men should or ought to do. As a heterogeneous concept, it is necessarily plural[17] as it does not exclude *ācāra*, customary practice, handed down from generation to generation within a community.[18] In fact, in Hindu society, a regulatory principle such as *dharma* can be enunciated only as applicable differently to different classes of human beings. *Dharma* thus is a socially consolidating scheme which encompasses both what obtains widely and also what ought to be done. It includes, as acceptable, wide ranging divergent practices (I.108-110) and even practices peculiar and restricted to places, classes and families are accepted (*MS* I.118).

Both in its generic sense (*sādhāraṇa*) and its specific (*viśeṣa*) senses, *dharma* contributes to the preservation, progress and welfare of human society, and in a wider sense of the whole world. This principle of *Dharma* is thus the over-riding principle; it is the touchstone of the value of all human pursuits and also their only valid goal. The *Bṛhadāraṇyaka Upaniṣad* says (1.4.11-14) that this *dharma* is stronger than even the ruling class and that there is nothing greater than dharma. *Dharma* is thus like the rule of law – something respected above the ruler and that bound the ruler also. If the society respects it, it protects itself; when the society starts violating it, it undermines itself (*Ṛgveda* VIII.1.5).

There is an imperative to this conception of *dharma* – it is a principle that needs to be upheld at all times but not by doing violence to others. Manu observes that in pursuit of *dharma* one must not cause trouble to any being (*Manusmṛti* II.238). Thus for example, though one must never compromise truth for being nice, yet truth should be spoken only if it causes no hurt (*Manusmṛti* IV.138). Again he says that it should be taught without hurting people (*MS* II.159) and declares that *dharma* which ends up unhappily and is derided by the world should be abandoned (IV.176). *Mahābhārata* again clinches the point by asserting that *dharma* is that which is attended by the welfare of the world and by noninjury to beings (XII.109.15).

VI

Dharma is a complex sociological construct. The *Purāṇas* attribute six clear, distinct meanings of this term:

(i) *kartavya*, duty or practice of the elders,

(ii) *manovṛttin*, tendencies of the mind/psychological properties such as anger,

(iii) *indrion kā kārya*, functions of the senses,

(iv) *guṇon ki kriyā,* action of the qualities (viz., 'burning' is the *dharma* of 'heat'),

(v) *vṛtti-anukūlakārya*, action according to innate ability (*dharma* of the agriculturist),

(vi) collective mode of communities or 'worlds' (viz., *laukika dharma,* worldly duties, *sāmājika dharma,* societal obligations, including that of the individual).

The synonyms of the word *dharma* shed further light on the ethical substance of this core concept of the *Dharmaśāstras.* The synonyms are:

(i) *puṇya* (the good), *śreya* (the preferred as against the desired), *sukṛta* (the good deed) according to the seminal Sanskrit thesaurus, the *Amarkoṣa*,

(ii) *nyāya* (justice),*svabhāva* (the given self as against the acquired one), *ācāra* (customary practice), *ahiṁsā* (non-violence) according to *Upaniṣads,*

(iii) *satsaṅga*, keeping company of the good, *ārhata,* wisdom according to the 11th-12th century *Jaina* thinker.

Three dimensions are quite clear – *dharma* as the primary **goal of life** (first of the four ends of life), **duty** according to one's position or status or condition in life (*dharma* of the eldest son or husband or mother or wife), and **conduct** both in the private and public sphere. In all the three senses, the concept has **a marked ethical inflection**.

Of these three, *dharma* as duty is central from the point of view of societal obligations and interpersonal relations.

VII

We can construct the *dharmaśāstric* conception of women in all the three dimensions:

(i) There is no difference between men and women as far as the goal of life, the first *puruṣārtha*, is concerned – both men and women seek liberation from here and now, *mokśa.*[19]

(ii) Duty of men and women differs on account of their 'bio-social' differences in the context of Indian society. Woman as a mother is the fulcrum of the core social unit called 'family' and ensures both nourishment and continuity of the network of relationships that is the first condition of the happiness of the individuals in a social framework.

(iii) Their conduct, *ācāra,* is also expected to be different for the same bio-social differences.

There is a general 'philosophy of womanhood' in this thought. Her fragility is recognized as also the duty of her father/brothers to marry her to a worthy man.[20] But she is the bedrock of the family.[21] In Indian thought, the source of happiness of the individual and the society is the network of human relationships and this network is centered in the 'family'. Therefore 'family' is the all important social unit around which all social structure is built. Wife-Mother is therefore the keystone of the social arch. She is *Lakśmī*, the one responsible for husbanding the resources.[22] As such she must be honoured.[23] No rites or rituals can be performed without her. No one can take away her *strīdhana*, gold and silver given to her by her father at the time of her marriage. In receiving respect in public, she takes precedence over father and teacher.

It is an amazing code considering that it was first codified almost 4,000 years ago. Its validity is established by its success in ensuring continuity of the Hindu way of life. Though modern Western influence has impacted sections of the educated, urban Hindus, the large masses still adhere to this *model* code.

A careful reading and a theory bound interpretation of texts will resolve many dilemmas that modern readers or thinkers experience when they read the *Dharmaśāstras*. For example, the condemnatory passages, according to the *Mīmāṁsā* rules of interpretation, are understood as praise of the opposite. We must also historicize the text and put it in the context of the times. Thirdly, we must clearly grasp the nature of these texts –

they are not prescriptive. They describe and accept widely divergent practices and also describe what ought to be and that too in relation to the 'cultured', the *Śiṣṭas*, the people whose example others follow.

There is no one law and a remarkable eclecticism marks the reasoned discourse about such controversial issues as widow remarriage and divorce. There is no dogmatism and three stand-points are present:

(i) recording what obtains in the world as a result of *kāma*, physical needs and desires,

(ii) conceding the facts that are in vogue, and

(iii) the personal or the ideal opinion.

And when we move from one *Dharmaśāstra* to the others, we find that the debate is a 'multi-logue' and several contending points of view are argued. There is therefore no substance in holding the texts responsible for whatever ills afflicted or afflicts Hindu women. On the contrary, all that is good about the situation of women can be traced back to the *Śāstric* enunciations and records with a remarkable sense of recognition. And some of them are even more modern than the modern societies as for example when they declare that a woman, married or unmarried, has a right to have a child from the man she wants to or when Kauṭilya composes two whole chapters (Chapter III.2-3) on marriage and women's rights and discusses at length crimes against women (Chapter IV.11) and devotes a whole chapter to 'Sexual Relations with Immature Girls'(Chapter IV.12) and says categorically that no man has a right to have sex with a women without her consent.

The conceptualization of women in fact takes place from three points of view: ontological, as individual and as social. As an individual, a woman is seen as fragile and delicate physically in a certain sense but emotionally and spiritually stronger than man. As a social being, she is central to the whole social structure in her bio-social role as mother.

It is the profound ontological conceptualization of women which is uniquely Indian. Ontologically, woman is a primal force, the *Śakti-tattva*, the energy principle. This needs to be reconciled to the *Sāṁkhya puruṣa-prakṛti* structure in which *prakṛti* is erroneously understood by modern commentators as the female principle. In fact, *prakṛti* is 'matter' and *puruṣa* is 'energy'–the word *puruṣa* in *Sāṁkhya*, etymologically, means 'that which inhabits the body', that is *ātmā* which is a spark of the universal creative energy, the '*parama-ātmā*' or *Brāhmaṇa* (of *Vedānta*). It may be noted parenthetically that the word *ātmā* grammatically is feminine gender. So *ātmātattva* is *Śakti-tattva. Strī-tattva* is a *dharma* of the physical body. Woman therefore in the Hindu *Śāstra* apart from being the source of life and happiness is recognized as a spiritual force as well – it is said that man is *yājñapradhāna*, action-oriented but woman is *tapapradhāna*, devotion-oriented.

To conclude, in Indian philosophy, the universe is seen as a vast pulsating life. That life is not manifest in all in one grade alone – it (consciousness, the expression of life) sleeps in metal, is awake in plants, moves and knows in animals and knows *that it knows in human beings.* Progress beyond man is not in the physical domain but in the cultural and social domain and then in the spiritual domain. As in physical, in the socio-cultural domain as well, higher levels or forms of being involve greater complexity and that complexity has the potential for anarchy – with the breakdown of any one part the whole will collapse. For growth and sustenance in the social-cultural domain, a close knit inter-dependent unity and coordination are needed to provide the individual the environment for his growth and elevation. The Hindu view of life therefore assigns functions to all the segments and to individuals – each has a *dharma* and to understand the *dharma* of one segment, one will need to look at the *dharma* of all parts of that system be it the family or the society. The *dharma* of women is contingent on the *dharma* of men and vice versa – no doubt about it at all.

Notes

1. This year the civil services topper is a girl, Ms. Mona Pruthi.
2. It is significant that in Indian history some of the greatest men are known by their mothers – '*Gautamīputra* Śātkarṇi', '*Dakṣiputra* Pāṇini'. The *Chāndogya Upaniṣad* narrative of Satyakām is an assertion of the primacy of the mother - the sage impressed with the truthfulness of his mother Jābālā tells him that henceforth he shall be known as 'Satyakāma Jābāli', Satyakāma son of Jābālā. In the form that Satyakāma is asked to fill up for his admission to the University, he is asked to name his mother only.
3. Article 15.1-3 ensures this.

4. Codified law consists of eight enactments and two amendments: (i) Hindu Widows' Remarriage Act 1856; (ii) Special Marriages Act 1954; (iii) Hindu Marriage Act 1955, Amendment Act 1976; (iv) Hindu Succession Act 1956; (v) Hindu Adoptions and Maintenance Act 1956; (vi) Dowry Prohibition Act 1961; (vii) Hindu Minority and Guardianship Act 1956; (viii) Hindu Widows' Property Act 1997, Amended 2005.
5. There are more than 2000 judicial decisions on record pertaining to these enactments.
6. This is how *Sāṁkhya* defines *mokśa* as the supreme well-being which is the goal of the four ends of life, the *puruṣārthas*. See *Sāṁkhyasūtra* 1.1.1-5
7. Some of the more important *Dharmasūtras* are of Gautam, Baudhāyana, Āpastamba, Vasiṣṭha, Viṣṇu and Hārīta.
8. Principal ones are of Nārada, Manu, Yājñavalkaya, Bṛhaspati, Kātyāyana and Pārāśara.
9. *Nibandhas* are glosses in major modern Indo-Aryan languages, Marathi, Kannḍa, Malayalam on *Dharmaśāstras*. Their logic of argumentation is founded on *Mīmāṁsā* rules of interpretation. Pursued by some of the best minds such as Medhātithi, Vijñāneśwara, Kullukabhaṭṭa, these were composed in different parts of India and functioned as law in the particular area. Most of this literature is lying around as unscrutinized, unpublished manuscripts.
10. So there is no absolutism in Hindu thought and practices. There is no one Hindu custom , no one Hindu injunction. Instead plurality, variation, is accepted and celebrated. Therefore, India is pluralistic not because so many races settled here but because Hinduism is intrinsically pluralistic and provided a 'Home' to so many diverse cultures.
11. Brahma, Daiva, Ārṣa, Prajāpatya, Āsura, Gandharva, Rākśasa, Paiśāca.
12. Manu allows this in one place but excludes at another place.
13. The almost universal acceptance of *niyoga* even for an unmarried woman shows a remarkable recognition of the psychic, physical and social need of a woman to have a child of her own. This also partly explains the ready acceptance of adoption in the Hindu society.
14. Patañjali in the first *āhnlka* of his *Mahābhāṣya* defines the cultured, ṣiṣta, as one "whose material goods are constituted by a jar of grain, who devotes himself to knowledge without any motive or purpose and excels in it, is *śiṣṭa*".
15. One of the unfortunate memory lapses of Indians – particularly the English-educated Indians is their complete confusion about the concept of *dharma*. In the often-repeated ideal of *dharma-nirpekśa*, *dharma* is equated with religion in the sense of an organized, church-based, priest-ruled belief system. Noth-

ing could be farther from the meaning of *dharma*. (The appropriate expression that captures the intended meaning is *matanirpekśa*.)

16. Akṛ-adi parasmaipada seit verb-root *(vide Pāṇiṇi's Dhatupāṭha)*.

17. It is important to remember that *dharma* is not laid down as something absolute or universal – it is constituted differentially for place, community, time and individuals.

18. *M S I*.107-10. There are immemorial customs peculiar to places classes, families, guilds, fringe communities and republican groups.

19. We will not dwell here on this profound concept of *mokśa*.

20. "...better she remain a spinster than she marry a worthless man". (*MS* IX.89)

21. In Indian thought, the source of happiness of the individual and the society is the network of human relationships and this network is centred in the 'family'. Therefore 'family' is the all important social unit around which all social structure is built. Wife-Mother is therefore the keystone of the social arch.

22. So in *Śiṣṭa* families, whatever a man earns, he hands it over to his wife.

23. "Where they are not honoured, all good acts become futile" (*MS* III.56).

4

Social Dimensions of the Discourse on Women and Sex as Reflected in *Manusmṛti* – the Earliest Known Indian Code of Law

Pushpa Tiwari

Dharmaśāstra texts are viewed by a group of modern scholars as the fountainhead of every evil plaguing the contemporary Hindu society. There are so many women academic-activist groups who celebrate their so-called modern emancipation by performing the annual ritual of burning the text of *Manusmṛti*. In contemporary politics and feminist agenda, the expression of such phrases as *'Manuvāda'* and *'Manuvādī'* have acquired, almost, a legitimate status. Such acts of academic violence notwithstanding, the continuity of *Dharmaśāstras* as a living tradition, warrants for revisiting the vast canvas of *Dharmaśāstra* texts for their proper understanding and contextualization.

Nowadays, it has become imperative on the part of policy makers to discuss the issue of sex education for and sex awareness among teenage students, so as to address the problem of sexual abuse and also that of sex related crimes and diseases like AIDS. Keeping this pertinent burning issue in mind I have chosen the theme of this paper. The aim of this paper is to situate the theme of this seminar in its historical setting through the process of correlating the textual tradition of *Dharmaśāstra* – particularly of *Manusmṛti,* with that of the archaeological evidences reflecting on the socio-cultural milieu of c.200 BC to c. 200 AD – the time frame generally accepted for *Manusmṛti.* While dealing with the discourse on women and sex as found in *Manusmṛti*, one cannot ignore the archaeologically revealed/discovered evidences constituting the concrete tangible material image of the society where the *Dharmaśāstra* texts were formulated to regulate the daily life. Present paper is a small step taken in that direction.

This paper proposes to investigate, scrutinize and isolate the discourse of *Manusmṛti* on women and sex, which is blended with the discourse on *Dharma* in general. What Manu states as the rights and duties of women also seems to point to the regulation of sexual behaviour of both male and female. The anxiety of *Dharmaśāstra* in this regard has often been interpreted as its agenda of gender discrimination and male dominance. But one must analyse them in their proper historical time frame to avoid simplistic misinterpretations and readings. By isolating the discourse on women and sex, one can have a comparative data on the theme, which may be further evaluated for the gendered symmetry or asymmetry.

A word of caution here. Do we intend to talk about the women of the whole of ancient India while discussing women in *Dharmaśāstra?* Do we propose to take into account the issue of social stratification of the content of these texts on *Dharmaśāstra?* Was the tradition of *Dharmaśāstra* treated as an autonomous category in ancient India? Do we intend also to have an understanding of the social background of these texts on *Dharmaśāstra* as an integral part of their critique? These questions constitute the theoretical framework within which *Dharmaśāstra* discourse on women ought to be situated.

Manu on Women and Sex

There are two perspectives visible in Manu's discourse on women and as its corollary on sex. Firstly, he gives them a position equal to that enjoyed by Gods themselves. He goes, even, to the extent of proclaiming that Gods shower their blessings only upon those families where women are worshipped (3.56)[1]. On the scale of social respect he accords the highest position to a mother who is thousand times greater than a father

(2.145).[2] Secondly, he propagates again and again that women should not be allowed freedom in the society. Her life is controlled at every stage of her life by a male relative such as her father in childhood, her husband in youth, her son/s in old age. Manu has categorically stated that women do not deserve freedom. These two apparently contradictory perspectives in Manu's discourse on women and sex create problems in their proper interpretation to reconstruct the historical reality.

This gets further complicated when we are confronted with the questions of nature and scope of *Dharmaśāstra* on the one hand, and on the other, with that of the historical reality itself. It is a well accepted fact that *Dharmaśāstra* was, and still is, a living system of law, "sharing features with each of the other literate traditional systems, but manifesting much that was peculiar to itself " [Derrett, J. Duncan M., Vol. 2, (1977)].[3] Derrett has rightly pointed out the dilemma arising from the modern practice of treating *Dharmaśāstra* as code of statutory laws which is "as if a statute had been passed requiring lemon-juice to be produced from oranges". Much confusion arose in colonial period because to the courts was imputed a complete judicial knowledge of the traditional Hindu law as if by magic, and both Britishers and Indians trained in English legal system never tried to find out what *Dharmaśāstra* actually said on a historical basis. Derrett has explained this as follows: "One error led to another, and, despite repeated lengthy and costly rehearsals, and reconsiderations of the law, poor *Smṛti* texts, which were never intended to be law in our sense, were enforced, in their Anglo-Hindu guise, as the common-law of the Hindus of India" (Vol. 3).[4]

Question of historical reality and its reconstruction through literary and archaeological data is equally complicated. What we call as historical evidences were never meant to be so by their original creators, be they authors or artists. They reflect on the historical reality of their times, or, they are the historical reality, these two approaches make the process of reconstructing the past a complicated task fraught with the risks of macro generalizations about India as a single undifferentiated entity. These theoretical issues become more relevant in reconstructing the many worlds of women through literary evidences as vast as *Dharmaśāstra* texts. The highly curious and complex nature of these texts further compound the problem. The basic problem in their interpretation is, whether what they propagate is mandatory, or directory? Much depends on the position taken by the scholar approaching these texts.

Manusmṛti is a *Dharmaśāstra* which has been clearly mentioned at the end of each chapter. A *Śāstra* may present new ideas and material or attempt to present the old material in new way. But it is beyond doubt, that authors of *Śāstra* largely drew on material provided by their predecessors.

If we take c.BC 200-c.200AD as the chronology for the final composition, compilation and crystallization of *Manusmṛti*, then we can have some speculation on the sociopolitical and sociocultural environment of the text, and also intention and motivation of its author. Maurya rule and its impact on Vedic-*śāstric* traditions, Suṅga-Kaṇva-Sātavāhana rule as the emergence of counterpoint to the ideology of their predecessors, and the foreign invasions and Mlechchha rule, it is in the backdrop of these historical elements that Manu seems to have composed his text. While analysing his law one must keep this in mind.

There are several methods to reconstruct past. In this presentation archaeo-historical method has been employed to situate Manu in proper historical perspective.

Manu has laid down rules and regulations governing the sexual behaviour of both men and women. They may, for convenience sake, be grouped in several categories:

(a) General rules involving social etiquette.

(b) Rules for special circumstances/unwarranted situations of sexual abuse.

(c) Rules relating to married life elaborating the do's and don'ts relating to sex.

Before proceeding to analyse these rules, it is imperative to discuss how Manu approaches the subject of women's sexuality. In the whole of *Manusmṛti* could find only one example where women per se are being condemned for their sexuality. In chapter two (verse 213) it has been said that it is the very nature of women to corrupt men. Hence, wise men are always alert in presence of alluring young women.[5]

Kulluk in his commentary on Manu explains this as follows:

स्त्रीणामयं स्वभाव:–यदिह शृङ्गारचेष्टया व्यामोह्या वयामोह्य पुरुषाणाम् दूषणम्।[6]

It clearly says that women by nature are prone to corrupt men through their sexual passion/erotic sentiment. Here women in general are condemned for their womanhood which is considered a negative attribute in the male oriented discourse of both Manu and his commentators. But Manu is not an exception in ascribing negative value on the womanhood. The so-called egalitarian religious traditions having reformative social agenda such as Buddhism and Jainism are equally male-oriented in their approach towards women. One can refer to eight *'Gurudharma'* which nuns were to follow strictly. They reflect gender bias and are highly discriminatory both in their content and spirit. Also, many Theravada scriptures have portrayed women as a monk's most dreaded threat. Jātāka stories are replete with the negative image of women. Anadabhuta Jātāka contains a highly derogatory reference on women in general.

> A sex composed of wickedness and guile, unknowable, uncertain as the path of fishes in the water, womankind hold truth for falsehood, falsehood for truth! As greedily as cows seek pastures new, women, unsated, yearn for mate on mate. As sand unstable, cruel as the snake, women know all things [bad].[7]
>
> (from Rhys Davids and K.R. Normon, ed., *Poems of the Early Buddhist Nuns (Therigatha),* Oxford: Pali Text Society, 1989).

All these references suggest that singular condemnation of Manu for gender biases reflected in his text will not help. Historically and sociologically analyzed facts suggest that it was patriarchy and its structural framework wherein all the religious traditions were enacting their socio-religious laws and precepts. So-called reformative agenda of heterodox religions, such as Buddhism and Jainism, was limited by and set within the patriarchal structure of society. Therefore, while discussing the discourse of Manu on women and sex, Brahminism per se will not be taken as the fountainhead of discriminatory social practices as has become the trend in all Marxist interpretations of ancient Indian scriptures and their social values.

A thorough examination of Manu's Code of Law makes it clear that the whole discourse is directed towards male members of society right from their birth to death. With few exceptions as mentioned above (2.213),[8] the most of the rules relating to social etiquette vis-a-vis women are meant to regulate male sexuality and desires. For example, in the second chapter, Manu directs a cultured wise man not to spend time alone even in the company of his own mother, sister and daughter as the array of sensory organs is capable of overpowering even a wise person. Here female sexuality is not being condemned rather the sensory organs in general are held responsible for incestual abuses.[9]

It seems that Manu was far ahead of his times in understanding the psychology of human sexuality in a way which is similar to that of modern psychologists like Freud and Jung. Modern electronic and print media worldwide have forced people to accept the menace and disease of incestual abuse very much present both in traditional and modern structures of family. Therefore, Manu's view on the matter of incest as cited above qualifies to be both rational and remedial.

In the category of rules relating to social etiquette Manu has laid down specific code of conduct for disciples residing in *Gurukul* with their teachers. They were living in the close contact of teacher's wives who were to be treated with equal respect. As celibacy (ब्रह्मचर्य) was the prerequisite for entering into *Gurukul* and the close proximity of young wives of a teacher could create obstacles and undesirable consequences in the maintenance of discipline and celibacy of young students, so Manu has dealt with this problem by laying down specific rules for students relating to their conduct with the wives – particularly young ones of their teacher. He has forbidden a Vedic student to apply oil, to bathe, to massage or to do hair and apply cosmetics to the wives of his teacher.[10]

Likewise, a twenty year old student is prohibited from touching the feet of the young wife of his teacher. It seems, Manu has taken care of every unforeseen situation relating to sexual behaviour by laying down specific laws and code of conduct as a system of checks and balances to ensure the sanctity of well-defined social-relations be they familial or institutional.

There are certain rules relating to sexual abuse. In chapter 8, which deals with *Vyavahāra* or court procedures, 18 types of human actions are listed for judicial trial. *Strīsaṁgrahaṇa* (स्त्रीसंग्रहण), i.e., sexual relation outside of marriage is one of the crimes listed in it. Manu states that a king should punish a person indulging in sexual relationship with a female other than his wife through such severe punishments as by getting his limbs severed (8.352).[11] The aim of such severe punishment system was to maintain the purity of the fourfold division of society by avoiding unwanted mixture of castes. Manu is more than concerned to protect the reputation of a virgin by providing specific law for the same:[12]

> When a man with a malafide intention asserts that a girl is not a virgin, and if he fails to prove his claim, then he should be punished with a fine of 100 *Paṇa* (पण) (copper coins).

Chastity and virginity are regarded as the highest virtues in a maiden in all traditional societies and Manu is no exception to it. According to him *Pāṇigrahaṇa* (पाणिग्रहण) is meant only for virgins (8.226)[13]. It is in this backdrop that Manu has provided specific laws to punish persons committing sexual offences against a virgin be they male offenders or females.

As a mature jurist Manu has discussed all the fines points of law by taking into account the complex nature of sexual offences. Verse 364 in chapter 8 is one such example:[14]

> A person who defiles an unmarried girl, i.e., a virgin against her will deserves immediate execution. If a person of equal status defiles a virgin with her consent, he does not merit execution.

Consensual and non-consensual sex is a very complex legal point which till date remains problematic in judicial system. In case of the above cited Manu's law, the term *'Kanyā'* (कन्या) further brings complication. Technically and legally *'Kanyā'* in *Manusmṛti* means a girl of 8 to 10 years' old child. If it is the case, then, the consent of a girl child in any kind of sexual relation seems illogical from legal point of view. On the contrary, if *'Kanyā'* suggests a virgin of any age, then, what Manu has said on consensual or non-consensual sex becomes an important legal point.

Manu has laid down several rules and punishments for persons indulging in adultery (8.352-388).[15] All these references prove that Manu has provided effective and adequate injunctions and laws to ensure the practice of socially and morally sanctioned behaviour in sexual sphere both by men and women. He does not seem liberal to either of them, although in some cases he provides harsher punishments to male offenders than the females for committing the same kind of offence. He is equally harsh to both the parties for indulging in pre and extramarital sex.

As per the beliefs and customs of his times, Manu has provided certain rules to control marital sex. Chapter 3 contains many rules relating to sexual union of husband and wife. Manu exhorts the married person that he should always have sex only with his wife during her season (ऋतु काल). In this context certain days are prohibited for sex on various grounds. One of the grounds was related to the sex-selection of the would-be child. Manu provides that[16]:

"Having sex on even nights gives birth to sons, on odd nights to girls. A person desirous of a son should have sex with his wife on even nights during her season."

This clearly suggests that sons were preferred over daughters and traditional system of sex-selection to get a son was very much present which has also been mentioned by Manu.

As I have mentioned earlier that in order to understand Manu's Code of Law a proper historical contextualization of both text and author is necessary. Chronologically the text belongs to c.BC 200 – c.AD 200. Various scholars accept the upper limit of this time frame more accurate than the lower one. Let us examine the historical geography as we find in *Manusmṛti*. In Chapter 2, Manu has used regional names like *'Brahmāvarta'*, *'Brahmarṣi'*, *'Madhya Deśa'* and *'Āryāvarta'* with their boundaries and landmarks. He describes the traditional conduct of the people of *Brahmāvarta* as the conduct of good people (2.17).[17] But in verse No. 19 he has described the sacred land of *Brahmarṣi* as follows:[18]

> Kurukṣetra, Matsya, Pāñcāla, Śūrasena – they constitute *Brahmarṣi Deśa* which is beyond *Brahmāvarta* but near it.

Verse 20 says:[19]

> All the people must learn their respective conduct from the *Brāhmaṇas* born in this land.

These references clearly suggest that Manu belongs to northern India which he has defined as the land sandwiched between western and eastern oceans, and *Himālaya* and *Vindhya* mountains, and is called *Āryāvarta*. Regarding the issue of *Manusmṛti's* authorship there are two different opinions among the scholars. One group suggests the composition of the text as a gradual process over the centuries by several compilers and copyists. Another view point is that of the unitary authorship of the text. Bühler (1886) is the first scholar to propose that *Manusmṛti* was authored by one author. Recently, Hiltebeited has proposed that *Mahābhārata* epic was written by a committee or team over a relatively brief period of time spanning "at most a couple of generation". (Olivelle, 2005). P. Olivelle, thinking on the same line of thought, has suggested that *Manusmṛti* is the result of "a conscious plan created by a single gifted individual" (2005). He further suggests that "if not by an individual, then it must have been composed by a "strong chairman of a committee" with the help of research assistants who carried out his plan" (2005). The purpose of the above references regarding the authorship of *Manusmṛti* is twofold. Firstly, to suggest that there reflects in the text a clear authorial intent of an individual author who belonged to some place in northern India probably in *Brahmarṣi* and/or *Madhydeśa*. Secondly, to bring out the fact that in the *Śāstric* tradition authors have heavily drawn upon previous scholarship. Therefore, while discussing the aspects of *Manusmṛti* one has to accept 'Manu the tradition' and 'Manu the individual author' – the man of high scholarship dealing with the socio-religious issues of his time. Thus, historical methodology of empirical research suggests that an author exists in a particular time-space from where he draws his subject matter and creates his text. This entails a deeper study of socio-religious-political-economic factors of that particular time-space where author-text exist. Archaeo-historical method further reinforces this empirical approach by adding a visual documentation of any time-space culture to the subject matter of any text.

Manu has clearly described the customs and practice of the region belonging to *Kurukśetra-Pāncāla-Mathurā* as the ideal customs to be followed by every human on earth. Here, I have tried to discuss the female forms of Mathura railing pillars of c.AD 100 – c.AD 200. These railing pillars belong to Jain and Buddhist *stupas*. No Brahmin temple using this kind of massive stone pillars have been discovered from Mathura or for that matter, from any there site belonging to Murya-Kushana time frame.

Female forms depicted in Mathura railing pillars are extremely beautiful, attractive and full of joy for life, vibrating with sensuous postures and emotions. They display an urban set-up full of luxury and various comforts. These life-size statues are wearing typical jewellery and ornaments of Kushan period. Their upper portion is bare displaying unnaturally, heavy, round breasts. Lower part is covered by a piece of cloth but their genitals are prominently displayed. From art point of view, they display high quality and expertise in the depiction of human anatomy. They are depicted on Buddhist, Jain railing pillars. These religions are ascetic in nature emphasizing upon the control of sensory organs and a complete segregation from women in general. It is a matter of sociological enquiry how and why Buddhist, Jain churches permitted the portrayal of this kind of tantalising, sensuous, semi-nude forms on their religious structures which was central to their religious customs and beliefs. *Stupas* were worshipped by the masses as the very symbol of Lord Buddha. Inscriptional records suggest that people took on pilgrimage to visit these *stupas* from for off places.

Manusmṛti belongs to c.200 BC – c.200 AD. Recent researches have narrowed down the lower limit as c.100 AD. As Manu himself has proclaimed that the customs and beliefs of the *Brāhmaṇas* belonging to

Mathura and adjoining *Kurukśetra, Pāncāla* regions, are the ideal customs which ought to be followed by every human, therefore, one can have a peep into the socio-religious background of the above mentioned time-space wherein, supposedly, Manu composed his text. It is against this backdrop of the openness relating to use of nude female forms in popular Buddhist, Jain religious buildings that Manu's famous dictum – 'न स्त्री स्वातन्त्र्यमर्हति' which has become cause celebre in the agenda of every anti-Manu discourse, ought to be situated. Manu is concerned with the four-fold division of society and its equilibrium. Historically, his time and society he lived in, were full of changes, both internally and externally due to foreign elements, boosting international and national trade and commerce, emergence of a complex urban culture emphasizing upon market economy and consumption of luxuries generated therein, which would have forced Manu to codify law to maintain the equilibrium of the four-fold division of society. As Buddhism and Jainism were strongly patronized by rich trading class and royalty, therefore, a conservative Brahmin like Manu seems to be anxious to maintain the ideals and customary laws based on Vedic ideology. Mathurā art of Kushan period makes it clear that Buddhist and Jain establishments not only compromised their non-worldly ideals but also propagated to construct more *stupas* displaying sensuous female forms. Art mirrors the prevalent way of life. A society open to the depiction of nude female forms in public places, would have been too elastic and advanced to sanction such portrayals.

We can conclude that *Manusmṛti* ought to be situated in its proper historical context, and archaeologically revealed historical facts should be taken in account, in the interpretation of this significant code of law. An archaeo-historical approach unravels the anxieties of the traditional society and provides a concrete socio-religious backdrop against which Manu was codifying customary laws. He was neither anti-female nor promale; he was a great scholar dealing with the problems of his society which were breaking and endamaging the fabric of traditional society.

This discourse on women and sex becomes more comprehensible both in meaning and intent by archaeo-historical methodology of reading a text.

Notes

1. Manusmṛti - 3/56.
2. Manusmṛti - 2/114.
3. Desert, J. Duncon, M. Vol. 2, 1977.
4. Ibid. Vol. 3.
5. स्वभाव एष नारीणां नराणामिह दूषणम्।
   अतोऽर्थान्न प्रमाद्यन्ति प्रमदासु विपश्चितः।। Manusmṛti - 2/213.
6. Kulluk, Manu.
7. Rhys Davids and K.R. Normon, (ed.) *'Poems of the Early Budhist Nuns'* (Therīgāthā) Oxford: Pali Text Society, 1987.
8. Manusmṛti - 2/213.
9. मात्रा स्वस्रा दुहित्रा वा न विविक्तासनो भवेत्।
   बलवानिन्द्रियग्रामो विद्वांसमपि कर्षति।। Manusmṛti - 2/215.
10. अभ्यञ्जनं स्नापनं च गात्रोत्सादनमेव च।
    गुरुपत्न्या न कार्याणि केशानां च प्रसाधनम्।। Manusmṛti . 2/211.
11. Manusmṛti - 8/325.
12. अकन्येति तु यः कन्यां ब्रूयाद् द्वेषेण मानवः।
    स शतं प्राप्नुयाद् दण्डं तस्या दोषमदर्शयन्।। Manusmṛti - 8/225.
13. Manusmṛti - 8/226.
14. योऽकामां दूषयेत् कन्यां स सद्यो वधमर्हति।
    सकामां दूषयंस्तुल्यो न वधं प्राप्नुयान्नरः।। Manusmṛti - 8/364.
15. Manusmṛti - 8/315-388.
16. युग्मासु पुत्रा जायन्ते स्त्रियोऽयुग्मासु रात्रिषु।
    तस्माद् युग्मासु पुत्रार्थी संविशेदार्तवे स्त्रियम्।। Manusmṛti - 3/48.
17. Manusmṛti - 2/17.
18. कुरुक्षेत्रं च मत्स्याश्च पञ्चालाः शूरसेनकाः।
    एष ब्रह्मर्षिदेशो वै ब्रह्मावर्तादनन्तरः।। Manusmṛti - 2/19.
19. एतद् देशप्रसूतस्य सकाशादग्रजन्मनः।
    स्वं स्वं चरित्रं शिक्षेरन्पृथिव्यां सर्वमानवाः।। Manusmṛti - 2/20.

5

Women and the Notion of *Kāma* in the *Dharmaśāstrīya* Discourse

Shalini Shah

This paper sets out to discuss what has been described in the ancient Indian tradition as *kāma* or sexual desire. *Kāma,* along with *dharma, artha* and *mokśa,* has been enumerated in our tradition as one of the four goals (*puruṣārtha*) of human life. What has prompted me to focus on just the analysis of the *kāma puruṣārtha* is due to my concern with the issue of women in general, and the social relations of the sexes in particular. In the *kāma* tradition, a woman seemed to have a far more visible (though not always subjective) role to play. Perhaps this was because within the Indian tradition unlike in the Greek for instance, *kāma* was conceived predominantly in heterosexual terms.

The philosophical ideas of a given culture are a significant medium through which sexual behaviour gets represented. Of all the philosophical discourses, the normative *Dharmaśāstrīya* discourse has always been the dominant, one. This is because the framers of this discourse, the *Brāhmaṇas,* have always enjoyed an unparalleled dominance in the ancient Indian context.

Sexuality is learned and it is learned in a societal context. And, if sexuality is a social construct, then, the laws by which the society is regulated were bound to leave their impact on the nature of Eros. All societies prescribe and codify sexual activity and in this way legitimize some sexual practices and not others.

The *ṣāstric* texts like the *Dharmaśāstras* are storehouses of ethics dealing with a series of interdictions regarding human sexuality. By the 7th century CE the creative period of Indian law was over. What we have in our period of study (7th-13th centuries CE) are several commentaries and digests on the earlier *Dharmaśāstras*, the most significant being Medhātithi's commentary *Manubhāṣya* on *Manusmṛti*[1] written in the 9th century CE. Aparāraka's commentary on the *Yājñavalkyasmṛti,* as also Vijñāneśvara's *Mitākśarā* on the same text, the latter composed in about the 11th century CE, are other important texts of the period. The most significant law digests in this period are *Kṛtyakalpataru* of Lakśmīdhara (12th century CE) and *Smṛticandrikā* of Devaṇṇabhaṭṭa (early 13th century CE).

The *Dharmaśāstras,* which were dominated by the householders' code of the reproduction of the specie at its core, were given to glorifying the status of the *gṛhastha* and pushing into the background the āśrama of *vānaprastha* and *sannyasa*.[2] Certain *Dharmaśāstras* even state that the latter *āśramas* are forbidden in the *kali* age *(kalivarjya).* Since the *Dharmaśāstrīya* laws were concerned with laying down norms for regulating society and not with its pleasures, hence, in the man-woman sexual relationship it was the procreative and not the erotic angle that was focused upon. In fact, the erotic was subordinated to the procreative. Thus, cohabitation was a duty enjoined upon both men and women and there were penalties if that did not happen. It was men's duty to see that women's *ṛtu* was not wasted.[3] The centrality of procreation in the *Dharmaśāstras* left a deep imprint on the conception of sexual love that did not bring forth progeny or had procreation as its aim. Such a love was to be deplored – *socyam maithunam aprajam* as stated in the *Mahābhārata*.[4] There was a gender implication of this *Dharmaśāstrīya* norm as well. The patriarchal normative tradition[5] justified man taking another wife if his first one could not give him children particularly sons. This practice of abandoning the spouse was not extended to women by the *Dharmaśāstra* writers. It is true that Manu[6] states and Medhātithi[7] agrees that a wife is not to blame if she shows aversion to a husband who is impotent (*klibambijam*). *Nāradasmṛti*[8] allows a woman to desert one husband if he was impotent and sexually unite with another. But since the trend in the *Dharmaśāstra* tradition is to disallow the remarriage of women[9] the medieval commentators and digests tend to interpret such practices as forbidden in the present Kali age.

The notion of sex that was driven for the reproduction of the species had heterosexual coitus as the ideal form of sexuality. Any deviance in the form of homosexuality (tellingly referred to as klibya, that is impotence) and lesbianism earned the ire of the *Dharmaśāstra* writers. According to Manu,[10] one who unites in sexual union with a man loses his caste. Medhātithi[11] agrees with Manu that such a man should perform atonement for this sin. As for lesbian lovers Manu[12] says that if the offender is a maiden herself she can get away with a lighter punishment (of lashes) without her crime being publicised. But if the offender was a mature woman, her guilt was to be publicly proclaimed and she had to be paraded on a donkey.

Another thing which comes through from the reading of the *śāstric* laws as far as women and their sexuality was concerned is that the control mechanism vis-a-vis female sexuality operated at two levels. First, at an ideological level female sexual prowess was greatly exaggerated. Manu[13] said and Medhātithi[14] confirms that this was women's inherent nature, they were wanton *(pramadā)*. Given this *strīsvabhāva*, women were dangerous and, therefore, had to be controlled and defended against. Yet at another level women were depicted as *abalā* who were forever needing protection of the males in the family, viz., father, husband and son, under whose tutelage, says Manu,[15] she had to be all the time. Medhātithi[16] says that women must always be guarded even when they are dependent. The *Dharmaśāstras* talk of two types of women – the *pativratā* who was chaste in thought, word and deed to her husband. As Manu[17] says, "she alone is sadhvi". This *pativratā* ideology with the weight of cultural force behind it was quite powerful in its insidious omnipotence. The second type of women described at length in *Nāradasmṛti*[18] were *svairiṇi/ bandhiki* who were loose, promiscuous women.

A patriarchal Brahmanical society concerned with the purity of the patrilineage and caste was bound to treat adultery as a sin. Thus, we find that the *Dharmaśāstrīya* writers were obsessively concerned with the upper caste womens' sexuality, be it a wife or a widow. Within Brahmanical patriarchy a widow was enjoined to be patient of hardships, self-controlled and chaste.[19] Medhātithi[20] says that a man who guards his wife well, will be able to keep his progeny pure, his family free of blemish or ill-fame, his own self protected (a paramour of the wife would not be able to murder him) and his religion too would be protected. Vijñāneśvara in his *Mitākśarā* commentary on *Yājñavalkyasmṛti* also takes the view that an unchaste wife was not entitled to be associated with the performance of religious rites.[21]

In a Brahmanical society there was also a caste connotation to female sexuality. Although ideally *Dharmaśāstra* writers wanted a same-caste union and *varṇasaṅkara* (progeny born of miscegenation) was anathema to them, in practical life the *Dharmaśāstras* accommodated *anuloma* (hypergamous union). They were, however, vehemently opposed to *pratiloma* (hypogamous union), where low caste men sexually united with higher caste women.[22] Because in this case the purity of the caste would have been compromised as caste status was perceived as being contingent upon the purity of the women in brahmanical patriarchy.[23] Sociologically speaking, the *pratiloma* union was more of a taboo says Kamla Ganesh[24] because it ran contrary to the social arrangements that were based on patrilineal descent, patrilocality and male authority. In a *pratiloma* marriage the wife could not live with her natal relatives since her children were of a lower ritual status. She could move into the husband's patrilineage, but as a member of a superior caste she would upset the hierarchy of domestic relations which were based on male dominance and female subordination. Since both inter-sex and inter-caste relations were equally hierarchized and expressed in a similar language of subordination, a direct conflict between the two was avoided by banning *pratiloma*. Interestingly, a system that had negative implications for the sexuality of elite women[25] had a positive one for the women of lower castes. *Śūdra* women thus always had a greater sexual autonomy for the risk of pollution through defilement was not present. And since it is reasonable to surmise that the *Śudra* castes far outnumbered *Brāhmaṇas* in the society, relatively independent women were also more numerous.

In spite of the *Dharmaśāstras* essentially presenting a picture of a patriarchal society, we can discover spaces or niches within these *ṣāstric* traditions where either patriarchy was not functional at all or was greatly diluted. Thus, we find eight forms of marriage listed in the *Dharmaśāstras*.[26] Even though the more acceptable forms of marriage (*brahma, daiva, ārṣa* and *prajāpatya*) were the ones where men's (father's/ husband's) *svāmya* or authority over women was established. The other four forms (*rākśasa, asura, paiśāca* and *gandharva*) were not excluded by the lawmakers and these were relatively non-patriarchal forms of marriage, where property rights and consent agency all point towards greater if not absolute control by women and their kin.[27]

The *śāstras* also note the presence of a variety of sons.[28] Thus, the *Dharmaśāstras* refer to *kānina* (son of a maiden), *sahoḍha* (son of a pregnant bride) and *paunarbhava* (son of a twice-married woman) were all accepted as part of family (*bāndhava*). The very manner of the birth of these sons allows a more lenient view of female sexuality within patriarchal society.

Not only was there a social scripting of sexuality but an economic scripting as well. Women's economic freedom and unfreedom also had a lot to do with their social/sexual behaviour. We have established in another context[29] how communal control over resources also spelt greater sexual freedom for women. That economic considerations were crucial in constraining female sexuality is particularly noteworthy in the context of widow's property rights, as enumerated in the *Dharmaśāstras*. *Kātyāyanasmṛti*[30] states that a sonless widow preserving the bed of her dead husband unsullied and residing with her elders and being self-controlled could enjoy her husband's property till her death. Kulluka, the commentator on *Manusmṛti*, opines that a chaste widow could never be deprived of her right to inherit the property of her husband.[31]

From the above analysis of the *Dharmaśāstra* texts, it would not be wrong to surmise that sexuality was not a somatic fact; rather it is intelligible only in relation to the warp and woof of the entire social fabric.

Notes

1. *Manusmṛti*, translated by D. Wendy and B.K. Smith (Penguin, London, 1991), III. 77.
2. P.V. Kane, *History of Dharmaśāstras*, Vol. II, Parts I & 2; second edition, (BORI, Poona, 1974), p. 424.
3. *Manubhāṣya*, of Medhātithi, translated by Ganganatha Jha, Volumes 1-5, (Calcutta University, 1920-1926), III.45; IX.4.
4. *Mahābhārata*, of Vyāsa, Critical edition in 19 volumes, (BORI, Poona, 1933-66), V.39.62.
5. P.V. Kane, *History of Dharmaśāstra*, Vol. 2, op. cit., p. 561.
6. *Manusmṛti*, IX.79.
7. *Manubhāṣya*, IX.79.
8. *Nāradasmṛti*, translated by J. Jolly, (Bhartiya Publishing House, Delhi, 1978), XII.62.
9. P.V. Kane, History of *Dharmaśāstra*, Vol. 2, op. cit., pp. 619-620.
10. *Manusmṛti*, XI.68.

11. *Manubhāṣya,* XI.174.
12. *Manusmṛti,* VIII.369-370.
13. *Manusmṛti,* II.213.
14. *Manubhāṣya,* II.213.
15. *Manusmṛti,* V.148.
16. *Manubhāṣya,* IX.3.
17. *Manusmṛti,* IX.29.
18. *Nāradasmṛti,* XII.50-54.
19. *Manubhāṣya,* V.156-160.
20. *Manubhāṣya,* IX.7.
21. A.S. Altekar, *Position of Women in Hindu Civilization,* third edition, (Motilal Banarsidass, Delhi, 1962), p. 313.
22. *Smṛticandrikā,* of Devaṇṇabhatta, translated by J.R. Gharpure, Bombay, Vol. 2, Part II, 1950, pp. 478-485.
23. Chakravarti, Uma, "Conceptualising Brahmanical Patriarchy in Early India: Gender, Caste, Class and State", *Economic and Political Weekly,* Vol. 28, No. 14, April 3, (Sameeksha Trust, Bombay, 1993), pp. 579-585.
24. K. Ganesh, "Seclusion of Women and the Structures of Caste", in M. Kṛṣṇaraja and K. Chanana (eds.), *Gender and The Household Domain: Social and Cultural Dimensions,* (Sage, Delhi, 1989), p. 89.
25. As Gananath Obeyesekere notes, the brahmanical ideal for high-caste women insisted on virginity in a bride, chastity in a wife and continence in a widow. This had the effect of extreme repression in women and such side effects as "sexual frigidity ... propensity to hysteria and masochistic tendencies owing to the internalisation of aggression" [G. Obeyesekere, Medusa's Hair, (Princeton University Press, Princeton, 1984), p. 431].
26. *Smṛticandrikā,* op. cit., Vol. I, 1946, pp. 149-153.
27. K. Roy, "The King's Household: Structure/Space in the Śāstric Tradition", *Economic and Political Weekly,* Vol. 27, No. 43, October 24-31, (Sameeksha Trust, Bombay, 1992), pp. 55-60.
28. *Manubhāṣya,* IX.158-160.
29. Shalini, Shah, "Gender and Sexuality in Ancient Punjab A Case Study of the Karṇa Parva in the Mahābhārat" in A. Basu and A. Tarneja (eds.) *Breaking Out of Invisibility: Women in Indian History,* (ICHR, Delhi, 2002), pp. 12-14.
30. P.V. Kane, *History of Dharmaśāstra,* Vol. 2, op. cit., p. 584.
31. Cited in A.S. Altekar, *Position of Women in Hindu Civilization,* op. cit., p. 257.

6

Re-reading *Dharmaśāstras* through Indian Eyes: A Feminist Perspective

Preeti Singh

Carole Pateman says that "the dichotomy between the public and the private... is ultimately what the feminist movement is all about".[1] Feminists have challenged all the Western mainstream theories on the ground that these theories ignore the private realm of life which is associated with woman and glorify the public realm of life wherein man is the sole actor. They argue, that though, gradually the fact that women are capable of acting in the public realm has got acceptance, sexual inequality still persists. They blame that the 'private' is not given proper recognition in the mainstream theories. None of the so-called liberal theories has raised the question of justice within the family, as according to them justice refers to public realm, where adult men deal with other adult men in accordance with mutually agreed upon conventions. Familial relationships, on the other hand, are 'private', governed by natural instinct.

The present paper is concerned with the question that whether the dichotomy between public and private also exist in ancient Indian sociological texts, i.e., *Dharmaśāstras*? The paper is divided into two sections:

1. The first section attempts to portray the dichotomy between public and private as prevailing in the Western philosophical tradition.

2. The second section investigates how far does the distinction between public and private exist in the *Dharmaśāstras.*

I

Western philosophical thought suffers from dualism in several dimensions; correlating with them is a further polarity between male and female.[2] Male is regarded as superior and female as inferior. The qualities and fields associated with men are regarded as superior to the qualities and fields associated with women. Separating public from private, particular from universal, human from divine, family from state, and male from female realms of experience and action forms a crucial aspect of Western philosophical tradition.

In Western philosophical and political traditions the public realm of the polis, state, city or republic becomes the site where people consent to or contest the laws, contracts, covenants, or principles of community that govern personal and social conduct. For Aristotle, man is "by nature an animal intended to live in a polis".[3] The private realm, defined by the hearth and home remains the loci of family identity. While the public realm has been the domain of the Western male subject, the private realm belongs to the wife, daughter, mother and sister. Men also function as fathers, sons, husbands, and brothers within the family but do not take these roles with them into public life where history, community, and state demand mutual recognition and progress towards rational and universal goals.

Crucial to the relegation of men and women to different realms were notions of the inherent characteristics of men and women. Men embody rationality, thought, justice, critical judgement, objectivity, sternness, individuality, and propensity for violence and acquisition. Women embody feeling, fickleness, cunningness, purity, subjectivity, spirituality, possessiveness, delicacy, dependence, sensuousness, and unbridled sexuality.[4] The contradictory nature of these qualities reinforced the unity and rationality of the male while at the same time prove the fickleness and fragmentation of the female and hence her 'natural' unfitness for public life. Aristotle opines that the citizens are the 'integral parts' of the polis while women, children, slaves, mechanics and labourers are the 'necessary conditions'.[5]

With the disjunction of public and private, male and female, the family (i.e., private) becomes inherently naturalized, depoliticized, and dehistoricized. Private is always regarded inferior to the public. The *idion*, or the private, in contrast to the public or common, was accorded a much lower status in Greek life. According to the Greek view of life, the private person or *idiot* was a being of lower purpose, goodness, rationality and worth than the *polites* or public citizens who belonged to and participated in the city.[6]

By arguing that a non-public quest for justice, given a debased public world, may be the superior life, Plato seems to confound the Greek order of things. In his claim that under those conditions when a certain sort of private life is the preferred life, indeed the seedbed for ultimate public righteousness and justice, one might presume that women, private beings by definition, would enjoy an enhanced dignity and status in the overall scheme of things. Unfortunately, this in not the result of Plato's scheme, what Plato requires for the creation and sustenance of the good man outside the good city is not the private world of household or *oikos* within which women, children, slaves, and servants carry on that everyday production and reproduction which sustain life itself, but another sort of private space exemplified by the symposium, that all-male forum for philosophic discourse, pedagogy, and social intimacy.[7]

For Plato the private speech of households lacks either the form of prose or the form of poetry and is therefore without meaning-unformed, chaotic, evanescent, the speech of *doxa*. Household speech could be neither heroic nor partake in the quest for wisdom at which the private, philosophic male speech of the dialogues aims.[8]

Moreover, the arrangements made by Plato which seem quite egalitarian are not aimed at bringing any kind of gender justice. For example Plato's motive for equal education of the sexes was not primarily considerations of social justice, or equality but was a mean to his ultimate aim of social harmony and unity. He argues that because woman's natural potential for virtue is inferior to a man's, she is a greater danger to social harmony than he. She is inclined to be secretive and crafty, because of her weaknesses.[9] She must not be left to her own devices or the state may lose control. Plato's insight here, is that the private realm in which women live lives of obscurity and retirement is not the best school for citizenship but a breeding ground of discontent.[10]

It seems clear that in Plato's view women cannot enter in public realm with their inherent qualities (what he calls 'secretive and crafty'). This would become possible only when they would leave their basic feminine qualities. Here, it is clear that his attitude towards both the woman as well as the private realm is condemnable.

Aristotle outdoes even his teacher in denigrating women and private realm of life. He absorbs women completely within the *oikos* or household, denies that women have any capability for public role, and precludes the possibility for female self-transformation over time. He regards man as form and woman as matter. To quote his words:

> Since the Form, is better and more divine in its nature than the matter, it is better also that the superior one should be separate from the inferior one. That is why whenever possible and so far as possible the male is separate from the female.[11]

He further says:

> Woman is 'as it were an infertile male', and even in regard to reproduction, 'a male is male in virtue of a particular ability, and a female in virtue of a particular inability.[12]

Aristotle's these teleological commitments suffuse his presumptions on public and private, women and politics. He begins with the claim that the good life is possible only in the 'final and perfect association' and for individuals, only through their participation in it. [13] In his opinion Man (meaning the male) is by nature an animal intended to live in a polis.[14] All associations aim at some good, but it is only in the polis that the highest good is attained. It follows that free citizens, polites, who participate in this goodness themselves attain good.[15]

As women were debarred from taking part in politics in the Greek city state, they did not have the right to partake in the full unfolding of goodness and reason. There is an 'essential difference' between greater (free, male) and lesser (unfree, female) persons although those two categories of persons are linked in relationships of necessary dominance and subordination. Aristotle justifies this relationship by finding a 'community of interest' between 'the naturally ruling element with the element which is naturally ruled' essential to the 'preservation of both'.[16]

He was of the opinion that women are inferior to men and it is the law of nature that the superior in goodness should rule over inferiors. As the private realm is associated with women, it is inferior to public realm. The household constitute a non-public sphere within which the female is subsumed and which therefore defines her. He opines that because the good at which the household aims is a lesser good than that which is the end of the polis, the wife-mother achieve only the limited goodness of the 'naturally ruled', a goodness different in kind from that of the naturally ruling.[17]

To quote his words :

> The ruler, accordingly, must possess moral goodness in its full and perfect form [i.e., the form based on rational deliberation], because his function, regarded absolutely and in its full nature, demands a master artificer, but all other persons need only possess moral goodness to the extent required of them [by their particular position].[18]

Thus, women are merely regarded as necessary condition of the state.[19] As the class or category 'Woman' was regarded as inferior to the class or category 'Man', and was deprived of the right of citizenship. In Aristotle's scheme women were *idiots* in the Greek sense of the word, persons who either could not or did not participated in the polis or the 'good' of public life, individuals without a public voice.[20]

The imbecillitus sexus of women fit them only for blank ruminations which put no strain on their limited faculties. Ideally, the good man and the good citizen are coterminous. Exclusively private persons, not fully rational, limited in goodness, women lived out their lives in the realm of necessity, a life deemed inferior in its essance, intent, and purpose to political life, but a functional prerequisite for the realm of freedom.

Similarly, Jermy Bentham also sees the relation between the sexes as that of superity and inferiority. He offers a few of the traditional encomiums to womankind: the female is more sensitive, delicate, moral, religious, and sympathetic than the male. On the other hand, man is stronger, hardier, intellectually superior, and firmer in mind to her. He believes that women should not enter the public realm as their affection is limited to their own children or to young children generally and so they cannot embrace the welfare of their own country, much less all human kind.[21] For him the family is sealed off from the public world and relations between the sexes are explored as if they were unrelated to public problems.

This discriminatory attitude can easily be seen in the thought of Rousseau also. Despite being a champion of equality, his answers to many of the dilemmas posed by the relationship between the sexes, and the public and private spheres, are frequently less than satisfactory to the contemporary feminists. In *Emile* he opines that men's and women's nature and abilities are not the same, and these biologically given differences define their whole role in society, with men becoming citizens and women wives and mothers. He writes: "Little girls always dislike learning to read and write, but they are always ready to learn to sew."[22]

His whole scheme of education was intended to give the training of rational citizenship to boys and to teach the art of pleasing a man to girls as if they were made for man's delight. Rousseau's following statement has earned the ire of feminist scholars :

> ... it is not enough that a woman should be faithful; her husband, along with his friends and neighbours, must believe in her fidelity... Nature herself has decreed that woman, both for herself and her children, should be at the mercy of man's judgment...worth alone will not suffice a woman must be thought worthy; nor beauty, she must be admired; nor virtue, she must be respected.[23]

Thus, in his view, women do not get their identity through the qualities they possess but it depends on how men perceive their qualities. Is it not the denial of woman's identity?

On the basis of his argument that man is different from woman by nature as he is rational being whereas she is emotional, he blames that woman pose a permanent threat to the political order. He opines that the natural morality of women fits them only for the 'natural society' of domestic life. He states: "Even if it could be denied that a special sentiment of chasteness was natural to women, would it be less true that in society...they ought to be raised in principles appropriate to it? If the timidity, chasteness and modesty, which are proper to them or social inventions, it is in society's interest that women acquire these qualities."[24]

For Hegel, the natural differentiation of the sexes translates into an ethical differentiation. According to him even if women were to enter the public sphere as many women in history have, they cannot have voice as citizens but must inevitably represent only the particular concerns of the family or children. To quote his words:

> The community creates for itself in what it suppresses and what is at the same time essential to it an internal enemy – womankind in general. Womankind – the everlasting irony of the community – changes by intrigue the universal end of the government into a private end, transforms its universal activity into a work of some particular individual, and perverts the universal property of the state into a possession and ornament for the family.[25]

According to Hegel, man, who is more dynamic, reflective and capable of steadfast endeavour is perfect for state management which requires him not only to learn and labour but to discipline himself in order to lead and control vast mass of men. On the other hand, woman who is passive and generally confined to the pursuit of more or less persons attains destiny as a person by exercising and cultivating her native capacity for service and sacrifice in looking after the family.

Freud also justifies women's confinement in the domestic sphere. To quote his words:

> For women the level of what is ethically normal is different from what it is in men. Their superego is never so inexorable, so impersonal, so independent of its emotional origins as we require it to be in men ... They show less sense of justice than men, they are more often influenced in their judgements by feeling of affection, of hostility ...[26]

Thus, all the above traditional thinkers have played important role in creating distinction between public and private. Even the contemporary scholars have adopted the same attitude. For them, private realm of life does not need scholarly discussion.

While commenting upon liberal theories feminists remark that liberals refuse to interfere in the family, even to advance liberal goals of autonomy and equal opportunity, for maintaining the public-private distinction. As Jagger writes that because the liberal right to privacy encompasses and protects the personal intimacies of the home, the family, marriage, motherhood, procreation, and child rearing, any proposal to interfere in the family, in the name of justice represents a clear departure from their traditional liberal conception of the family as the centre of private life. As the liberal feminist emphasis on justice comes increasingly to overshadow its respect for so-called private life, one may begin to wonder whether the basic values of liberalism are ultimately consistent with one another.[27]

Even Rawls, who is well-known for his theory of justice have adopted the same gendered attitude and reinforced the opinion that family is one of the social institutions to be evaluated by a theory of justice, he simply assumes that the traditional family is just, and goes on to measure just distribution in terms of the 'household income' which accrues to 'heads of households', so that questions of justice within the family are ruled out of court.[28] Susan Moller Okin rightly remarks that the judgement that the family is 'non-political' is implicit in the very fact that it is not discussed in most of the works of political theory today.[29]

However, the distinction between public and private, as present in Western philosophical discourse, has following characteristics:

(i) It perceives different qualities of man and woman as superior and inferior.

(ii) Women are considered as suitable for private domain and inefficient for public realm of life.

(iii) Private realm which is associated with woman is regarded as inferior to public realm which is associated with men.

In fact, the domestication of women or confinement of women in private sphere is not discrimination but to perceive private as valueless is real discrimination. Because for smooth functioning of any society, some kind of division of labour is required but problem arises only when the society starts to discriminate between different kinds of work as superior and inferior.

Thus, even if men and women share the unpaid domestic labour, this would hardly count as genuine sexual equality, if the reason why it was unpaid was that a particular culture devalues 'women work' or anything feminine. Sexism can be present not only in the distribution of domestic labour, but also in its devaluation. And since the devaluation of house work is tied to the broader devaluation of women's work, then part of the struggle for increased respect for women will involve increased respect for their contribution to the family.

Therefore, the need of the hour is not only to allow women to cross the boundaries of the family, but to give proper recognition to the family. So all the male-centric theories need to be revised.

II

In the philosophy of *Dharmaśāstras* man and woman are conceived as complementary to each other. This fact gets corroboration in the theory of human origin as described in the *Dharmaśāstras*. As Manu says that dividing his own body Prajāpati became half male and half female.[30] Yājñvalkya, in the *Bṛhadāraṇyaka Upaniṣad,* has clearly explained the psychological unity of the husband and the wife. He says that the man who was originally one, cleft himself into two because he felt no pleasure in loneliness and wished for a second; these two became the husband and the wife. The two separately are like half of a shell; together they are one whole.[31] We are told in the *Rāmāyaṇa* that Vasiṣṭha asked Sītā to remain at home and rule the kingdom in place of Rāma and argued that the wife is the very soul of him who marries her.[32] Manu states that to be mothers were women created and to be fathers men; religious rites therefore are ordained in the *Veda* to be performed by the husband and wife together.[33]

Dharmaśāstras accept that there is a vital structural difference between man and woman. The two are different from each other from top to toe. Each one is suited for different types of work. Man is intended by nature to do all the rough and hard work for earning bread while woman is designed for household affairs, duties less strenuous but requiring a good deal of love and affection, which none but she alone can bestow. Thus man and women are regarded as different from each other but their relation is not of superiority and inferiority but of complementarity. Radhakrishnan's following view depicts the *Dharmaśāstric* ideal of the relation between man and woman:

> Women cannot do something which men can. Their physiology prevents this. That, however, does not prove any inferiority on their part. We must do the things for which we are made and do them well.[34]

Dharmaśāstras have not the least idea of any inherent superiority of one in relation to other while assigning different types of work to man and woman. It is only a kind of division of labour, that men and women are required to do different jobs suited to their respective physical and mental capacities. Bhagwan Das explains the idea behind the division of labour as prescribed in *Dharmaśāstras:*

> And for the time being the difference of sex lasts, the vocations of the two are accepted as different in the same way as the functions of the two halves of one brain and of the head and the heart in the same body.[35]

Thus, public (men) and private (women) are regarded as supplementary to each other. *Dharmaśāstra's* ideal is gentleman and gentle woman each filling a distinct place in the domestic and the social scheme, never entering into conflict with each other but ever supplementing the qualities of each other and ever making life's way smoother for each other.[36]

From the above account, there remains no doubt that in the philosophy of *Dharmaśāstras* man and woman are regarded as different but complementary. Because of their different qualities women are considered as suitable for private realm of life whereas men for public realm of life. Now, the question arises that what was the position of private realm of life in the social scheme of *Dharmaśāstras.* From the esteemed position given to the order of the householder (i.e., *Gṛhasthaśrama*) it seems clear that private realm of life is regarded as the source of energy for public realm of life.

The āśrama system is the very base of Hindu social system. Individual's life is divided into four *āśramas*. Though all the *āśramas* are regarded as equally important, *Gṛhasthāśram* is given greater importance than the other three.

Dharmaśāstras are divided among three groups on the subject of *āśrama* system. They are the *Vikalpa,* the *Badha,* and the *Samuccaya* schools. The supporters of the *Vikalpa* school of thought hold that after the *Brahmacaryāśram,* a man has full option in choice of the *āśramas* he may become a householder after he finishes his student life or he may become a *parivrājaka* immediately after finishing his studies.[37] Vaśiṣṭha is the prime supporter of this view.[38] Jabala also puts forth this view as an alternative to that of the *Samuccaya*.[39]

The theory of *Badha* is advocated by Baudhāyana and Gautam. They are of the opinion that there was really one *āśrama*, the *Gṛhasthāśram*, and that all other *āśramas* are inferior to it.[40] Baudhāyana names the four *āśramas* and informs that it was the *asura* Kapila who being jealous of the Gods, made these distinctions which a wise man should pay no heed to.[41] Baudhāyana appears to hold that there was really only one *āśrama,* the *Gṛhasthāśrama,* the Kapila devised the scheme of the four *āśrama* to harm the gods as those who adopted the *Vānaprasthāśrama* or became a *parivrājaka* could not perform any *Yajña* and due to that the gods lost the offerings they received from men in that proportion and consequently became less powerful.

The third is the theory of *Samuccaya.* According to it, a person should resort to the *āśrama* one after the other in order and should not omit any one or more of them and pass on to the next. Āpastamba is supporter of this view who states that if a person lives in all these four *āśramas* according to the rules of law without allowing himself to be disturbed by anything, he will obtain salvation.[42]

Thus, the followers of the *Vikalpa* theory do not attach much importance to the *Gṛhasthāśram* whereas the followers of the *Badha* theory eulogise it to such a height that they hold that there is one and only one *āśrama* that is the *Gṛhasthāśram*.

Dharmaśāstras are full of such verses in which the order of householder is regarded as the most important. Manu says:

> As all living creatures subsist by receiving support from the air so all the orders subsist by receiving support from the householder. Because the men of the three orders are daily supported by the

> householder with sacred knowledge and food, therefore, householder's is the most excellent order. The duties of this order which can not be practised by men with weak organs must be carefully observed by him who desires imperishable bliss in heaven and constant happiness in this life.[43]

The sage also says:

> The student, the householder, the hermit and the ascetic, these all spring from the order of the householders. And, in accordance with the precepts of the *Veda* and of the *Smṛti's* the housekeeper is declared to be superior to all of them; for he supports the other three. As all rivers, both great and small find a resting place in the ocean, even so men of all orders find protection with the householder.[44]

It is said in the *Mahābhārata* that the life of a householder itself is very superior and sacred and gives scope for fulfilment of life's mission.[45] The order of householder is regarded as the order wherein the three *puruṣārthas,* viz., *Dharma, Artha* and *Kāma* can be achieved simultaneously. Prabhu rightly remarks :

> "The *śāstrakāra's* praise for the *gṛhastha* as the best *āśrama* emanates, we must not fail to notice, from the point of view of the best in 'social values' of the *āśramas*. Otherwise, in general, since each *āśrama* is regarded as an essential stage for the development of the individual, it is the best in its own place, and any comparison of merits between them on absolute grounds would be surely beside the point. But, from the point of view of a particular aspect, viz., *Dharma, Artha* and *Kāma* as well as of its direct contact with the society and the consequent direct contributions made by it to the society."[46]

One point which is significant to note is that the logic of Western scholars for confining women to private realm of life is that as the private realm of life is based on narrow interests so women are suitable for it as they can never think in the broader interest of whole humanity. But none of the *Dharmaśāstras* has perceived the private realm of life as an institution based on narrow interests. Moreover, in the philosophy of *Dharmaśāstras* private realm of life is regarded as a place where all the public responsibilities get fulfilled. Unlike Plato who in his communism regarded family as an impediment in the attainment of ideal state wherein individual would be free from any kind of parochialism, *Dharmaśāstrakārs* perceive it (the order of householder) as the institution where one learns the practice of self-control, self-sacrifice and public welfare. Prabhu rightly writes :

> The *gṛhasthāśrama* proves another kind of field for a life of *yajña*. At its best it is, in a sense, the fully dedicated life. Here it is one's duty to practise *artha* and *kāma* in terms of *karmas* in strict accordance with the *dharmas*, the meaning and value and the justification of which he has learnt in the first *āśrama*. He can partake of *artha* and *kāma*, of the material and the physical pleasures available on earth, but without any feelings of covetousness, greed or lust, taking only his due share in these pleasures in strict accordance with the *dharmas* of this *āśrama*. The *gṛhastha's* life has also to be a continuous stream of giving (*dāna*), a life of self-service and dedication of his best and utmost for his elders, children, wife (who also is sharer in his service to others) and other members of his family (*kula*), his dependents and strangers (*atithi*), through his acts of fulfilling his social obligations (*riṇas*). ... Here, therefore, a *karma-yajña* consistent with and in accordance with dharma has to be practised as fully as possible by the individual.[47]

Performance of five types of sacrifices, viz., *Brahma Yajña, PitṛYajña, Deva Yajña, Bhūta Yajña,* and *Nṛ Yajña,* are prescribed for the householder.[48] These expiatory sacrifices are performed in terms of the execution of certain social and human duties. Thus, teaching and studying are to be presumed as expressive of the *brahma yajña,* which is offered to the memory of distinguished and learned sages of the past (*ṛṣis*); the offering of water and food known as *tarpaṇa* and offered at the *śrāddha* ceremony forms the sacrifice to the spirit or memory of the ancestors (*pitṛ-yajña*); oblations offered to the sacred fire (*homa*) have reference to the sacrifice to the gods (*deva yajña*); offering of food to alleviate and propitiate the spirit which are supposed to influence human being constitutes the *bhūta-yajña* and the hospitable offering of food and shelter to guests and strangers (*atithi yajña*) has to be performed in a spirit of sacrifice to man (*nṛ-yajña*).[49] Every *gṛhastha* along with his *gṛhi* must offer these five sacrifices as the sages, the ancestors, the gods, the spirits and the strangers look up to them in expectation of these offerings.[50] By performing these sacrifices the householder secure permanent happiness.[51] Thus, these sacrifices are performed at private realm with the aim of universal happiness. So where is the distinction between public and private?

Since private is not regarded as inferior to public in the philosophy of *Dharmaśāstras*, detailed rules have been laid down by the *Dharmaśāstrakārs* for regulating private matters. Thus, there is very rare possibility of exploitation of women in the private realm of life in the guise of privacy. To illustrate, *Dharmaśāstras* laid down rules even concerning very intimate relations between husband and wife. Even mating of husband and wife is not regarded as a private matter. But as a duty to be performed for continuing of progeny. Detailed rules have been laid down regarding the foetus-laying-ceremony (i.e., *garbhādhān saṁskāra*).[52] This ceremony is performed at the consummation of marriage. It is in continuation of the pledge taken by the marrying parties at their wedding, viz., to fulfill the obligation of continuing the family line. Thus, the mating of husband and wife as identified with the foetus laying ceremony suggests that mating is conceived as a part of the obligations of the married couple towards family and the community.[53] Kane writes:

> To modern minds it appears strange that intercourse should have been surrounded by so much of mysticism and religion in the ancient sutras. But in ancient times every act was sought to be invested with a religious halo; so much so that according to *Hiraṇyakeṣi Gṛhyasūtra* 1.7.25.3 Atreya held that *mantras* were to be repeated at each cohabitation throughout life, while Badarayana prescribed that this was necessary only at the first cohabitation and after each monthly course.[54]

Moreover, the time when a husband should approach his wife does not depend on his arbitrary will. *Dharmaśāstrakāras* were not of the opinion that husband can approach his wife according to his arbitrary will. As Yāj prescribes:

> Remembering the vow of women, being faithfully devoted to one's own wife and being influenced by desire proportionate to (hers), one can know (his wife), even at any other time except the menstrual period, for it is laid down in *Smṛtis* that women should be protected by every means.[55]

Commending the above view of Yāj, Sati Chatterjee rightly writes that this in a starting flash, forbids what is mentioned as rape in wedlock in feminist parlance of our time.[56]

They also lay down rules on the issues like when a wife can be deserted? On which grounds wife can be superseded? She would be entitled to what types of benefits in case of supersession? All these questions corroborate the fact that in the philosophy of *Dharmaśāstras* the private sphere is not regarded as a realm beyond justice.

One point may be raised against the above view that as the opinion of the *Dharmaśāstrakāras* was that there should be no legal proceeding between husband and wife, how can it be said that they consider the private realm of life as a place where court could intertwine.

Jois opines that as according to *Dharmaśāstrakāras* a dispute between husband and wife should not be brought before the king or any other people's court for adjudication,[57] the *Strīpumdharma* can properly be called an *Ācāra Saṁhitā* (code of conduct) and not as law enforceable in courts. If any dispute arose between husband and wife, it used to be settled by the assembly of either relatives or elderly members of the caste.[58] Derrett observes:

> Matrimonial disputes came before the king's court only in highly exceptional circumstances. They were dealt with within the family, the caste, the village, subject to the spiritual supervision of the *Rājagurū́* or Pandit whose duty it was to see that *Varṇāśramadharma* was observed in the kingdom. Just as *pañcāyats* today deal with irregular unions, sexual misbehaviour and matrimonial discord, so too in ancient times, problems between husband and wife were not to be handled by the civil and criminal administration.[59]

Thus, though they were of the opinion that dispute between husband and wife should not be subjected to legal procedure yet they recognized importance of such private issues and emphasized the need of solving these matters through informal machanisms. Emergence of family courts in modern India proves the relevance of the view of *Dharmaśāstrakāras.* They prohibited legal proceedings between husband and wife not because they considered these matters as less important but because these very delicate issues needed to be handled very passionately and delicately.

Thus, the watertight compartment between public and private does not exist in the *Dharmaśāstras*. Further, private is not regarded as inferior to public but as more important where public responsibilities get fulfilled. In this private realm which is even important to public realm woman plays the key role. None of the *yajñas* can be performed alone by men.

It is said in the *Mahābhārata*:

> Wife is the very source of the *puruṣārthas* not only of *dharma*, *artha* and *kāma*, but even of *mokśa*. Those that have wives can fulfill their due obligation in this world; those that have wives can be happy and those that have wives can lead a full life.[60]

The duties for which the order of householder is regarded as most important cannot be performed without the wife. Therefore, Manu says that for conceiving progeny, wives, the light of the household, the repositories of bliss and auspiciousness should be honoured with presents of apparels and ornaments. No distinction exists between the wife and the goddess of fortune in the household. Wife is the manifest source of procreation and bringing up of children, and of the performance of the duties of everyday life as well.[61] He says:

> Giving birth to children, performance of religious sacrifice, nursing, excellent love, and the acquisition of heaven by one and his manes are contingent on his wife.[62]

Thus, wife is not regarded as poor being who is dependent on his husband's mercy but as the pivot of the family. It is said in the *Mahābhārata* that the house full of sons, daughters, and daughters-in-law, is quite empty for a person if his wife is not there to supervise it; she is surest solace to her husband; she is the friend who never forsakes him in adversity; in fact a home without a wife is worse than a forest in point of dreariness.[63] Medhātithi in his commentary on Manu explains how the householder is incapable in fulfilling his duties either private or public without the support of his wife: "they (the wives) are like effulgence in their homes. It is well known that there is no comfort at home in the absence of the wife. Even when there is plenty of wealth, if the wife is absent, the householder is not able to attend the feeding and other needs of the friends and relatives that may happen to come in as guest. In fact they are as powerless as poor men. For this reason there is no difference between the goddess of wealth and women in their homes. Wives serves the fulfilment of the visible and invisible ends of men. For example when desire for sexual intercourse arises in a man, there is the possibility of his having recourse to any and every woman; but intercourse with maidens and wives of other men being prohibited, the said desire comes to be accomplished only through his own married wife. The married wife thus serves a visible end. Then again there is the saying that every religious act shall be done by the husband and wife together, which shows that it is only as accompanied by his wife that a man is entitled to the performance of religious act and thus it is clear that the accomplishment of the invisible purpose of a man also is dependent upon his wife."[64]

Thus, Medhātithi while making above statement does not appear less feminist than Carol Pateman who argues that this public man looks so shining, so smiling and so enlightening because a messy content of the body all the time looks after his needs.

Conclusion

In the conclusion three points can be made: first, unlike the dominant Western philosophical discourse the *Dharmaśāstrīya* discourse do not make any watertight compartment between public and private; second, private is not regarded as inferior to public rather the existence of the public is considered as dependent on the private; third, woman is in the centre of the private. Thus, there is no point in making the remark that "*dharmaśāstras* have relegated women to a secondary position by confining them to the private sphere." Such remark comes out when one studies these texts through Western eyes. Therefore, there is a need to study these texts holistically in their particular sociocultural context. What is required is to evolve an indigenous methodology to study these texts and to analyse the position of women in it.

Notes

1. "Feminist Critiques of the Public/Private Dichotomy" in A. Phillips (ed.) *Carole Pateman, Feminism and Equality,* Blackwell, Oxford, 1987, p. 103.
2. See Coole, Diama H., *Women in Political Theory: From Ancient Misogyny to Contemporary Feminism.* Wheatsheaf Books, Sussex, 1988, pp. 1-2.
3. Barker, *The Politics of Aristotle,* New York, Oxford University Press, 1962, p. 4.
4. For Hegel, Antigone represents womanhood and family in both the polis of the pagan world and in modern life: "... Family life is expounded in Sophocles' Antigone... as principally the law of woman, and as the law of substantiality at once subjective and on the plane of feeling, the law of inward life ... . This law is thereby displaced as a law opposed public law, to the law of the land. This is the supreme opposition in ethics and therefore in tragedy: and it is individualized in the same play in the opposing natures of man and woman". (... in T.M. Knox, 1990, p. 63) *Encyclopedia Britanika,* Chicago, The University of Chicago Press.
5. Barker, p. 108.
6. Jean Bethke Elshtain, *Public Man, Private Woman,* Princeton University Press, Princeton, New Jersey, 1981, p. 23.
7. Ibid., p. 23.
8. *The Republic,* Book 2, 366 a-367a.
9. *The Laws,* pp. 262-63. See also the discussion by Christian Garside Allen, "Plato on Women", *Feminist Studies,* pp. 131-138.

10. Elshtain. op. cit. P. 36.
11. *Generation of Animals,* II, 932a, ef. 1, 727 b and II 738 b.
12. *Generation of Animals,* I, 729a, 731a (trans. A.L. Peck, Loeb Classical Library, London, 1970).
13. *Politics,* p. 4.
14. Ibid., p. 5.
15. Cf. MacIntyre, *Short History of Ethics,* p. 63, "The good of man is defined as the activity of the soul in accordance with virtue or if there are a number of human excellence or virtues, in accordance with the best and most perfect of them".
16. *Politics,* pp. 2-3.
17. Ibid., p. 34.
18. Ibid., pp. 35-36.
19. Ibid., p. 108.
20. Ibid., p. 11 ff.
21. Jermy Bentham, *The Principle of Morals and Legislation*, New York, Hafner Publishing 1965, pp. 58-59.
22. *Emile*, p. 331.
23. *Emile*, 1969, p. 325 (trans. Boxley).
24. *A Bloom Politics and the Arts: A Letter to D' Alembert on the Theatre,* tr. Ithaca, Cornell University Press, 1968, p. 87.
25. Hegal, *Phenomenology of Spirit,* (trans.) A.V. Miller, Oxford: Clarendon, 1977, para 475, p. 288.
26. Freud, "Some Psychical Consequences of Anatomical Distinction between the Sexes" in the Standard Edition of the *Complete Psychological Works*, trans. J. Strachey, London, Hogarth Press, 1961, Vol. 7, p. 342.
27. Jaggar, A, *Feminist Politics and Human Nature,* Rowman and Allanheld, Totowa, NJ, 1983, p. 199.
28. See Rawls, *A Theory of Justice,* Oxford University Press, London, 1971, pp. 128 and 146.
29. Susan Moller, Okin, "Gender, the Public and the Private" in Devid Held (ed.) *Political Theory Today,* Cambridge, Polity Press, 1991, p. 71.
30. Manu, I. 32.
31. Br. Up. 1.4.3.
32. Rāmāyaṇa, II. 37, 23-24.
33. Manu, IX. 96.

    Sabara forcefully propounds the view that, in the matter of Dharma, Artha and Kāma husband must have the association of his wife. Sabara pp. 979-981 on Jamini VI (1)-101.

34. Swami Madhavanand and Majumdar, K.C. (eds.) *Great Women of India*, Advaita Ashrama, Calcutta, 1997 'Introduction', p. XV.
35. Das, Bhagwan, *Science of Social Organisation,* p. 450.
36. Ibid., Vol. II, p. 452.
37. Ranade, A. *Constructive Survey of Upniṣadic Philosophy,* pp. 60-61.

    see also Keith, *Religion and Philosphy of the Vedas and the Upaniṣads,* Vol. II, p. 587.
38. Vas. VII. 3.
39. Jab. Up. IV.
40. Gaut. III. 1-35.
41. Bau. D.S. II. 6.29-31.
42. Āp. D.S. II. 9.21.2.
43. Manu. III. 77-79.
44. Manu.VI. 87, 89, 90.
45. Mbh. Śāntiparva. II. 27.
46. Prabhu, P., *Hindu Social Organization,* Popular Prakashan, Bombay, 1995, p. 95.
47. Prabhu, p. 98.
48. Manu. III. 68-69.

    These five sacrifices are intended to expiate the sins committed by a *gṛhastha,* and which as a gṛhastha, he cannot but help committing, at the five "slaughter-houses", as it were, which exist in each home, viz. the hearth *(chulli)*, the grinding stone *(peshni)*, the broom *(upaskarah)*, the pestle and mortar and the water-vessel. While using these implements and tools in the home, he would wittingly or unwittingly cause destruction of so many creatures, like ants, worms etc.
49. Manu. III. 70 and 81; Yaj I. 102, Asw. G.S. III . I. 1-4.
50. Manu. III. 80.
51. Manu. III.79-81; Yaj. I. 23 and 104.
52. See Atharva V. 25.3 and 5; Br. Up. VI. 4.21; Asv. G.S. I. 13.1; Par. G.S. I.11, s.B.E. Vol. 29, pp. 288-90; Ap.G.S.8.10-11, S.B.E, Vol. 30, pp. 267-268; Gobhila II.5 (S.B.E. Vol. 30, pp. 51-52) Hir. G.S. I.7, 23.11 to 7, 25'; Manu. III.46; Yaj. I. 79.
53. See Prabhu, p. 219.
54. Kane, *History of Dharmaśāstras* Vol. II, Pt.-I, p. 203.
55. Yaj. I. 81.
56. See Chatterjee, Sati, "Ontological Status of Women in the Dharmaśāstras : The Positve Perception and the Negative" in Chandrakala Padia (ed.). *Feminism, Tradition, and Modirnity,* IIAS, Shimla, 2002, p. 222.

    Yāj's this text also gives recognition to woman's sexuality.

57. दम्पत्ती विवदेयातां न ज्ञातिषु न टाजनि,

58. Jois, Rama, *Legal and Constitutional, History of India,* Universal Publication, New Delhi, 2000, p. 253.

59. *The Death of Marriage Law* by J. Duncan M. Derrett, p. 58.

60. Mbh. Adi. 74, 40-41.

61. Manu. IX. 26-27.

62. Ibid. 28.

63. Mbh. XII. 4.4; XII. 144.16; III. 58.29.

64. Medhātithi on M. IX. 26-27.

7

My Hours with Manu and Some Unlikely Answers

Devapriya Roy

Let me start by being entirely honest. My hours with Manu were wrought with difficulty. My knowledge of history, society and culture was anything but specialized; not knowing Sanskrit myself I could only work with translations; and more than anything else I was largely limited by age and experience. Then, there was a fervent search to locate an apt methodology to analyse the text. Thankfully, soon enough, a certain gentleman, Mr I.A. Richards, came to my rescue!

Now, I.A. Richards, the chief proponent of Practical Criticism or New Criticism of the 1920s, had started an interesting exercise in his classrooms. He would come to class, distribute a poem printed on sheets of paper to the students, and without disclosing the name or particulars of the poet ask them to engage closely with the text and come up with their own readings. The method has its advantages. Since one does not start with any 'given', the text opens up to a wide range of possibilities, becoming a dynamic site of 'unlikely dialogue', across time and space. My methodology in dealing with the broad theme of 'Women in the *Manusmṛti*' has been somewhat akin to that of the New Critics. I looked at George Buhler's English translation of the text, as well as the Bengali version of the same, edited by Dr. Manabendu Bandopadhyay. Indeed, the Bengali one captures the essence of the Sanskrit original much better, since many of the words have absolutely no counterparts in English, but have remained in some form of the other in the vernaculars.

Undoubtedly, the *Manusmṛti* or the *Manusaṁhitā* is one of the most controversial of the *Dharmaśāstras*. But first let us ask ourselves, what is a *Dharmaśāstra?* And indeed, what is *dharma?* The second verse of the very first chapter of the *Manusmṛti* defines *dharma* as that through which *śreya* is achieved, or in other words, the means to *śreya* is *dharma (dharman no baktumaharsi*[1] *)*. So now we are led on to ask, what is *śreya* then? This brings us to the famous story of Naciketā and Yama, as narrated in the *Kathopaniṣad.* As one of the boons granted to him, Naciketā asks Yama to reveal to him the mystery of death :

"There is doubt in regard to a man who has departed, some (holding) that he is and some that he is not. I would be instructed by thee in this knowledge."[2]

Yama hesitates, and then requests Naciketā to ask for something else:

It is not, indeed, easy to understand; so subtle is this truth. Choose another boon, O Naciketā. Do not press me.[3]

But when Nachiketā perseveres, Yama begins his profound discourse on Death. At any point of time man is faced with two choices –that between *śreya* or what is good and must be done, and *preya* or the pleasant which continuously beckons. (Yama said): "Different is the good, and different, indeed, is the pleasant. These two, with different purposes, bind a man. Of these two, it is well for him who takes hold of the good; but he who chooses the pleasant, fails of his aim."[4]

But what makes the discourse of *śreya* and *preya* very complex and subtle is the fact that *śreya* is not merely doing one's duty, but there is an entire philosophy of joy which underlies it, and actually leads to the choice of *śreya* over *preya.* Indeed as Yama goes on to inform Nachiketa, for one who lives by *śreya,* there is no death. We must not lose sight of the various connotations of śreya, including its deeper philosophy of joy, as we consider dharma in general and the *Dharmaśāstras* in particular.

Now, indeed the *Dharmaśāstras* are enûnciatory texts which deal with the codes and mores, the social, political and legal aspects of human life. And yet, there is more to the work than this. In the first chapter of the *Manusmṛti* we find 'the great sages' approach Manu and ask him:

"Deign, divine one, to declare to us precisely and in due order the sacred laws of each of the (four chief) castes (*varṇa*) and of the intermediate ones."[5]

It is to be noted that Manu starts, not by answering this specific question but by going on to describe the creation of the universe, the presence of 'Svayambhu' or the divine self-evident and goes on right up to the creation of the first human, and then finally to the birth of the male and female principles. What does this have to do with the specific question asked to Manu about the *varna* system? Indeed, one must think through this. By talking about the universe and its creation, not only is there an attempt to seek some kind of divine legitimacy for the rest of the document but more importantly one locates therein an attempt to provide metaphysical precepts to social practices. The key to unlocking the *Manusmṛti* lies in understanding these metaphysical precepts, and indeed through the prism of these, we might seek to re-read the social practices, and correct them where faulty.

I would deal with some specific examples regarding the position of the female within the realms of sexuality. My argument is that while the *Manusmṛti* is quite clearly concerned with the day to day aspects of marriage and sexuality (for instance it seems to privilege reproductive sex over unproductive, pleasure-oriented sex), there are verses within it which deal with the philosophical aspects of sexuality. Significantly, these throw new light on the position of women within the metaphysical framework of the tradition.

According to Manu

"This (universe) existed in the shape of Darkness, unperceived, destitute of distinctive marks, unattainable by reasoning, unknowable, wholly immersed, as it were, in deep sleep."[6]

"In order to understand the essence better we might consider some of the adjectives used in the Sanskrit original – a-*pragyatam* or beyond the range of direct perception, a-*lakśaṇam* or beyond inference or signs, a-*pratakyam* or beyond reason or logic, and a-*bigyeyam* or beyond words. Indeed, these go on to signify a world which, prior to the definitions and divisions of modernity, is fluid, one, and beyond gender."[7]

Then, the divine Self-evident (Swayambhu, himself) indiscernible, (but) making (all) this, the great elements and the rest, discernible, appeared with irresistible (creative) power, dispelling the darkness.

Then,

> He, desiring to produce beings of many kinds from his own body, first with a thought created the waters, and placed his seed in them.[8]

This metaphor of the seed and the receptacle (water/soil), the first example of a male and a female principle immanent in the cosmos, is recurrent throughout the *Manusmṛti*. For instance, Chapter IX, Verse 33 declares:

> "In this sacred tradition the woman is declared to be the soil, the man is declared to be the seed; the production of all corporeal beings (takes place) through the union of the soil with the seed."

Water (narah) becomes the amniotic fluid to the first *Puruṣa* (here, puruṣa is not used in the sense of male, but human in general, since it refers to the residence of the soul), who resides for a whole year within the cosmic egg. And finally the duality of male/female or Śiva/Śakti, inherent in nature, is achieved when:

> Dividing his own body, the Lord became half male and half female.[9]

To me this becomes the fundamental pivot around which the hermeneutics of the *Manusmṛti* must revolve. Only then may we evolve a strategy of reading that would privilege an indigenous model of feminist thought.

In the realm of sexuality, the idea of one body, divided into two, and ever desirous to be one again forms the central concept. *Kāma* is the desire for this union which at its ecstatic best, is likened to the divine. Within the Indic tradition desire has been granted legitimacy ("Not a single act here (below) appears ever to be done by a man free from desire"[10]), and *kāma* is one of the four *puruṣārthas*. And indeed both man and woman are equal partners in the ideal sexual union, which is the physical manifestation of a metaphysical yearning. There is a wide pervasion of these concepts in texts like Vātsyāyana's *Kāmasūtra,* Jayadeva's *Gītagovindam* and the later *Vaiṣṇav Padas*. For instance, we might look at *Caṅḍidāsa's pada,* describing Rādhā's lament as she pines for her soul mate:

> Radhar ki hoilo antare byatha
>
> Bosiya birole thakoye ekole
>
> Na shune kaharo katha

Sadai dheyane dekhe meghpane
Na chole nayaan tara
Biroti ahaare ranga baas pore
Je mata joginee para.
(Oh what was the anguish that seized Radha's soul!
Sitting all lonesome, Away from everyone,
Unmindful of the words of all.
Meditating all day
On the dusky clouds far away
Her eyelids did not move.
Forgetting what was to be done
Dressing herself in saffron
Like a joginee she sat all aloof.[11])

Rādhā's pining for her Krișṇa, is not merely on the plane of mortal needs but is a profound yearning of cosmic proportions, of the human halves seeking their wholeness.

A close reading of the *Manusmṛti* yields evidences of this:

Thus (says the *Veda*), and learned Brāhmaṇas propound this (maxim) likewise, the husband is declared to be *one* with the wife.[12]

There are also the concepts of the 'offspring of desire' articulated in Verse 107, of Chapter IX and of *gandharva vivāha* in Verse 32 of Chapter III:

The voluntary union of a maiden and her lover one must know to be the gandharva rite, which springs from desire…

Very often we find that corruptions have crept into human practices, and a wide chasm is present between the worlds of egalitarian precept and faulty practice. As far as the position of the woman is concerned, nothing can be more true! We find, in the *Manusmṛti*, in spite of the essential equality between man and woman in creation, various contradictory notions exist about the position of women in society. However, there should be no hesitation in us to completely reject that which common sense and indeed, the 'egalitarian' philosophy underlying the text itself find unfair, cruel or plain irrelevant to our times. Indeed I would like to conclude with a story about the *Manusmṛti* which resonates with this very idea.

According to the *Nāradasmṛti,* Manu had written one lakh *ślokas,* divided into twenty-four chapters in his original *Dharmaśāstra.* Reading this text Nārada felt that its length was definitely a deterrent, and he edited it accordingly, bringing it down to 12,000 verses. It was subsequently given to Mārkaṇḍeya who revised it into 8,000 ślokas, and finally it was Bhṛgu who gave it the present form of around 4,000 verses[13]. Indeed, this exemplifies the fact that the tradition of *Dharmaśāstras* in particular, and of *Hinduism* in general, is not static but is rather subject to the needs and requirements of its age. Thus, we see that even the 'much maligned' *Manusmṛti* contains the basic egalitarian and deeply philosophical precepts that must be evoked in order to evolve a vibrant, Indic model of feminism where woman, where deprived, would be readily restored to a position of equality.

Notes

1. Bandopadhyay, Manabendu, Trans. and Ed. *Manusaṁhitā,* Kolkata, Sanskrit Pustak Bhandar, 2003.
2. Manu. Ch. II, Verse 4.
3. Verse 20, Section 1, *Katha Upaniṣad* (Radhakrishnan 603).
4. Verse 21, Section 1, *Katha Upaniṣad* (Radhakrishnan 604).
5. Verse 1, Section 2, *Katha Upaniṣad* (Radhakrishnan 607).
6. Manu. Ch. I, Verse 2.
7. Manu. Ch. I, Verse 5.
8. Manu. Ch. I, Verse 6.
9. Manu. Ch. I, Verse 7.
10. Manu. Ch. I, Verse 7.
11. Manu. Ch. I, Verse 7 (Italics mine).
12. Manu. Bühler's Translation.
13. Related in the Prologue, *Manusaṁhitā*, p. 3.

II

Diverse Images of Women in *Dharmaśāstras*

8

Mahābhārata through the Eyes of Women

Kavita A. Sharma

If we look at *Mahābhārata* through the eyes of women, the central issue that stands out is one of sexuality. Yudhiṣṭhira, the newly anointed king after the war, requests Bhīṣma lying on his bed of arrows, to tell him about the disposition of women who were supposed to be the root of all evil and were regarded as exceedingly frail.[1] This is a strange request from a man trying to learn about statecraft but obviously one that troubles him and which even Bhīṣma finds at first difficult to answer. So he does not give him a direct reply to begin with but takes recourse to the re-counting of discourse between Nārada and the celestial courtesan Pañcacūḍā.[2]

Women's sexuality is seen as a potentially extremely destructive force in front of which the mightiest of men are rendered helpless. Yet, it can be put to great use once it is subordinated and regulated. Hence, women are divided into two classes: the utterly destructive because of their unbridled sexuality and the chaste wives and mothers. Within this polarity lie the ambiguities of *Niyoga* or levirate, polyandry and a woman's freedom to take the initiative in approaching a man. There are also ambivalences with regard to the relationship between the wife and the husband's brother. All these indicate the changing social structures at different points of time as *Mahābhārata* evolved for about a thousand years before reaching its present form. It also shows variations of region, class and caste. On the one hand, it is absolutely legitimate to forcibly abduct a woman for marriage, but on the other, a woman has the freedom to reject a suitor at her *swayamvara* in spite of being bound by conditions laid down by her male relatatives as Karṇa is by Draupadī.

Bhīṣma explains the division of women into the two categories of chaste and unchaste. At one time he says, women were as virtuous as men and so in the course of natural progress, both began to reach the status of deities. This alarmed the gods who went to Brahma for help as they did not wish to lose their superior position in the hierarchy of creation. Brahma, then created women with the aid of an Atharvan rite and implanted in them the desire for the enjoyment of all kinds of carnal pleasure at the time of their creation itself. Thus, those who were created from illusion became sinful while the others remained chaste. Brahma then created Wrath as the companion of Lust and men yielding to the power of both desired women intemperately causing evil.[3]

Bhīṣma uses a woman, Pañcacūḍā, to denounce women in the strongest possible terms. She describes them to be at the root of all sin. They are, according to her, extremely lascivious and always ready to bestow favours on any man who comes their way even if he is an invalid or an idiot.[4] They cannot be restrained continues Bhīṣm, even by the Creator himself. He buttresses his arguments by citing Ṛṣi Devasarman's words to his disciple, Vipula. The Ṛṣi divided women into two classes – those who were virtuous and those were not. The virtuous women were the mothers of the universe and highly blessed. They upheld the earth with all its waters and forests and so needed to be protected and cherished. Those who were not, destroyed the entire race and could not be restrained or protected.[5]

The question then arises, wherein lies the virtuousness of women. The idea of chastity and virtue were conjoined with the subordination and regulation of the sexuality of women by men. This creates a dominant patriarchal structure although some matriarchal customs survive as in the case of Mādri where Bhīṣma has to give gifts to her father in return for her hand for Pāṇḍu.[6] The patriarchal structure is also hierarchal and these two paradigms operate both in the public and private sphere. In the public sphere the hierarchical structure is seen in the superiority of the two rulings classes – the Brahmins and the Kṣatriyas – between whom an equation has to be established so that they do not challenge each other's hegemony and create conflict. Interestingly, this is done again through the agency of women.

Parśurāma, the son of Ṛṣi Jamadagni, angered by the death of his father, set out on a conquest of the world with the aim of exterminating Kṣatriyas. When he had annihilated all of them, the Kṣatriya women began to approach the Brahmins in order to have offspring from them. These were regarded as virtuous motives and hence no sin accrued to them.[7] Thus the Kṣatriya race was revived and the Kṣatriyas and Brahmins got related by ties of blood. A division of functionality was established between them so that both the requirements of governance could be fulfilled: rule by sagacity and action through war. These two got intermingled in Droṇa, a warrior Brāhmin who avenged his insult by Drupada by ruling over half his kingdom obtained as gurudakṣiṇā from Arjuna.

Within the patriarchal framework women acquire chastity not necessarily through fidelity to one man but by allowing their sexuality to be regulated by men whether as wives or daughters. Kuntī, for example, the daughter of Śūrasena, was given away by him to his dear friend and cousin, Kuntībhoja, who was childless. It was customary in those times for heirless kings to invite Brāhmins to their house to seek their favour and blessings for sons. The daughter of the house would serve them looking after all their needs and even share their bed if they so desired in order to please them. Kuntī was thus appointed by her adoptive father Kuntībhoja to serve Durvāsā Ṛṣi, who pleased by her conduct, bestowed on her a *mantra* that would enable her to call upon any man or god that she might desire. As curiosity she called upon Sūrya, who begat Karṇa on her and whom she abandoned as she was not married at that time.[8]

The scope of chastity seems to have got progressively narrowed as patriarchy gradually became more and more firmly entrenched. Pāṇḍu talks of a time when women were not immured within their houses nor were they dependent on their husbands and relatives. They were free to go wherever and to whomever they wanted and were still considered virtuous because that was the accepted customary usage. However, their freedom was curtailed by Śwetaketu, the son of the ascetic Uddālaka. One day a Brāhmin came and invited Śwetaketu's mother to go with him in the presence of Uddālaka his father. She readily agreed but Śwetaketu did not like it and got angry in spite of his father telling him that there was nothing wrong with it, as that was the sanctioned practice. Śwetaketu laid down rules of conduct for women by which they were obliged to adhere to one man and it became sinful for them to deviate from this, as did Dirghatamas in another story. However, Śwetaketu also made it imperative upon men to treat a chaste and loving wife well otherwise they would be guilty of sin. Further, he prohibited women from raising offspring from another man at the behest of their husbands.[9] Thus morality got circumscribed.

In times of greater sexual freedom, women too could approach men on their own and it was imperative upon the men so approached to gratify their wishes. For example, Gaṅgā approached Pratipa, Śāntanu's father in the form of a beautiful woman when she sat on his right thigh. She desired him for a husband but Pratipa pointed out that the right thigh was meant for daughters and daughters-in-law so he promised to ensure that he would get her married to his son. Consequently, Śāntanu later married Gaṅgā.[10] Arjuna was punished for not responding to the advances of Urvaśī and had to spend his time as a eunuch in the court of Virāta surrounded by women.[11] Hiḍimbā too approached Bhīma when the Pāṇḍavas were in exile. Bhīma hesitated as he was guarding the sleeping Kuntī and his brothers. They were, however, aroused because Hiḍimbā's brother arrived and challenged Bhīma to a duel in which Bhīma finally defeated him. The commotion woke them all up and Yudhiṣṭhira learning of Hiḍimbā's wishes gave Bhīma permission to go and gratify her. As a result Ghaṭotkaca was born who rendered great service during the *Mahābhārata* war.[12]

In between complete freedom and complete fidelity to one man lay the system of polyandry. After Arjuna won Draupadī in the *swayamvara,* the five brothers took her to Kuntī who inadvertantly said that they should share equally whatever they had brought. She realized her blunder when she saw Draupadī but then the question arose on how to both fulfill Kuntī's words and also ensure the virtue of Draupadī. The problem was referred to Yudhiṣṭhira who was the embodiment of *dharma.* At first he pronounced with great impartiality that since Arjuna had won Draupadī he should marry her. However, Arjuna could not marry before his elder brothers, Yudhiṣṭhira and Bhīma. Finally, however, realizing that Draupadī's extraordinary beauty had generated desire in all of them including himself and that this could be a cause of discord among them he decided that Draupadī would be their common wife.[13] Later, after the marriage, Nārada advises the Pāṇḍavas to work out rules of cohabitation with Draupadī as otherwise it would lead to a conflict.[14]

Drupada is aghast when Yudhiṣṭhira asked him for his consent to his proposal and says that this was against dharma to which Yudhiṣṭhira shrewdly replied that it was difficult to decide what was *dharma* and what *adharma.* It was very subtle and its real implications lay beyond them. Here they simply had to follow the path trodden by their ancestors. Besides their mother also desired this. A discussion on polyandry followed. Yudhiṣṭhira referred to the authority of the *Purāṇas* in which the virtuous Jatila had married seven rishis simultaneously. Also, an ascetic's daughter born of a tree had united herself with ten brothers all called Prachetas. Moreover, this was expedient because an elder brother could not approach his younger brother's wife but the reverse was acceptable. Therefore, Yudhiṣṭhira concluded that Draupadī should agree to his suggestion as the path of *dharma.*[15]

There is the story of the rishi Utathya and his wife Mamatā narrated by Bhīṣma to Satyavatī in this context. Mamatā was already pregnant from Utathya and the child had studied the *Vedas* while in her womb, foreshadowing Abhimanyu's learning the techniques of the *cakravyūha* in the womb of Subhadrā. Vṛhaspati, her husband's younger brother, approached her. Although Mamatā told him of her condition, he could not resist her beauty and united with her. When the child in the womb protested that he had already occupied the space within and that there was no room for another, Vṛhaspati cursed him with blindness as he had been interrupted during a pleasure common to all living beings. Hence the child Dirghatamas was born blind.[16] The episode foreshadows the later disabling of Pāṇḍu which prevented him from cohabiting with his wives because of his interrupting the mating of deer.[17]

Vyāsa also supports Yudhiṣṭhira and narrates two stories to show that Draupadī was in any case destined to marry all the five brothers. They seem to be contradictory but the conclusion arrived at in both cases is the same. According to the first, a beautiful daughter of an ascetic performed penances to propitiate Śiva who appeared before her. In her impatience, she asked him for a husband five times and so Śiva granted her five husbands in her next birth. In the next story Śiva was playing dice with Pārvatī when he was arrogantly disturbed by Indra who described himself as the lord of the world. As a penalty he was split into five and sent to earth as the five Pāṇḍavas. Sri Indra's consort followed as Draupadī and so although she was to marry the five brothers, they were in essence one. Hence, in one story it is Śiva's boon and in the other his wrath but the conclusion is the same.[18] Draupadī's silence on as important an issue as her marriage is strange and out of character. Two explanations can be given. One is that she may have been familiar with the custom of polyandry and may not have had serious reservations about it.

The second is that she herself may have been Drupada's daughter from a woman other than his wife or alternately a product of a levitate relationship. The description of her extraordinary birth as an adult from the sacrificial fire may only be an attempt to gloss over these possibilities. If any of these alternatives are correct, her silence is understandable.

It is curious that Kuntī should desire that Draupadī marry all the five brothers. When Pāṇḍu had wanted her to beget sons for him through levirate relationships she had initially opposed the idea but on his citing ancient authorities in his favour she had ultimately agreed.[19] She informed Pāṇḍu of the boon given to her by Durvāsā Ṛṣi by which she could summon anyone she liked. She had three sons through Dharmarāja, Vāyu and Indra but when Pāṇḍu wanted more she said that a woman having relationship with four men was considered an outcaste and one with five a harlot.[20] But then, of course it can be argued that in case of Draupadī it is a marriage and in the other levirate relationships.

Levirate seems to have been an accepted custom. Pāṇḍu himself cites several instances. Madayanti, wife of Saudasa, commanded by her husband went to Ṛṣi Vasiṣṭha and got a son called Asmaka by him.[21] The daughter of Saradandayana, a warrior woman begot three sons for her husband from a Brāhmin ascetic.[22] In any case Pāṇḍu himself was begotten of a levirate relationship between Vyāsa and his mother Ambālikā.[23]

A similar discussion had taken place between Bhīṣma and Satyavatī when he had refused to beget children on the widows of his brother Vicitravirya Ambikā and Ambālikā because of an earlier vow of celibacy that he had taken for Satyavatī herself. He, however, suggested that Śāntanu's line could be saved by requisitioning the services of some Brāhmin ascetic. The Kṣatriya race itself, he reminded her had been revived by the union of Kṣatriya women with Brahmins after Parśurāma's extermination of them. He also narrated the story of King Vāli who asked the blind sage Dhirgatamas to beget sons on his wife Sudeśṇā. At first she did not go to him looking down on the blind old man. Instead she sent her nurse on whom he begot eleven sons. When Vāli realized that they were not his children he once again requests Sudeśnā to go to the Ṛṣi and this time he begot five sons on her.[24] This foreshadows Ambikā's substitution of the maid for cohabitation with Vyāsa the second time round resulting in the birth of Vidura.

Satyavati confesses to the existence of Vyāsa, a great ascetic and her premarital son from Pārāśara Ṛṣi. He is then chosen by Bhīṣma to father the children from Vicitravirya's widows. This foreshadows Kuntī's premarital son Karṇa from Sūrya. Pāṇḍu mentions twelve kinds of sons admitted by religious institutions of which the first six could be regarded as both kinsmen and heirs while the latter six as only kinsmen. The first six were the son begotten by one's own self upon ones wife; the son begotten upon one's wife by an accomplished person from motives of kindness; the son begotten on one's wife by a person for pecuniary considerations; the son begotten upon the wife after the husband's death; the maiden born son; and the son born of an unchaste wife. The latter six were: the son who is given; the son bought for a consideration; the son begotten upon a wife of lower caste; the brother's son; and the son received from a pregnant bride.[25] This is obviously an effort to provide for the care and legitimacy of children whether born in or out of wedlock. Since the maiden born son could also be the heir to the throne, it can be argued that if Kuntī had had the courage like Satyavatī to confess about Karṇa, the carnage of the *Mahābhārata* war need not have taken place at all. Yudhiṣṭhira says as much at the end of the war when he comes to know the truth about Karṇa.[26]

Hence, relationship with a man other than a husband was not precluded for a chaste wife provided it had the acquiescence of the husband and was for the purpose of begetting sons. The position of a chaste wife was of primary importance as no family could come into existence without her. She was vital for bringing forth the much needed sons and for making a home. Her primary duty was dependence upon and obedient service to the husband. Since marriage took place in front of the holy fire, the husband was the wife's highest deity and her whole being should be devoted to pleasing him.

The duties of a chaste wife are expounded over and over again in *Mahābhārata*. As is the usual technique in the epic, different characters are used to say the same thing in different situations in order to lay down the *dharma* or the moral principle. Thus Saṇḍili tells Sumana the duties of a chaste wife.[27] Pārvatī lays down the code of conduct for her at the behest of Mahādeva who assures her that it would become universal law since she formed half the part of his body. The duties of a woman says Umā are created through kinsmen in the rites of marriage. In the presence of the mystical fire, a woman becomes the associate of her husband in the performance of all righteous deeds. This makes her the equal partner of her husband.[28] It is not clear whether a woman has the right to dissociate herself from the unrighteous actions of her husband. The question is not far removed from the issue raised by Draupadī after the game of dice about whom did Yudhiṣṭhira lose first, himself or her.[29] It raises the whole question of the status of a wife and the extent of her husband's rights over her. The question is a tangled one involving two issues: the rights of a master over a slave and the rights of a slave over his wife. It is unanswerable because if Yudhiṣṭhira loses his rights over Draupadī by virtue of his slavery then she is left entirely at the mercy of the Kauravas and if he doesnot he has a right to stake her. By losing her too, however, he has put her in the clutches of the Kauravas. This incident parallels that of Nal and Damayantī.[30]

It is ironical that Draupadī saves the Pāṇḍavas in this situation instead of being protected by them.[31] This parallels the episode of the *Gandharva Aṅgaparṇa* whom Arjuna imprisoned and who was saved by his wife Kumbhinasi.[32] Ironically, Yudhiṣṭhira at that time had said that it was not worth Arjuna's while to slay someone who had been saved by his wife and who therefore had no prowes. When Dhṛtrāṣtra intervenes because he fears the consequences of the indecency that has taken place and grants Draupadī three boons, she asks nothing for herself. With the first, she asks for Yudhiṣṭhira's freedom and with the second that of the others as she feels that once her husbands are free and armed, the rest can be retrieved. She thus saves the Pāṇḍavas from degradation winning even Karṇa's admiration. No woman, he says, has done before what Draupadī has accomplished.[33]

But, none other than Draupadī also discourses upon the duties of a wife. After the second game of dice, when the Pāṇḍavas are living in exile in the forests, they are visited by Kṛṣṇa and Satyabhāmā. Draupadī and Satyabhāmā meet as long standing friends and Satyabhāmā half in jest inquires of her how she manages the five Pāṇḍavas to make them all so obedient to her and solicitous of her welfare. Was it the practice of some vows, or asceticism, or beauty or the recitation of some *mantras* that made her in such complete command of them she asks. The suggestion that asceticism or the practice of some vows could lead to such a situation is curious in this context but although Draupadī gently rebukes her by saying that all the practices mentioned by Satyabhāmā were of wicked women, the kind of routine that Draupadī has laid for herself speaks of great discipline. She says that she has controlled all vanity, desire and wrath and serves them all together with their wives without jealousy, with great devotion and without any sense of degradation. She never thinks or looks at another man and does all that a chaste wife should.

Hence, her husbands have become so obedient to her. Satyabhāmā apologizes for her levity and Draupadī then proceeds to tell her how to win Kṛṣṇa's heart. A wife she says, must be able to convince her husband that she truly loves him and him alone. She should be his confidante not divulging anything that he says to her whether it is meant to be confidential or not. She should keep aloof from anyone who is hostile or deceitful towards him. She should not converse with any man, not even speak to her sons in private. She should also associate only with women who were high born and devoted to their husbands. Finally she should ornament herself and make herself beautiful for him.[34]

However, all the obligations are not on the wife alone. Some space has been created for a wife's rights within this framework. When a chaste wife deviates, the fault is of the husband. For example, in the case of Dirghatamas, who acquires a young and beautiful wife, Pradweshi in spite of his blindness because of his great learning. Realizing the legitimacy of the practice of *niyoga,* he began to enter into such relationships beyond the limits of propriety. The other Munis were indignant and cast him off. His own wife was dissatisfied with him and told him that she would not be able to support him the way she had been doing. A husband, she says was, called *bhartṛ* because he supported a wife and *patī* because he protected her. He had done neither and so she was unable to look after him any longer.[35]

In the patriarchal framework of *Mahābhārata* then, women gain status as wives and mothers through which relationships their sexuality is regulated but which also gives them a voice that cannot be easily dismissed. Since sons are of vital importance as a means of gaining worth both in private and public domains, they are a cause of intense rivalry among women.. For example, Vyāsa pleased with the services of Gāndhārī blesses her with the boon of a hundred sons. She conceives but does not deliver in spite of one year having passed when she hears of the birth of Yudhiṣthira making him the oldest son in the clan and thus giving him rights to the throne that would eventually give Kuntī a higher status than her. Maddened by her grief at this news and impatient of the long gestation period, she strikes violently at her womb delivering a ball of flesh as a consequence. In despair, she is about to throw it away when Vyāsa arrives and admonishes her for what she has done. He then asks her to get pots filled with clarified butter while he divides the ball of flesh into a hundred and one parts, each the size of a thumb and puts one in each pot to be opened by Gāndhārī after two years. A daughter called Duhssalā is born from the hundred and first part because Gāndhārī had also desired a daughter during her pregnancy as there was a special affection for a daughter and son-in-law. Besides the sons of a daughter could access to worlds otherwise unattainable.[36]

A similar jealousy is seen between Mādri and Kuntī. Mādri, although superior in birth to Kuntī, feels inferior because she has no sons. The only way she could have offspring was through Kuntī's help but hesitates to ask her, the two being rivals. On Pāṇḍu's request Kuntī gives her the *mantra* but Mādri invokes the two Aświns simultaneously giving birth to the twins Nakula and Sahdeva. Kuntī is infuriated because she perceives that Mādri has cheated her and was trying to get more sons than Kuntī herself thereby gaining in status. She consequently refuses to give her the invocation the second time in spite of Pāndu's pleading.[37]

Although women gain status through husbands and sons, they create a remarkable space for themselves within the limits set for them almost subverting the patriarchal order. Kuntī, for example, is politically very aware and guards the interests of her sons. She takes them to Hastināpur after Pāṇḍu's death so that they can be trained and educated with the sons of Dhṛtarāṣtra and their claim to the kingdom cannot be easily overlooked, thus, sowing the seeds of discord from childhood itself. She accompanies her sons to Varnavata and later spends a year in the forest with them after their escape from the fire in the Lākśāgṛha undergoing all the hardships. Later, she unites the five brothers in an inalienable bond by giving them a common wife in Draupadī. Aware of the power that an intelligent woman can exercise if she conducts herself with acumen, she charges Draupadī with the care of her sons. After the game of dice, Kuntī is unable to accompany them in their thirteen years of exile, but, she wisely chooses to stay with Vidura rather than at the palace where she would be more vulnerable to court intrigues.

When Kṛṣṇa comes on his peace mission, he first meets Kuntī who laments before him all the miseries that have befallen her right from her childhood when her father gave her away to Kuntībhoja and since when she has never had any peace. However, nothing has hurt her more, she says, than the present separation from her sons whom she has not seen for almost fourteen years. She is very clear that the kingdom has to won and retained by them. Her message to Yudhiṣṭhira is that it is better to die than to live a life of dependence. To Bhīma and Arjuna, that the time had come for which Kṣatriya women bore sons. If they allowed the opportunity to slip, then although they might be respected now they would be regarded with contempt by the world later. When the hour comes, even life must laid down, if required. She reminds Nakula and Sahdeva that all objects of enjoyment must be won by their own prowess. Interestingly, her message to Arjuna is that he must tread the path pointed out to him by Draupadī perhaps because she fears that left to themselves they might settle for a compromise. She tries to arouse Kṛṣṇa and her sons through him of the unprecedented insult to Draupadī in the Kuru court and is confident that at least Bhīma and Arjuna will not forget it.[38]

When the peace mission fails, Kṛṣṇa once again goes to meet Kuntī before his departure to the Pāṇḍavas. Now her message is chiefly to Yudhiṣṭhira as he is the oldest and the future course of action turns mainly on him. She tells Kṛṣṇa to tell him that his virtue was now declining rapidly because of his inaction. A Kṣatriya must depend on the prowess of his arms. She reminds him of the royal sage Muchukunda who was gifted the earth by Vaisravana but who declined to accept it because he desired to enjoy only that sovereignty which was won by his own prowess. A sixth part of the virtue practised by well-protected subjects went to the king, she expounds, while the virtue that he himself practised conferred godhead on him. However, a king who perpetrated sin through his own actions went to hell. It was necessary for a king to rule wisely but firmly. He could not take recourse to the excuse of the vagaries of time. The kind of *yuga* that his subjects experienced depended on the king himself because the king's sins affected the world as much as the world's affected him. The king himself enjoyed heaven or hell according to the *yuga* that he allowed to get established. A weak hearted king given to compassion always remained instable and never acquired any merit. She makes an emotional appeal to Yudhiṣṭhira that is most likely to move him by saying that what could be a cause for greater grief than that she, his mother should be deprived of friends and be living at the mercy of others.[39]

In this connection Kuntī narrates the story of Vidulā who was a well educated and brave princess. She rebuked her son Sanjaya who lay prostrate and depressed after being defeated by the king of Sindhus by saying that he could not be her son if he gave way to such despair. He was more of a eunuch than a man if he was unable to carry the burden of his affairs on his own shoulders. She exhorts him to abandon his fears and to stop delighting his foes by grieving over his defeat bereft of all sense of honour. Instead, he ought to think big and not be gratified by small gains. He must range like a hawk ranges the sky and make himself known by his deeds. He must fight in the battlefield and thus free himself from the debt he owed to the duties of the Kṣatriya order. If he could not display prowess, what was the meaning of his life. Even when one's roots are cut off, says Vidula, one should not give way to despair but act mustering up all his strength and courage. Hearing the words of Vidulā her son regained his valour and won his kingdom back. Similarly, Yudhiṣṭhira should now act as only a man who lives by the prowess of his succeeds in winning fame in this world and a blessed state in the next.[40]

Her message to Arjuna is that at the time of his birth there had been a prophecy that he would vanquish in battle all the assembled Kurus. Aided by Bhīma he would conquer the whole earth and his fame would touch the very heavens. With Vāsudeva as his ally, he would slay the Kurus and regain his lost paternal share of the kingdom. Endued with great prosperity, he would, with his brothers perform three great sacrifices. To Bhīma her message is that the time had come for which a Kṣatriya lady brings forth sons. Those who have hostilities to wage never become cheerless and are also never satisfied until they have exterminated their foes. To Draupadī she says that she is greatly blessed, of noble parentage, endued with great fame and that her conduct towards the five Pāṇḍavas had indeed been worthy of her. To the sons of Mādri, Nakula and Sahadeva , her message is that they must value only enjoyments acquired by their own prowess more than life itself. Draupadī was humiliated in front of their eyes and how could they forgive that insult. Kuntī says that it did not grieve her when they were deprived of their kingdom or when they were defeated in the game of dice. What grieved her most was that Draupadī weeping in the midst of the assembly had to hear the cruel and insulting words hurled at her and in spite of being wedded to such powerful protectors found none in her hour of need. She says for Arjuna that he must always follow the path pointed out by Draupadī. Kṛṣṇa , she says, knows well that Bhīma and Arjuna were capable of defeating the very gods. Was it not an insult to them that their wife Draupadī was dragged into the assembly hall and disrobed? She also exhorts Kṛṣṇa to make them recall the cruel and harsh words that Duhśāsana had said to Bhīma in the presence of all Kuru warriors.[41]

Kuntī's chief aim is to spur her sons to battle. She even swallows her pride and goes to Karṇa to reveal to him the truth about his birth so that he becomes an ally to her sons. That she thinks would ensure the defeat of the Kauravas. Karṇa spurns her in the harshest terms possible but promises her that the decisive battle would be between him and Arjuna guaranteeing that she would always remain the mother of five sons. She is forced to be content with this partial gain because it at least ensures the life of her other four sons, Karṇa being the most feared warrior in the Kaurava camp[42].

At the end of the war, Kuntī watches the funeral pyres burning on the bank of the Ganges. She cannot contain her grief. Weeping, she discloses to Yudhiṣṭhira that the great warrior Karṇa was actually their older brother, her premarital son from Sūrya. It is curious why she should make a public acknowledgement of her son now when no tangible good could come out of it any more. Perhaps, she feels, that it is the least she can do after all the injustice her silence has done him. Overwhelmed by grief Yudhiṣṭhira performs the last rites of his elder brother. If only Kuntī had told him there would have been no war he says as Karṇa might have been acceptable to both sides. He curses her that henceforth no woman would able to keep anything secret, an action very out of keeping with his generally compassionate and forgiving nature and completely lacking in any understanding of Kuntī's motivations.[43]

When Yudhiṣṭhira is finally crowned king and has ruled for several years, Dhṛtarāṣṭra and Gāndhārī prepare to retire to the forest to spend the last years of their lives. They have been treated well by Yudhiṣṭhira but Bhīma constantly insults and humiliates them. In any case it has become irksome for them to go on living at the mercy of the Pāṇḍavas whom they have harmed so much. Kuntī, Vidura and Sañjaya decide to accompany them. It creates great consternation among the Pāṇḍavas who together with Draupadī try to stop Kuntī. She has suffered all her life they say. Why did she have to make them fight if she had to leave it all. Now that finally that the kingdom had been won, it was time for her to enjoy it. But she remains unshaken in her resolve. Yudhiṣṭhira reminds her repeatedly that it was she who had spurred them on to fight but Kuntī is not to be persuaded. She has no regrets in her life she says. She has lived the life of a queen and enjoyed all the material pleasures of a householder. She has done all she could to ensure that the house of Pāṇḍu remained unblemished. She did not want anything for herself. The time had now come to serve the older people, Dhṛtarāṣṭra and Gāndhārī, which she had never found the opportunity to do before. All that she had set out to do had been fulfilled and she would now she says like to practice austerities, serve her in-laws and attain heaven. In the forests she looks after them faithfully and perishes with them in the forest fire, unbending in her resolve at the end as she had always been in her life[44].

Just as Kuntī plays a pivotal role in the affairs of the war, so does Gāndhārī. She has been as much a victim of patriarchy as Kuntī. She was betrothed to Dhṛtarāṣtra without being told of his blindness simply because he came from a much bigger and wealthier kingdom than her father's and such an alliance might have been politically expedient. When she comes to know about it she binds her own eyes ostensibly so that her husband may not feel inferior to her, but it could also have been in sheer rage at the injustice done to her. By this act she becomes a constant living reminder of it. Dhṛtarāṣtra has neither the moral courage as her husband and king nor the sagacity or humility to persuade her to remove it. Her lifelong anger is so intense that her mere glance burns the toe nail of Yudhiṣṭhira when he goes to see her after the war.[45]

Gāndhārī had tried to dissuade Duryodhana from war. When he rejects Kṛṣṇa's appeal for peace and Dhṛtarāṣtra feels helpless in front of him, he calls Gāndhārī to the court as she is wise and the only one who can influence Duryodhana at this juncture. She blames him for following Duryodhana's counsel in spite of knowing his wickedness. Duryodhana, she says, is completely possessed by lust and wrath and was now a slave to delusion. As a consequence, he was incapable of being turned back from his path by Dhṛtarāṣtra who was now reaping the fruit of having made over the kingdom to an ignorant fool of wicked soul possessed by avarice and having evil counselors. Why was the king indifferent earlier, she asks to the situation between persons related so closely to each other and about which discussion was about to take place that day. His enemies would laugh, she says, at the conflict in the family. Who was there, she asks, who would use force for a problem that could only be solved by conciliation.[46]

On being sent for by Gāndhārī, Duryodhana returns. She tells him that if he makes peace he would earn the blessings of all his elders including her. Nobody, she says, succeeds in acquiring, keeping or enjoying a kingdom by his own desires alone. Only one who has his senses under control can enjoy a kingdom. Lust and wrath are the greatest enemies of a king and it is only by conquering these foes that a king can bring the earth under his subjection. It is easy to win a kingdom but without binding the senses to profit and virtue, no one can retain it. If the senses are restrained, intelligence increases but if they are not controlled, they are like unbroken and furious horses capable of killing an unskillful driver. One who tries to conquer his counselors without conquering his own self and to conquer his foes without conquering his counselors, is soon vanquished and ruined. He who conquers his self as he would his enemy, will conquer his counselors and his enemies. Prosperity worships a person who has conquered his senses and his counselors, who punishes transgressors, who acts after deliberation and is possessed of great wisdom. Lust and wrath are his prime enemies. However, a king who can conquer them together with avarice, boastfulness and pride can rule over the whole earth. A king desirous of gaining wealth and virtue and vanquishing his enemies, should always be engaged in controlling his passions. Influenced by lust or wrath, he that behaves deceitfully towards his own kinsmen or others, can never win many allies. She, therefore, advises Duryodhana peace with the Pāṇḍavas. When he rejects her advice, Gāndhārī can only concludes that let victory be his on whose side was righteousness.[47]

At the end of the war, Dhṛtarāṣtra orders that all the ladies including Gāndhārī and Kuntī be brought to the battlefield. It is a world drowned in tears and lamentations as the women tried to identify their husbands, brothers, fathers, sons and other near ones. Kṛpā tries to console Gāndhārī by telling her that the Pāṇḍavas and the other kings too had suffered the death of their loved ones. Even Draupadī's sons had all been wiped out. She asks sarcastically for the new king. Yudhiṣṭhira together with his brothers comes to her. In all humility he stands before her with his head bowed acknowledging that he has done her irreparable harm and asking her for her forgiveness. She is completely unprepared for this. Afflicted with grief she had at first wants to curse them. Vyāsa restrains her and advises her to show forgiveness. He points out that whenever Duryodhana had asked her for her blessings she had never actually blessed him but had always said that let he who had righteousness win. It was only her own words that had been fulfilled. Gāndhārī recognizes that she should cherish the Pāṇḍavas as her own sons but cannot reconcile to the unrighteous way in which Bhīma killed Duryodhana whom he could not have otherwise defeated. Bhīma himself praises Duryodhana's valor but points out that he too had acted unrighteously not once but several times including showing his thigh to Draupadī and humiliating her. Hence, he says, it became his duty to avenge the humiliation of Draupadī. He also explains his conduct towards Duhśāsana during the war and once again reminds Gāndhārī of his behaviour towards Draupadī in the court after the game of dice. Conceding the validity of their position, she comforts the Pāṇḍavas in their grief like a mother and weeps with Draupadī as both lament the loss of their sons. However, she has the greatness to acknowledges that it was perhaps through her fault that the entire race had been destroyed. She is referring to the ill omens at the time of Duryodhana's birth and the prophecy that he would be the cause of the destruction of the Kauravas. She had been advised to destroy him as an individual must be sacrificed for a family, a family for a village, and a village for the integrity and truth of the self. She had not heeded the advice overpowered by her love for her first born. Also, she tacitly acknowledges that somewhere within her there was the temptation and desire to have the status of a queen mother rather than allow Kuntī to gain that position.[48]

While lamenting this vast destruction, Gāndhārī comes across Kṛṣṇa and repeatedly points out to him the heroes lying mangled and slain in the battle. She can forgive the Pāṇḍavas but not Kṛṣṇa because he who could have prevented the war remained indifferent to the carnage that would ensue. She curses him by saying that he would be slayer of his own kinsmen thirty-four years later and then perish disgracefully in the wilderness. The women of his race would lament even as these Kuru women were now wailing

Kṛṣṇa unmoved replies that there was no one in the world except himself who could destroy the Vrishnis and that he was trying to bring that about himself. She had only aided him in his task by uttering the curse. He tells her bluntly that there was no point in her grieving as she herself was the cause of that vast carnage. She had encouraged Duryodhana knowing that he was wicked, envious and exceedingly arrogant. All that she was doing now was try to transfer the guilt to him. In any case by mourning for something that had already occurred a person only increased his own grief. A princess like Gāndhārī afterall bore sons only for war. At this time Dhṛtarāṣtra restrains Gāndhārī and asks Yudhiṣṭhira to ensure proper funeral arrangements for all those who had died, the number being one billion six hundred and sixty million and twenty thousand.[49]

The person on whom the entire war turns is Draupadī. At the time of her birth itself there had been a prophecy that she would be the cause of the destruction of many Kṣatriyas[50], The war is as much to vindicate her honour as to retrieve the kingdom. Draupadī is an independent woman in the patriarchal world. Exiled after the game of dice she dwells in the forest but still performs all the duties of a queen fulfilling the laws of hospitality when the ascetics and others come to visit them, giving advice to Yudhiṣṭhira and participating in all the deliberations among the Pāṇḍavas and with Kṛṣṇa. She is as much a subject to the intrigues of the

Kauravas as her husbands – an indication that they consider her a force to reckon with.

For instance, Duryodhana sends Durvāsā Ṛṣi, known for his temper, with his ten thousand disciples to the Pāṇḍavas. Yudhiṣṭhira invites all of them for a meal following the laws of hospitality the onus of which falls on Draupadī. Greatly worried she calls on Kṛṣṇa her unfailing ally, friend, and soul mate. She had been give a pot by Sūrya from which unlimited quantities of food could be got but only till it was cleaned and put away. This Draupadī had already done. Kṛṣṇa arrives and asks her for food. Puzzled, she explains that she has already cleaned up the pot but he insists that she bring it to him. He finds a small grain of rice and a bit of vegetable sticking to it. Consequently, he grants her the boon that the hunger of all the Ṛṣis would be satisfied as there was still food in the pot. Durvāsā Ṛṣi and his disciples who had gone to bathe before the meal miraculously find themselves satiated.[51]

Endowed with a fiery beauty, accomplishments and intellect, she is irresistible to men and hence is constantly attacked and humiliated. Jayadratha, passing through the forest on his way to get married sees Draupadī standing alone outside her cottage while the Pāṇḍavas had gone for hunting. He is immediately enchanted and carries her off by force in spite of being warned by Dhaumya, the priest of the Pāṇḍavas. Meanwhile, Yudhiṣṭhira intuitively sensing something wrong persuades his brothers to abandon the hunt and return to their cottage. Dhatreyika, Draupadī's maid tells them of her kidnapping and urges them to follow the direction taken by Draupadī's abductors. The Pāṇḍavas retrieve Draupadī after defeating Jayadratha. While Yudhiṣṭhira returns to the cottage with her, Bhīma and Arjuna pursue and catch the fleeing Jayadratha. Bhīma would have killed him but is prevented by Arjuna because Yudhiṣṭhira would not have permitted it since he was Duhssala's husband and hence in a way also their brother-in-law.[52]

On another occasion when Kṛṣṇa visits them in the forest, Draupadī traces the animosity between the Pāṇḍavas and the Kauravas right from their childhood. She points out the injustice done to them and to her and asks why was it necessary for her to burn in grief for so many years. She belongs to a great race, has had an extraordinary birth, is the beloved wife of the mighty Pāṇḍavas, and the daughter-in-law of the illustrious Pāṇḍu, yet she has been seized by her hair in the open court in front of Pāṇḍavas and humiliated. Weeping she says that she has no husbands, sons, friends, father or brothers and now not even Kṛṣṇa as he sits unmoved by her insult. She deserves to be protected by him because of their relationship, his respect for her, their friendship and his lordship over her. Kṛṣṇa gives her his word that the wives of the Kauravas would weep even as she was weeping then beholding their husbands dead on the ground weltering in blood and covered with arrows. He promises her that she would one day be queen again as he would exert all his powers on behalf of the Pāṇḍavas. Arjuna also reassures her and Dṛṣṭadyumna her brother promises to slay Droṇa. Śikhaṇḍin will kill Bhīṣma he says, Bhīma Duryodhana and Dhananjaya Karṇa.[53]

Draupadī is an active participant in all the deliberations of the Pāṇḍavas. Her position on the issue is the same as Kuntī's. One evening, sitting with all of them in the forest she analyses the events with Yudhiṣṭhira and blames chiefly Duryodhana, Karṇa, Śakuni and Duhśāsana for them. She tries to exhort Yudhiṣṭhira to action contrasting his rightful position as king with his present situation in the forest. Painting a detailed picture of their fallen state she wonders why his wrath does not blaze up at the sight of the misery of his brothers and why is he not moved to anger at her own plight. She had heard that no Kṣatriya was without anger but Yudhiṣṭhira seemed to be an exception. However, she points out, a Kṣatriya who did not exert himself at the opportune time was disregarded by others as his duty was not to forgive but to slay his foes. Giving him examples of the conduct of others in similar situations, she exhorts to Yudhiṣṭhira to immediate war.

Yudhiṣṭhira tries to give her another perspective. Anger, he points out, was at the root of all sin and destruction as it obscured all ethics and morals. A wise man forgives and does not allow anger to overtake him or cloud his judgement even when persecuted by his enemy. There could be no peace or prosperity in a world of anger. Hence, a wise man, he says, should follow the path of tolerance, peace, forgiveness and patience.[54]

Draupadī does not agree and regards it as an aberration of Yudhiṣṭhira's mind. Acts, she says, produce consequences that are inevitable. Emancipation from desire is mere folly. Disagreeing with Yudhiṣṭhira, she points out, that no man can attain prosperity in this world by the virtues of gentleness, forgiveness, straightforwardness or fear of censure. The proof of it was the calamity that had overtaken Yudhiṣṭhira himself in spite of his virtues and his willingness to sacrifice all his wealth, his brothers, his wife and even himself for the sake of his principles. Even in the forest, solitary, haunted by robbers, divested of his kingdom Yudhiṣṭhira was clinging on to his virtues. Yet, she taunts him some perversity must have attracted him to the vice of gambling in which he had lost his kingdom, wealth, weapons, brothers and Draupadī herself. It could only be explained she felt by accepting that all men were subject to the will of god, and never to their own wishes. If god ordained everything, and man was not independent even for a moment he could not be the master of his weal or woe. Thus god himself was responsible for all actions and human beings were his mere puppets. If this be true then god seemed to behave viciously and in anger towards human beings as was evident from the distress of Yudhiṣṭhira and the prosperity of Duryodhana. God then becomes stained with the sin of every act of man, she argues. It follows that if the sin of the act done does not attach to the doer then the individual must exert his might and act and she could only grieve for those who had no strength or courage.[55]

Yudhiṣṭhira tells Draupadī that she speaks like an atheist. He says that he only does his duty and does not worry about the fruits of actions. He performs sacrifices and does charity because it is duty. He acts virtuously not because he wants any reward but because it is his innate nature. A man who sought reward for his virtues was only a trader in virtues and would earn no merit by them. Nor would a man who doubted dharma. He who disregarded it in favour of his own reasoning was a fool because he could only see the external world capable of gratifying his senses and was blind to everything else. For him, says Yudhiṣṭhira, only those who had their minds under control and were content with little would reap the fruits of their virtuous acts. Neither the origin nor the consequences of virtuous acts or of transgressions were known to anyone except to those evolved beings who had destroyed all aspirations and lived according to their vows and asceticism, who had burnt all their sins and had acquired minds where peace and holiness dwelt. Therefore, he tells Draupadī, even if she could not see any rewards of virtue she should not doubt dharma or the gods. He advises to do her duties without insolence, firm in the belief that all acts in this world have their consequences and that virtue is eternal.[56]

Draupadī is not convinced. She says that she does not disregard god or *dharma* but her point is that every conscious creature in the world must act. Lives of living beings were shaped by the acts of former existences and hence they were different from each other. Birds and beasts acted untaught by anyone but life without action was impossible even for them. Man differs from other creatures, she says, as he alone is capable of conscious action. She therefore, urges Yudhiṣṭhira to act. One must act she says, both for protecting one's own self and also for increasing one's wealth because otherwise it would soon be exhausted. Those who believe in destiny or chance she says are the worst among men and are soon destroyed. Only those who believe in the efficacy of their actions are laudable. God as the ordainer, judging the actions of past lives shapes the present but man working with the aid of his intelligence is free to be the cause of all that he accomplishes. It is because a person is himself the cause of his work that he is applauded or censured for his failure or success which would not be possible if man was not responsible for his actions. Possessions are obtained by man either because of chance or destiny or through exertion. There is no other way. She therefore, urges Yudhiṣṭhira to war by saying that a man of action generally meets with success while the idle not only fail but are also overpowered by adversity. At this moment, she points out, misery had overtaken them but could be removed through Yudhiṣṭhira's actions. One can only know the consequences after one acts and so should not be deterred by thinking of the outcome. Even if the act resulted in failure one could be absolved from blame, but if no exertion was made, there could be no success. Success in the world, concludes Draupadī, depends on acting according to time and circumstances.[57]

When the thirteen-year exile is over, Yudhiṣṭhira sends a peace message to Duryodhana requesting him to give them only five villages with which they would be content. Duryodhana refuses even this, but, Yudhiṣṭhira persists and sends Kṛṣṇa with a last peace proposal. Draupadī is disturbed and reminds him of all the injustices done by the Kauravas to the Pāṇḍavas and that even the offer of accepting only five villages had already been rejected. Duryodhana was obviously not willing to part with anything of the kingdom and as such peace was neither possible nor worth having. The Kauravas now did not deserve any mercy she says. She tells Kṛṣṇa that if sin is incurred by slaying someone unjustly there was equal sin in not slaying one who deserved to be slain. She reminds him of her great humiliation and ignominy and points out that it was she who had won for the Pāṇḍavas their life and liberty with their chariots and weapons only to be exiled again. Morally too, she was the daughter-in-law of both Bhīṣma and Dhṛtrāṣṭra and yet she had been made a slave. How could they all talk of peace she asks. If the Pāṇḍavas do settle for peace she says, her aged father with his warlike sons, her own sons and Abhimanyu would fight for her as she would not rest until she saw Duhśāsana's arms splintered into atoms.[58]

Other women, too, play significant public roles. After the war is over, Yudhiṣṭhira as king is persuaded to perform the *Aśvamedha* yajña. After completing the due ceremonies, Vyāsa commands Arjuna to protect the horse and follow it to conquer the entire world while Bhīma stay to protect the kingdom and Nakula and Sahdeva to look after the guests. As Arjuna follows the steed, defeating any king that comes his way, a great battle occurs between him and the Saindhavas who still live after the slaughter of their clan in Kurukṣetra and who are determined to avenge the killing of their king Jayadratha by Arjuna. Great destruction takes place and the Saindhavas begin to lose when Duhssālā their queen, the daughter of Dhṛtarāṣṭra and the wife of the slain Jayadratha takes her grandson in her arms and meets Arjuna. The brave prince approaches Arjuna for the safety of all the Saindhava warriors while Duhssālā weeping reminds Arjuna that the prince is his grandson as he is the son of Suratha, Jayadratha's son and hence like Parikṣit. Sūratha, she tells him, died of grief on hearing how his father had been killed by Arjuna and also on being once again confronted by an impending war. Duhssālā orders the Saindhavas to cease the battle and seeks Arjuna's protection appealing for mercy.[59]

During the same time Arjuna goes to Manipura where his own son from Chitrāngadā, Vibhruvāhana is the ruler. Vibhruvāhana comes to greet him with all humility accompanied by Brāhmins and treasure. Arjuna, however, does not approve of this and asks his son to fight him as he has come as protector of Yudhiṣṭhira's sacrificial horse and not as his father. Ulūpī, the daughter of the snake king, another of Arjuna's wives and the stepmother of Vibhruvāhana, unable to tolerate these words pierces the earth and comes to the battlefield. She asks Vibhruvāhana to fight Arjuna in which battle Arjuna is defeated and falls own dead. On hearing of this, Chitrāngadā, Vibhruvāhana's mother comes there, her heart burning with sorrow at the thought of her slain husband. She begs Ulūpī to revive Arjuna their common husband which Ulūpī does. Arjuna gets up as if from sound sleep and is surprised to see both his wives there. Ulūpī tells him about all that has happened and that she had to bring it about for his own good. He had erred in overthrowing Bhīṣma by using unrighteous means through sheltering behind Śikhaṇḍin and would have been cursed by the Vasus to hell with the permission of Gaṅgā herself. Ulūpī, learning of this had requested her father's help who had pleaded with the Vasus. They had then modified their curse to the vanquishing of Arjuna by his own son.[60]

Arjuna also goes to Gāndhāra and fights the ruler who is Śakunī's son. His mother is filled with fear and come to meet Arjuna with all the aged ministers forbidding her son to fight any more. Peace is established and Arjuna, recollecting Gāndhārī and also for the sake of Dhṛtarāṣtra tells the ruler of Gāndhāra that he would spare his life because of them but then hostilities between them had to cease.[61]

Thus, the world of *Mahābhārata,* when seen from the point of view of woman, is one of power structures, both in the private and public spheres, totally controlled by men. They can attain a voice in this world through their status as wives and mothers acting through their husbands and sons. Independent women are branded as unchaste because their unbridled sexuality can so easily destroy this carefully constructed power structure. As wives and mothers, the sexuality of women is subjugated and regulated to fulfilling the societal demands of producing as many sons as possible. However, women manage to create space for themselves within these limitations and become powerful figures capable of changing the course of events. Hence, they become a force to be reckoned with through their own intelligence, acumen and endeavour. It is more often the men rather than the women who appear at crucial moments to be indecisive, lacking in sagacity and in need of support to move them to action.

Notes

1. The text used in this paper is the *The Mahābhārat of Kṛṣṇa* – Dwaipāyaṇa Vyāsa, trans. Kisari Mohan Gangulai, Delhi. Munshiram Manohar Lal 5th edn. 1991.Vol. XI, Anuśāsana Parva, section XXXVIII, p. 4.
2. Ibid.
3. Ibid., Section XL, pp. 7-8.
4. Ibid., Section XXXVIII, pp. 5-6.
5. Ibid., Section XL, pp. 9-10.
6. Vol. I, Ādi Parva, Section CXIII, pp. 238-239.
7. Vol. I, Ādi Parva Section, CIV, p. 224.
8. Vol. I, Ādi Parva, Section CXI, pp. 235-236.
9. Vol. I, Ādi Parva, Section CXXXII, p. 254. See also, Vol. I, Ādi Parva, Section CIV, p. 225.

10. Vol. I, Ādi Parva, Section XCVII, p. 208.
11. Vol. II, Vana Parva, Section XLVI, pp. 101-103.
12. Vol. II, Vana Parva, Section XIII, pp. 32-33.
13. Vol. I, Ādi Parva, Section CLXLIII, p. 381.
14. Vol. I, Ādi Parva, Section CCX, p. 409.
15. Vol. I, Ādi Parva, Section CLXLVIII, p. 389.
16. Vol. I, Ādi Parva, Section CIV, pp. 224-225.
17. Vol. I, Ādi Parva, Section CXVIII, pp. 245-246.
18. Vol. I, Ādi Parva, Section CLXLIX, pp. 389-393.
19. Vol. I, Ādi Parva, Section CXXI, pp.252-254. Also Section CXXII, pp. 253-256.
20. Vol. I, Ādi Parva, Section CXXIII, p. 259.
21. Vol. I, Ādi Parva, Section CXXII, pp. 254-255.
22. Vol. I, Ādi Parva, Section CXX, pp. 252-252.
23. Vol. I, Ādi Parva, Section CV, pp. 229-230.
24. Vol. I, Ādi Parva, Section CIV, pp. 225-226.
25. Vol. I, Ādi Parva, Section CXX, p. 251.
26. Vol. III, Strī Parva, Section XXVIII, pp. 42-43.
27. Vol. XI, Anuśāsana Parva, Section CXXIV, pp. 254-255.
28. Vol. XI, Anuśāsana Parva, Section CXLVI, pp. 314-318.
29. Vol. II, Sabhā Parva, Section LXVI, p. 126. For the Nala and Damyanti episode, see LXXIX.
30. Vol. II, Vana Parva, Section LIII, pp. 114-163.
31. Vol. II, Sabhā Parva, Section LXX, pp. 139-140.
32. Vol. I, Ādi Parva Section CLXXII, pp. 344-346.
33. Vol. II, Sabhā Parva, Section LXXI, pp. 140-141.
34. Vol. III, Sabhā Parva, Sections CCXXXI – CCXXXII, pp. 472-476.
35. Vol. I, Ādi Parva, Section CIV, pp. 224-225.
36. Vol. I, Ādi Parva, Sections CXV & CXVI, pp. 241-244.
37. Vol. I, Ādi Parva, Section CXXIV, pp. 260-261.
38. Vol. IV, Udyoga Parva, Section XC, pp. 185-187.
39. Vol. IV, Udyoga Parva, Section CXXXII, pp. 255-257.
40. Vol. IV, Udyoga Parva, Sections CXXXIII – CXXXVI, pp. 257-265.
41. Vol. IV, Udyoga Parva, Sections CXXXVII, pp. 265-266.
42. Vol. IV, Udyoga Parva, Sections CXLIV – CXLVI, pp. 278-282.

43. Vol. VII, Stree Parva, Section XXVII, p. 43.
44. Vol. XII, Āśramavasikā Parva, Section XVI, pp. 26-27.
45. Vol. VII, Stree Parva, Section XV, p. 22.
46. Vol. IV, Udyoga Parva, Section CXXIX, p. 248.
47. Vol. IV, Udyoga Parva, Section CXXIX, pp. 249-251.
48. Vol. IV, Udyoga Parva, Section CXXVIII, pp. 245-248.
49. Vol.VII, Stree Parva, Section XVIII–XVV, pp. 27-44.
50. Vol. I, Ādi Parva, Section CLXIX, pp. 341-342.
51. Vol. III, Vana Parva, Sections CCIX–CCLXI, pp. 514-517.
52. Vol. III, Vana Parva, Sections CCLXV–CCLXX, pp. 520-530.
53. Vol. II, Vana Parva, Section XII, pp. 33-34.
54. Vol. II, Vana Parva, Section XXIV, pp. 59-62.
55. Vol. II, Vana Parva, Section XXX, pp. 62-64.
56. Vol. II, Vana Parva, Section XXXI, pp. 65-67.
57. Vol. II, Vana Parva, Section XXXII, pp. 67-70.
58. Vol. IV, Udyoga Parva, Section LXXXII, pp. 168-171.
59. Vol. 13, Aśwamedha Parva, Section LXXVIII, pp. 133-135.
60. Vol. 13, Aśwamedha Parva, Sections LXXIX–LXXXI, pp. 135-141.
61. Vol. 13, Aśwamedha Parva, Section LXXXIV, pp. 144-145.

9

Women in *Manusmṛti*

Vinita Chandra

The *Dharmaśāstra* constitute a vast body of literature, comprising of the *Dharmasūtras, smṛtis* and later digests. *Manusmṛti* is considered as the first and most authoritative work among all the *Dharmaśāstra* texts. Also, *Manusmṛti* has evoked more responses and reactions than any other *Dharmaśāstra*. Most of the times, these responses have been of an extreme nature. Manu has been scathingly criticized by many for sowing the seeds of gender and caste oppression in the Indian society. The author of *Manusmṛti* is criticized for tightening the noose around Hindu women's lives, shrinking the social space afforded to them and imposing severe restrictions upon them. On the other hand, there are others who consider *Manusmṛti* as the foundational document of Hindu way of life and seek to justify all the indictments laid down in it.

An objective analysis of *Manusmṛti* seems imperative. A few questions deserve to be answered before anything is commented upon *Manusmṛti*. Important among these are – whether the text reflects the true picture of the times, or the line of thinking that is reflected in it was a response or reaction to the then prevailing social, economic, political and religious conditions. So, firstly, the laws and indictments laid down by Manu need to be studied in the context of the social, economic and political developments of the time. Besides, one finds that what is being prescribed is not in consonance with reality. Several deviations from the norms laid down can be found. This demands a detailed study of the content of the text and its comparison with the picture which emerges upon a study of other sources.

The first part of the present paper shall throw some light on the political, economic, religious and social conditions prevalent in the society during the time of the composition of *Manusmṛti* and study the indictments laid down in the text regarding women in that context. The second part shall mark out some deviations from the norms as propagated on the basis of a study of some of the epigraphs of that period.

I

The period of the text is now unanimously accepted to be circa 2nd century BC to circa 2nd century AD. Political events in this period became diffuse. The Mauryan period presented a relatively uncomplicated picture with a centralized monarchy. However, during this period, with the disintegration of large kingdoms, a number of small kingdoms and tribal republics rose.

The Śuṅgas established the rule of their dynasty, usurping the throne from the last Maurya ruler, sometime around 185 BC. They were followed by the Kaṇvas and then the Āndhras. Petty kings ruled the region after the withdrawal of the Āndhras. This period also witnessed the reappearance of the tribal polities in Punjab, Haryana and Rajasthan. Another powerful kingdom that rose out of the ruins of Magadha was Kaliṅga under Khāravela, who was a powerful monarch and a devout Jaina. In the Deccan, the Sātavāhanas appeared as successors of the Mauryas in the first century BC and ruled for more than four centuries. They were sometimes called the Āndhras or the Āndhrabhṛtyas, leading to a doubt of their having a low origin. In the south, this period was marked with frequent conflicts between the Ceras, Colas and Pāṇḍyas. In the farther south, this was a period of transition from the chiefdoms to the kingdoms, with the formation of the states. The north-west was caught in the turmoil of happenings in central Asia. The north-western provinces of the Magadha Empire were wrested by the Indo-Greeks in the beginning of the second century BC. The Greeks were not the only foreigners to have entered and influenced India in this period. The Pārthians, Śakas and Kuśāṇas were the other people who entered India turn by turn.

As shall be discussed later, the influx of foreigners must have lead to loosening of the varṇa structure, and several indictments in *Manusmṛti* might be a result of the effort to preserve it.

Though the political scene seems to present a situation of chaos, the period is marked with brisk economic activity and a fabulous expansion in trade and industry. As Romila Thapar writes, the dynasties of this period had a relatively quick turnover, yet beneath these changes the most stable factor was trade.[1] There was an extraordinary growth of both inland and external trade during this period. Thus, there was also a corresponding increase of imports and exports, opening up of new markets, elaboration of urban settlements and consequent improvement in the level of prosperity. Also characteristic of this period was the opening up of the remote parts of the country and the discovery of new channels of communication. From an economic point of view, the most important development of the period was the thriving trade between India and the Roman Empire. External trade was carried on not only with Rome, but also with Egypt, South-east Asia and China. The period also witnessed remarkable growth in arts and crafts. Production and exchange were facilitated through the institution of *śreṇi*. The artisans were organized under their headman, the *jyeṣṭha*, who perhaps enjoyed the favour of the king. Among other functions, the guild also had judicial functions. There were judges and the disputes related to the members of a guild were settled by them. The court monitored the behaviour of the members of the guild and ensured the customary usage of the guild, the *śreṇi-dharma*. That the guild also intervened in the personal matters of the members is clear from the regulation that, in order to join the Buddhist order as a nun, a married woman had to seek the permission of the guild. It is interesting to note that in the ninetieth verse of Chapter 5 in *Manusmṛti*, it is laid down that libations are not to be offered to women who have joined some heretical sect. Among others put in the same category were those women who lived with many men through lust, who had caused an abortion, had killed their husbands, or drank spirituous liquor. It is clear that joining heretical sect commanded strong disapproval in *Manusmṛti*. However, with the approval of the *śreṇi*, women could join those sects. It is also important to note that the trading community were the patrons of Buddhism and Jainism. Manu's disapproval arose out of an anxiety to preserve the importance of the Brahmanical religion.

During the period under study, there were significant developments in the field of religion. One of the main aspects of the religious history of this period is the emergence of neo-Brahmanism more or less in the form in which we know it in later periods or even now. Neo-Brahmanism emerged as a mass of beliefs, opinions, usages, religious creeds and observances derived from the manifold sources, heretic or popular, Vedic or non-Vedic, native or foreign, Aryan or non-Aryan, orthodox or dissenting. It seems to have been an attempt at synthesis, the process of which stretched over a long period, though it assumes a tangible shape in the epic literature. The principal sects that emerged were Vaiṣṇavism and Śaivism. Others were the Bhāgavatas or the Pañcarātras, the Śākta, Saura and Gāṇapatya. During this period, Jainism prospered in different centres. Jainism received patronage from some rulers, but largely by the merchant community. In some respects, this period witnessed the greatest activity of the church and marked the heyday of the faith. The rapid extension of Buddhism after the time of Aśoka to various parts of India resulted in the rise of Buddhist sects of which the number is given as eighteen. Buddhism also received widespread royal patronage.

Religion played no less a role in determining the direction of the social responses. The prosperous community of the merchants patronized Buddhism and Jainism. There are references to donations being made by the guilds to the monks in the literature of the time. Also, many of the foreign ruling dynasties patronized Buddhism and Jainism. Buddhism in particular, reflected more flexible attitudes towards the social stratification. A sharpening of stratification at the theoretical level observed in the texts like *Manusmṛti* may have been a response to such flexibility. Theoretically, the varṇas were precisely and clearly defined, but this seems to have been far from the social reality.

The changes on the political and economic scene influenced the social scene of the period under study in a significant way. It was both, the political chaos and flourishing trade, which brought the foreigners in India. The influx of large hordes of people from Western and Central Asia resulted in a new and alien population. Those who came were initially alien in custom and belief, but the mutations that had occurred among them and among the host societies expanded the cultural experience of both.[2] Also, thriving economic activity gave rise to the prosperous classes of artisans and merchants. The situation became complicated initially and gave birth to reactions in the then society. This is corroborated by the gloomy prophecies made in the Brahmanical literature of the period.[3] It would have been difficult to find a place for the new emerging classes in the extant social structure. *Varṇāśrama* system formed the core of Indian society earlier. Though the *varṇāśrama* were never marked with tight compartmentalization, and it was perhaps this which gave way to further adjustments. An attempt to come to terms with the new elements within the social structure can be found in the acceptance of the foreign rulers as 'degenerate Kśatriyas'. No doubt that the foreigners too had a significant role to play in this as they too made attempts at assimilation into the new society. They adopted conciliatory propaganda measures to smoothen the hostility of the indigenous society.[4] Another such attempt at reconciliation is found in the theory of *varṇasaṁkara* (mixed castes) which were said to have originated out of the anuloma and pratiloma marriages. This category was perhaps formed to include those of the lowest *varṇa*, who had gained economic opulence due to a spurt in the economic activity and would have tried to improve their caste status by associating with the newcomers.

Due to unprecedented growth of trade and commerce, urbanism reached a high point during the first centuries of the Christian era. Many towns emerged as centres of crafts and commerce and became hubs of economic activity. The urban population seems to have been very fluid and this might have been the reason for which the urban life seems to be downplayed in the *dharmasūtra.* The attempt made by the lower in the social rung to exploit the demands of urban life to improve their social status, coupled with the influx of foreigners, might have generated fear psychoses in the Brahmanical class. This explains the continuous reiteration in the *Manusmṛti* of the inherent superiority of the Brāhmaṇas as compared to the other classes. To provide authority to what is said in the text, a divine origin was ascribed to it.

An analysis of the social conditions of the time presents a picture where the influx of foreigners and a spurt in economic activity, coupled with developments in religion, set a process of transition in the society. The pressure of the circumstances threatened the disintegration of the existent social order. Attempts at reconciliation led to an increase in the social mobility. However, a closer analysis reveals that the threads of the initial social fabric were loosened and the social reality was far removed from the normative models set by the Brahmanical texts.

Manu on Women

All that Manu laid down for women now needs to be analysed in the backdrop of these conditions. What seems to be an attempt to control women perhaps was an attempt rather to preserve the older order in a situation where the threads of the older fabric were getting loosened.

When in Chapter 2, Manu lays down the standards for naming a woman,[5] perhaps he wants to prevent the names of native woman from being confused with those of foreign and tribal women. In the same chapter, nuptial ceremony is considered to be the same as initiation for women, serving the husband equivalent to residing in the house of teacher, and the household duties are considered as the worship of daily fire.[6] This might well be criticized by the critiques as an attempt to keep women illiterate and confined to the household. However, to me it seems that it was because early marriage of girls made it impossible to reside in the house of the teacher. An anxiousness to marry girls at an early age might have resulted because of the fact that there was an influx of foreigners, which could have made the girls vulnerable or even if not that, at least susceptible to having married in the foreign population.

Again, women were held in high regard as female relations. Later there is reference to women turning heretics. Perhaps women were respected within the family structure to prevent them from doing so and thus go out of the Brahmanical order. Similar attempt to restrict the sphere of women's activities is evident in verses 147-151 of Chapter 5. Independence of women might have been feared because of their moving out of the Brahmanical order. The vehemently criticized verse saying women should never be independent,[7] is followed by another which says that she must not seek to separate herself from the father, husband, or sons; by leaving them she would make both families contemptible.[8] Further, in the next verse, woman is advised to remain cheerful, clever in the management of household affairs, careful in cleaning utensils and economical in expenditure.[9] Perhaps women tried to be independent by separating themselves from the family and joining heretical sects. So this was an attempt to limit them to the married household life, offering no scope for deviations. In the same nerve, perhaps, wifehood was exalted and husband made the God for the woman, for whom norms of ideal wifehood were laid down.[10] Duty as a wife was considered so important that it was laid down that by violating her duty towards her husband, a wife is disgraced in this world, after death she enters the womb of a jackal, and is tormented by diseases, which is the punishment for her sin.[11] Why widowhood was considered baneful,[12] and remarriage condemned, needs more to be answered.

Again, while mentioning the characteristics of maidens who should or should not be married to[13], one finds that the details have certainly something to do with the social conditions. For example when he forbids marrying a girl from a family without a male heir, it is out of the fear of her being made the appointed daughter *putrikā;* or when a girl with red hair, or bearing the name of a constellation, tree, snake etc. is considered unfit for being married to, perhaps this is to prevent marrying girls of foreign or tribal or mixed origin in an indirect way.

All attempts at preventing adultery were made. In Chapter 9, the second verse lays down that day and night women should be kept in dependence by the males of their families, and if they attach themselves to sensual enjoyments, they must be kept under one's control. Her father protects her in childhood, her husband protects her in youth, and sons protect her in old age; a woman is never fit for independence.[14] It was thus laid down that women need to be both controlled and protected. Perhaps, the chaotic condition in the political arena giving rise to fluid social situation made adultery very common. Women were to be protected from the incoming foreigners. Verse five states women should be guarded. Perhaps the idea of keeping women guarded originated out of a fear of admixture of castes, which becomes pronounced in the seventh verse when it is said that he who carefully guards his wife, preserves the purity of his offspring, virtuous conduct, his family, himself and his means of acquiring merit. Adultery is condemned for the same reason in verse 353 of Chapter 8. It says, by adultery is caused the mixture of *varṇa* among men, from which sin follows and cuts up the roots, causing the destruction of everything. It is important to note that an attempt to prevent adultery by males is also evident in Chapter 8, verse 352. Acts which are considered adulterous and the punishments for them are defined in the following verses.[15] It is said that he who violates an unwilling maiden shall suffer corporal punishment, but a man who enjoys a willing maiden shall not suffer corporal punishment, if his caste be the same as hers.[16] In a similar nerve, it is said that if any man forcibly contaminates a maiden, two of his fingers shall be instantly cut off, and he shall pay a fine of six hundred *paṇas*.[17] It is notable that rape was considered a crime and corporal punishment was laid down for it.

Notably, even in cases of adultery, *varṇa* hierarchy had its own role to play. The king shall not take any fine from a maiden who makes advances to a man of high caste, but he should force a maiden who courts a man of low caste to live confined in her house.[18] Again, corporal punishment is prescribed for a man of low caste who makes love to a maiden of the highest caste.[19] It is again evident that adultery was feared more because it threatened *varṇa* structure, which was already undergoing turmoil due to other factors cited earlier.

Varṇa hierarchy had an important role to play even in the case of marriages. Accordingly, it is laid down that "a *Śudra* woman alone can be the wife of a śūdra, she and one of his own caste (the wives) of a *Vaiśya*, those two and one of his own caste (the wives) of a *Kśatriya*, those three and one of his own caste (the wives) of a *Brāhmaṇa*".[20] It can be noticed that women of the lower *varṇa* can be taken as wives by the men of higher *varṇa*. However, the reverse of this is not permitted. It seems that since it would have been impossible to restrict inter-caste marriages completely, a concession in this way was granted. Further, the marriage of twice-born men with Śūdra women is discouraged, and testimony of various authorities is given in the support of this. Again, this was an attempt to protect the varṇa structure which was getting fragile.

Another thing which draws attention is the impurity associated with everything related to women's sexuality say menstruation or miscarriage. Why and how this whole concept of impurity in those times originated is a subject for detailed study. But it seems to me that in this context it came as a corollary to the disapproval of adultery. At one place, it is said that it is the nature of women to seduce men in this world, and their ability to lead astray not only the fool, but also the learned; and it is directed that one should not sit in a lonely place even with one's mother, sister or daughter.[21] Besides, one finds that while at one place, it is said that it is women's nature to seduce men (verse 213), in verse 215, it is recognized that the senses are powerful and master even a learned man. Perhaps the sexuality of women was feared as it had the capacity to cause men and even women themselves to go astray; thus leading to admixture of varṇas.

II

The epigraphs belonging to that period, which were records of donations made, serve as indirect evidences regarding the position of women in that period. They also mark out deviations from the norms set by the text. Some of these are discussed in this part of the paper.

Deviations from the Norm of Ideal Wifehood

Bedsā Cave Inscription of Mahādevī Sāmadinikā[22]

The inscription refers to the gift made by Sāmadinikā. The whole text of the inscription is devoted to establishing the identity of the donatrix. She is referred to as the Mahādevī, the Mahārathini, daughter of Mahābhoya and the wife of Āpavedataka. The reference to her wifely status comes in the last among the constituents of her identity. It seems that it was added as an afterthought when the whole text of the record had already been finalized and perhaps incised as well. It is surprising that the husband figures without the dignity of a single epithet or even the common honorific śrī, while the identity of the wife is highlighted by no less than three royal titles. This marks a deviation from the norm set by Manu, where the wife is asked to worship the husband, and her entry to the heaven is said to be dependent upon her service to her husband.

Kanheri Cave Inscription of Mahārathinī Nāgamūlanikā[23]

The inscription belongs to the post-Sātavāhana period. It is clear from the titles attributed to Nāgamūlanikā that she belonged to a family of Mahābhojas on her father's side, though was given in marriage to a Mahārathī, a person of lesser rank in political hierarchy. Perhaps this is the reason that he finds no mention in the record. Our knowledge of his official rank is based merely on the assumption that she derived the title Mahārathinī from her wifely status in relation to a Mahārathī husband. The utter exclusion of the husband and his family from the phraseology of the record again marks a deviation from the norm of ideal wifehood.

Nāsik Cave Eulogy of Queen Gautamī Balaśrī[24]

The inscription is meant to record the grant of a cave by the queen, and a village, to meet the expenses of structural decoration, by her grandson. It is in fact a triple eulogy, that of the queen herself, her son and her grandson. The identity of the queen is defined in terms of her motherly status with reference to Sātkarṇi, who is praised for all his virtues, powers and achievements, so much so that he appears to have been a paragon of perfection. It is noteworthy that he is mentioned by his metronymic alone at the beginning of the panegyric and his proper name is inserted only at the end. Significantly, his patronym or paternal *gotra* figures neither in this inscription nor in his own, though one of the epithets given to him is 'ekabahmanasa' meaning 'peerless Brāhmaṇa'. One wonders whether he inherited his varṇa credentials from his mother or father. In fact, the name of his father is conspicuous by its absence in this record as also in those of his own. Further, an ideal Brahmanical widow is marked out of the description given for the queen. It is curious that the identity of the queen-mother has a lengthy eulogy of her son as the fundamental constituent of her identity, whereas her husband remained absolutely unnamed and unhonoured. Such an ignorance of the husband is in contradiction with the ideal laid down by *Manusmṛti*.

Deviation from the Norm Regarding the Name of Women

According to Manu, the names of women should be easy to pronounce, not imply anything dreadful, possess a plain meaning, be pleasing and auspicious, end in long vowels and contain a word of benediction.[25] Names of women figuring in many of the inscriptions seem to go against this norm. The names Ayakotusiri and Vijhathavisiri are not easy to pronounce, and the names like Nāgavasusiri, Nāgasiri, Śivanāgasiri (all mentioned in Nagarjunikonda Memorial Pillar Inscription of the Ikṣavāku Queens),[26] Nāgamūlanikā (Kanheri Cave Inscription)[27], Śivaskandanāgaśrī (Vanvāsi Nāga-image Inscription)[28], Nāganikā (Nāneghāt Cave Inscription)[29], seem to have been derived from a snake and inspire terror. Nor do any of these names contain a word of benediction.

Deviations from the Norm of Prohibition upon Cross-cousin Marriages

Nagarjunikonda Āyaka-pillar Inscriptions of Mahādevīs Bapisiri and Chathisiri[30]

The queens figuring in the two records are sisters married to the reigning king. But their connection with the royal family is mentioned not only as been derived from their wifely status in relation to the king, but also as the daughters of his father's uterine sister. This marks a case of cross-cousin marriage. This is considered as a punishable act in *Manusmṛti,* where a lunar penance is prescribed for such a sin.[31]

The above instances of deviation are, though sporadic, but reveal that the injunctions were neither strictly enforced, nor completely followed in the society. The injunctions of the text were more normative in nature and not a few number of times were far removed from the social reality.

Conclusion

Some of the inferences which can be drawn out of the discussion in the paper are that the indictments laid down in the *Manusmṛti* were a response to the political, social, economic and religious conditions that arose during that period. It was an attempt at preserving the older order. Whatever was laid down was not followed in practice essentially. The sphere of influence of *Manusmṛti* was limited. Whether whatever was said in the text was right or wrong, should be criticized or eulogized, is something I disapprove of discussing on the ground that *Manusmṛti* should be seen as a document expressing the line of thinking that developed among a section of the society as a response to certain circumstances.

Notes

1. *Early India,* Penguin, 2002, p. 245.
2. Sastri, K.A. Nilkanta, *A Comprehensive History of India,* Vol. II, p. 223.
3. The *Gārgī Saṁhitā* states that at the end of the *Kali* age people of all four castes will observe a similar moral code and wear similar clothes (*GS, Yuga Purāṭa,* 100-101). The *Viṣṇu Purāṇa* goes further to say that in the *Kali* age people of all castes would become like *śūdras* (*Viṣṇu Purāṇa,* VI. 1,53). The *Mahābhārata* also echoes similar sentiments (*Mbh, Āraṇyaka P.*, 188.29).
4. Thapliyal, Uma Prasad, *Foreign Elements in Indian Society- 2nd century B.C. to 7th century A.D.*, Munshiram Manoharlal, 1979, pp. 129-130.
5. Manu, II, 33.
6. Ibid., II, 67.
7. Ibid., V, 148.
8. Ibid., V. 149.
9. Ibid., V, 150.
10. Ibid., V, 153, 157-62.
11. Ibid., V, 164.
12. Ibid., V, 157-161.
13. Ibid., III, 4-11.
14. Ibid., IX. 3.
15. Ibid., VIII. 354-363.
16. Ibid., VIII. 364.
17. Ibid., VIII. 367.
18. Ibid., VIII. 365.
19. Ibid., VIII. 366.
20. Ibid., III. 13.
21. Ibid., II. 213-215.
22. *A.S.W.I.*, Vol. IV, No. VI (3).
23. Ibid., Vol. V, No. 29.
24. *H.I.S.W.K.*, Part II, No. 18.
25. Ibid., II.33.
26. *E.I.*, Vol. XXI, No. 11 (L).
27. *A.S.W.I.*, V, No. 29.
28. *H.I.S.W.K.*, Pt. II, No. 37.
29. *A.S.W.I.*, Vol. V, No. 1, A-B.
30. *E.I.*, Vol. XX, No. 1 (C2, C4).
31. Manu, XI. 172.

IV

Dharmaśāstras and the Socio-Political Panorama

10

Social Status of Women in *Dharmaśāstras*

Anjali Chatterji

While the need for the analysis of traditional texts for enhancing our insight into Indian institutions and culture is undeniable, the methodological limitations of the work done so far in this direction needs to be considered.

Manu, the greatest lawgiver, says in one of his famous verses that by *Śruti* (revelations) is meant the *Veda* and by *Smṛti* (tradition) the *Dharmaśāstras* which has been translated by G. Bühler as "Institute of the Sacred Law".[1]

The *Smṛti* literature, as an important branch of ancient Indian Sanskrit literature, deals with every aspects of Indian life. However, the word *Smṛti* is used in restricted sense and as defined by Manu. The word *Dharmaśāstra* is also used in two senses: one extended and the other restricted. In its extended use *Dharmaśāstra* means what Manu said, specially all legal texts and commentaries *(bhāṣyas)* and digests *(nibandhas)* written in Sanaskrit. But out of these some earlier ones are written in prose and thus came to be known as *Dharmaśutras* and the later ones beginning from *Manusmṛti* are written in verse and these metrical *smṛtis* are sometimes called *Dharmaśāstras*. The term *Dharmasūtra* generally used in connection with the works of Āpastamba, Gautama, Vasiṣtha and Baudhāyana while *Dharmaśāstras* include their works as well as the metrical *Smṛtis* and their commentaries and the digests also.

Some of the important commentaries are Medhātithi and Kullakas on Manu and Vijñāneśvara's on Yājñavalkya known as the *'Mitākśarā'*. The later *Smṛtis* are generally extant of which the most important are the *Manusmṛti* and *Yājñavalkyasmṛti.* But *Manusmṛti* unlike *Yājñavalkyasmṛti* is more than a legal code, while the later *Smṛtis* like those of Nārada, Bṛaspati and Kātyāyana are really texts on *Vyavahāra* or formal law and legal procedure.

It is very difficult to determine the age of the *Dharmasūtras* or the metric *Smṛtis.* According to P.V. Kane, the *Dharmasūtras* of Āpastamba, Baudhāyana, Gautama and *Manusmṛti* are very ancient and were composed centuries before the Christian era. Some were composed in the first centuries of the Christian era such as the *Smṛtis* of Yājñavalkya, Nārada, Pārāśara and rest of the *Smṛtis* fall between the period from 400 AD to 1000 AD.[2]

It is obvious that objective description of social reality is not the primary purpose of these ancient texts. Many of these texts such as the *Dharmasūtras* and *Smṛtis* are of prescriptive nature and others like the *Purāṇas* and the epics particularly though have mythological and literary intent, the customs reflected in the narrative parts of the epics are, more or less corresponding to the age of the *Dharmaśāstras* as well as the age of *Manusmṛti*.

The history of Indian women has been endowed with an impressive past which is basically constituted with two elements – one is defined as the vedic age and the other one associated with *Manusmṛti.* The *Vedas* are the earliest textual sources which are by definition sacred and by extension Sacrosanct. *Manusmṛti* is the most well-known prescriptive text of early India.

It is said that "if Pāṇini has determined the Sanskrit for all time, Manu has determined Hindu code of conduct for all time".[3] Manu became the law giver and his name became a byword for what was righteous and proper. His dictums handed down in a mass of floating verses of rules and observations, were governing the life and conduct of people, and that they were invoked as authority is known from early literature.

The status a society assigns to women largely depends upon the basic structure of that society. Almost all the *Smṛtikāras* have discussed the status of woman. Manu's famous dictum runs thus "Her father protects her in childhood, her husband protects her in youth and her son protects her in old age".[4]

"Reprehensible is the father who gives not his daughter in marriage at the proper time; reprehensible is the husband who approaches not his wife in due season and reprehensible is the son who does not protect his mother after her husband's death."[5]

All these verses mean that woman is very precious social unit and as such must be guarded with great care during all the stages of her life. Thus, her status was co-related to her phase of life. It changed from daughterhood to wifehood.

Due to strong patriarchal society the birth of a girl was considered as a misfortune. No doubt, the birth of a female child was less welcome than that of the male, but it did not arouse cries of dismay as is generally believed. The *Atharvaveda* contains charms and rituals to ensure the birth of a son reference to that of a daughter.[6] In one of the early *Upaniṣads* such as *Bṛhadāraṇyaka Upaniṣad,* we find a ritual for having the birth of a learned daughter in addition to the rituals for the birth of sons.[7] This ritual, of course, did not become popular as that of *'Puṁsavana'* which is the chief sacrament for having male child. It is to be performed when the stars are of the male gender.[8] Thus, the desire to secure male child finds strong expressions in the *Gṛhyasūtras.*

As in the *Pāraskar Gṛhyasūtra,* we find that the wife was praised for bearing a son, the hope of the family. The husband recited the following verses in her honour: "Thou art ida, the daughter of Mitra and Varuṇa, thou strong woman hast born a strong son. Be thou blessed with strong children thou who hast blessed us with a strong son."[9] In fact the birth of a son heightened woman's status.

It is to be noted that at different stages of life a variety of *Saṁskāras* are to be performed and they reflect the status of a woman both in the home and in the society. When great sacrifices could not be performed by every individual, the *Saṁskāras* which were domestic sacrifices gained importance. Śaṁkha-Likhita writes that "purified by the *Saṁskāra* and always practising eight virtues of the soul, one gets fame, merit and heaven … ."[10] Medhātithi voices the same expression that the purpose of the *Saṁskāras* was the attainment of heaven and even *Mokśa,* i.e., liberation.[11]

The *Saṁskāras* were a guide that directed the life of an individual in accordance with the process of growth. Now, the question arises that whether the rituals and *Saṁskāras* which are prescribed by *Smṛtikāras* were to be performed both by the boys and girls or by the boys only?

Again, a question comes whether these *Saṁskāras* were to be performed by all the castes or by the twice-born?

The answer is to be found in *Āśvalāyana Gṛhyasūtra* where it is laid down that the *Saṁskāras* from *Jātakarma* (ceremonies on birth) to *Cūḍākarma* were to be performed in the case of the twice-born with *vedic mantras* if the child was a male and that in the case of girls, the same ceremonies were to be performed but without the *mantras.*[12] It clearly indicates that from the time as early as that of *Āśvalāyana Gṛhyasūtra* distinction between the boys and girls was made in the matter of ritual. For girls no Vedic *mantras* were needed. Veda Vyas declares that there were ten such *Saṁskāras* which *Śūdras* had to perform but without uttering the *mantras.*[13] Naturally, a question comes into mind why these *Saṁskāras* were performed without the *mantras* in case of the birth of a girl child or in case of *Śūdras*? The reason of forbidding the recitation of *mantras* could be that it was needed for the purification. A person who is born impure or for whom purification was not necessary, in that case, there was no need to recite *mantras* for them.

A woman had to perform from her birth till death rituals and *Saṁskāras* which reflects her position directly or indirectly in the family as well as in the society. One of the important *Saṁskāra* was *Upanayana* i.e. to take admission in the Aryan community and its sacred literature. To impart education to the children and to help them in setting in life are the two main duties of parents. The girl should be nurtured, brought up and educated in the same way as diligently as the boys. And the parents were well discharged with reference to the daughter, could be found in *Ṛgveda*. It clearly indicates that woman were by no means kept uneducated and ignorant of the larger life of the world. Till about the beginning of the Christian era *Upanayana* or the ceremonial initiation into Vedic studies was as common in the case of girls as it was in the case of boys. The Vedic age held that *Brahmacarya* discipline and training was as much necessary for girls as it was for boys.[14] It was apprehended that if the most important religious *Saṁskāra* of *upanayana* was not performed in the case of girls, women would be automatically reduced to the status of *śūdras*, how could then *Brāhmaṇa*, *Kṣatriya* and *Vaiśyas* be born of them?[15] Thus *upanayana* of women was absolutely indispensable, if the cultural tradition of the different Aryan classes was to be preserved. There was no prohibition against girls following the same full course of education as the boys of their caste-class and implicit permission was availed of in cases here and there, is amply proved by the classical stories of learned women. Pārāśara says that "in very early times girls were also invested with the sacred thread – at least some who showed special inclination for study".[16] Gobhila says "At the *upanayana* of the girl, she should be brought to the teacher duly dressed and with the thread on (in distinction from the boys who went with upper body bare and received the thread from the teacher)."[17]

According to Hārīta, "there are two classes of girls: (1) the *Brahmavādinīs,* students who received the sacred thread, constant reminder of the holy vows, tend the sacrificial fire and study the *Vedas,* and (2) the *Sadyovadhūs* who are given the sacred thread somehow only symbolically and that too immediately before marriage."[18]

After their *upanayana* girls used to follow a discipline more or less similar to the boys. But in case of begging for alms they did it within their own parental homes.

A *Brahmavādinī's* ideal of life was spiritual well-being. A *Sadyovadhū's* on the other hand was dedicating herself to the welfare of her family and spending her time mostly in daily domestic duties of an ordinary kind. Even then there was no real opposition between the status of a *Brahmavādinī* and that of a *Sadyovadhū.* The Vedic tradition of culture and education also continued during the age of Pāṇini, i.e., in the 5th century BC. Those *Brahmavādinīs* who themselves taught were reverentially called *'upādhyāya'* or *'upādhyāyī'* and *'ācārya',* while the *Sadyovadhūs* who were wives of teachers were called *'upādhyāyani'* and *'ācāryāṇi'.*

As the *Brahmavādinīs* used to devote themselves seriously to the *vedic* studies some of them figure among the authors of Vedic hymns. Śaunaka in his *Bṛhaddevatā* (5th century BC) a work on *Ṛgveda* has mentioned the names of as many as twenty seven *Brahmavādinīs* or women seers whose hymns were thought to be fit for being included in the *Ṛgveda.*[19] The brightest example of a *Brahmavādinī* one can find in Gārgī who earned immortal fame for her highly learned philosophical discussions with the great sage Yājñavalkya.[20] It has been recorded twice in the old and celebrated *Bṛhadāraṇyaka Upaniṣad.* The glorious example of a *Sadyovadhū* is also found in the same *Upaniṣad.* When Yājñavalkya at the verge of his retirement from the world desired to divide his property between his two wives – Maitreyī and Kātyāyanī, Maitreyī refused to accept it by profound utterance that "what should I do with that through which I cannot be immortal?"[21] She asked for the knowledge of becoming immortal. She was thus given choicest gift of knowledge by her husband in a most illuminating discourse on the unity of the self.[22] References are to be found about the girl's school and learned women when Panini wrote *Aṣṭādhyāyī.*[23]

The epic age records many strata of societies in which Vedic religious and philosophic education is mentioned to have been imparted to women. In the commentary on *Gobhila gṛhyasūtra,* we are informed that "the women folk should be taught, for without such study, they cannot perform *Agnihotra.*"[24] And *Agnihotra* surely was performed by the ladies in the epics.[25] Kauśalyā, the mother of Rāma had been offering oblations into the sacrificial fire deity, daily uttering the sacred Vedic mantra herself.[26] A magnificent example of a *Brhamavādinī* could be found in *Rāmāyaṇa,* i.e., Anūsuyā, the wife of sage Atri, she reached such heights of spiritual perfection by deep meditation as are rarely reached by even great seers.[27] Even in the *Mahābhārata* we find instances of highly learned ascetic women. Mention may be made of Sulabha who belonged to the clan of Rājarṣi (kingly sage) Pradhān and the daughter of Śāṇḍilya – both of them have mastered the *Vedas* and attained perfection and austerity.

Coming to the period of Brahmanical age (1500 to 1000 BC) one can find fast disappearance of Vedic education from amongst women. Scholars have given many reasons for that and one of the reasons was that the volume of Vedic studies became very extensive and the lengthy commentaries written on texts needed many years to specialize in the subject. Moreover, as Dr.Altekar opines that "the spoken dialect of the age had begun to differ considerably from the language of the Vedic hymns and the theory had found universal acceptance that to commit a single most minor mistake in the recitation of the Vedic *mantras* would produce most disastrous consequences to the reciter. As a natural consequence, society began to insist that those who wanted to undertake Vedic studies must be prepared to devote a fairly long period of about twelve to sixteen years to the task... ."[28] As the marriageable age of the girls everywhere was lower than that of the boys they could hardly find time for their Vedic studies. Consequently, as Hārīta relates that only a few *Brahmavādinīs* used to devote themselves seriously to the vedic studies after the *upanayana.*[29] Similarly, regarding Vedic sacrifices which became very complicated, voices raised that they could be performed only by those who had studied its minutest intricacies. Thus, many sacrificial duties that could be once discharged by the wife alone came to be assigned to male substitute in the age of the *Brāhmaṇas.*

Though she continued to perform the evening sacrifice down to the beginning of the Christian era, she was not allowed to recite the Vedic *mantras* for that occasion.[30] Now, as women had to take purely formal part in sacrifices, the *upanayana* of girls began to become a mere formality in course of time. And that formality of the sacrament somehow had gone through just before their marriage.

The *Smṛti* school, on the whole, was inclined to curtail the earlier religious rights and privileges of women. While Manu began to advocate that girl's *upanayana* may be performed but no Vedic *mantras* should be recited on the occasion.[31] *Upanayana* without Vedic *mantras* being recited in and taught after the ritual, was somehow contradiction in terms. Thus, Yājñavalkya straight away advocates its prohibition[32] since it was just a formality now. Therefore, an attempt was made to systematize this situation in the *Manusmṛti* where women were denied access to the *upanayana.* It was reinforced by suggesting substitutes: for women marriage ceremony was portrayed as equivalent to the initiation of the male, serving her husband is equal to the service of a teacher, staying with her husband is equal to the stay in *āśrama* and the performance of household duties was identified with the worship of the sacred fire.[33]

Thus, during the period of *Smṛtis,* which was the period of codification of social laws, women were bracketed with the *śūdras* as they were denied access to the sacred learning. To most of the *Smṛti* writers like Pārāśara, Nārada, Gautama, Baudhāyan, Śaṁkha, Samvarta, Atri etc. marriage and household works are everything for girls. Therefore, their *upanayana* was replaced by the *vivāha-saṁskāra.*

In any society, marriage is one of the major institutions around which interpersonal relationships tend to crystalize for the purpose of the continuance of society by bringing up children and the upliftment of the two by self-restraint, self-sacrifice and mutual co-operation. All the *Gṛhyasutras*, *Dharmaśāstras* and *Smṛtis* give importance to the *vivāha saṁskāra* or marriage through which not only to beget progeny but to ensure that on one's death son should perform the *śrāddha* rite which would in turn ensure heaven. Thus, the marriage is the most important of all the Hindu *Saṁskāra* as it is the origin and centre of all domestic sacrifices. In the Vedic age it was given religious sanctity. In the epics too, marriage as a prelude to life of the greatest importance, i.e., domestic life, gradually became an obligatory sacrament.[34]

In the case of women, however, the question of marriage has been inseparably associated with her status. When women by virtue of their intellectual education and religious status had a voice in shaping their future, marriage was not imperative for them. Thus, Sulabhā and others could forego marriage and lead a life of asceticism and independence.[35]

However, with the passing of that religious status and the disappearance of sacred learning their independence was lost. Absolute dependence on menfolk (which came to be the order of the day) led to compulsory marriage. The status of religious partner of the husband was gained by women through the sacrament of marriage.

Therefore, the question of marriageable age for girls is one of the most debatable points in ancient social history. In the *Ṛgveda*[36] as well as in the earlier *Gṛhyasūtras*[37] post-puberty marriage is generally referred to. A perusal of the marriage hymn shows that the bride was fully matured and quite grown-up at the time of marriage. She is expressly described as blooming with youth and pinning for a husband.[38] Again, we find in the two verses of *Ṛgveda* which refer to the natural age of the wife.[39] These references clearly indicates that the Vedic society was in favour of grown-up marriage.

Even *Baudhāyana Dharmasūtra* laid stress on marriageable age by saying that she should be married after attaining puberty.[40] Vasiṣṭha too is agreed to that.[41] It seems that during the period of the *Sūtras* child marriage was not popular, puberty was the main concern regarding the age of marriage. Perhaps progeny might have remained as the important part of the marriage.

However, coming to the period of *Smṛtis,* we find that the *Smṛtikāras* of the period between 500 AD to 1000 AD began to encourage marriages much before the time of puberty. They held that a girl should be regarded as having attained puberty at the age of ten and therefore her marriage should not be postponed beyond that age. It was considered a crime committed by a father or brothers of an unmarried girl who was permitted to attain puberty at her father's house.[42] In that case they all – the father, the mother and the elder brother go to hell.[43]

The great lawgiver Manu is strongly against marrying a girl after attaining puberty. He has given a girl three years time after puberty to choose her husband herself if her parents or guardians fail to arrange a match for her.[44] From this statement of Manu it can be inferred that a girl has the right of choosing her husband after gaining maturity. In another place he says that "a man who takes a girl, that has reached the age of puberty should not give marriage money to her father for by hindering the natural exercise of the female functions, the father would loose her ownership."[45] It seems that though the marriage at puberty age gets confirmation by Manu, he is in favour of pre-puberty marriage. Because in the same chapter verse 94 recommends that a man of thirty should marry a girl of twelve years and a man of twenty four years, who is in a hurry to become a householder should marry a girl of eight years.[46] Manu's prescription of marriageable age of a girl thus do not exceed the age of puberty. *Viṣṇusmṛti* also supports Manu in prescribing the age for marriage. He also has given three years to her to wait for her own choice of marriage.[47] Manu was willing to allow a girl to remain unmarried even to the end of her life if a proper husband could not be secured.[48] Commenting upon the statements of Manu regarding the marriageable age of a girl, Kulluka says that the verses are not intended to lay down a hard and fast rule but merely to give instances of suitable ages.[49] It seems that during the *Smṛti* period pre-puberty marriage became the order of the day. Yājñavalkya also insisted that girls should be married before the age of puberty otherwise every month their guardian will be guilty of the destruction of an embryo.[50]

The *Smṛtikāras* like Pārāśara and Samvarta were in favour of pre-puberty marriage. Samvarta puts it as "A girl of eight years is called *Gaurī* (and therefore the most suitable one for marriage), of nine years *Rohiṇi* and that of ten years *Kanyā*".[51] Kulluka interprets that a girl becomes marriageable at the age of eight years.[52] He further holds that a girl should be given in marriage before puberty begins, if her father fails, he is liable to be censured.[53] *Bṛhad-yamasmṛti* also shows his preference of marrying her before puberty.[54] The marriageable age of a girl as given by Dakṣa, Aṅgirās and Pārāśara varies from eight to twelve.

Probably, the analogy of *upanayana* also played an important role in lowering the marriageable age. As Dr Altekar opines that "Parents anxious to ensure a rapid progress of their sons in education were advised to perform their *upanayana* at the age of five, marriage was the substitute for *upanayana* in the case of girls and so it could well be performed at the same early age."[55]

According to the interpretation of later *Smṛtikārs* that learning of *Vedas* will be absolutely of no use to her. Moreover, for learning the *Vedas*, she shall have to go to a teacher and shall have either to mix freely with the male students or separate arrangement shall have to be made for the girl students. As the learning of *Vedas* will require about at least nine years and if a woman begins to learn them at the age of eight by the time she finished her education, she will be mature and will be in the possession of knowledge which is useless in her future existence as a mother and wife. Thus, the age for the marriage of a girl has been brought down to eight and that marriage has been declared as the *upanayana* ceremony of a girl. From the age of eight to the age of maturity, she goes to the house of her husband which is equivalent to the residence of the teacher (*gurū*) and she is to learn the householder's duties and the knowledge about the rearing of children from her mother-in-law and other womenfolk of the joint family. Here, in the house of her husband she learns the most essential duties and knowledge which is necessary for leading a happy householder's life.

Therefore, the most central and common identity envisaged for women was wifehood. In fact, the nature of wifehood was elaborated at length. The ideal process for becoming a wife involved a certain denial of women's personhood, implicit in the notion of *kanyādāna*.

A wife is considered as *'Ardhāṅginī'*, i.e., half of her husband so she has to stay at home as half of the body (namely that of husband).[56] Manu says that there is no difference between the wife and the goddess of fortune, as the wife is also worthy of worship, illuminator of the home and full of bliss due to giving birth to children.[57]

The highest possible praise for woman could be found in *Manusmṛti*:

(a) "Where women are honoured there the gods are pleased; but where they are not honoured, no sacred rites yield rewards."[58]

(b) "Between wives (*Striyah*) who are destined to bear children, who secure many blessings, who are worthy of worship and irradiate (their) dwellings and between the goddess of fortune (*Striyah* who reside) in the houses (of men) there is no difference whatsoever."[59]

(c) "Production of children, the nurture of those born and the daily life of man (of these matters) woman is visibly the cause."[60]

(d) "Offspring, the due performance of religious rites, faithful service, highest conjugal happiness and heavenly bliss for the ancestors and one-self, depend on one's wife alone."[61]

These verses and many others show the high respect with which women were treated in the society upto the period of the *Smṛtis*.

The usual remark that Manu treats women with scorn do not appear in the above-mentioned verses. The great lawgiver (when creating them) allotted to woman (a love of their) bed, (or their) seat and (of) ornaments, impure desires, wrath, dishonesty, malice and bad conduct.[62] This verse amongst others, is considered to be the most conclusive evidence that women are treated very badly by Manu. But, Dr M.V. Patwardhan while supporting Manu says that "these are the characteristics of the womanhood of all the world and not of a Hindu woman alone. Moreover to say that salt has a salty taste does not mean that it is a malicious remark about the salt, but is to state its correct qualities so that it can be properly used."[63]

The contents of wifehood are developed systematically in the *Manusmṛti*. The wife was expected to be thrifty and do her housework cheerfully,[64] to be faithful to her husband, to consider her husband as own-self, to bear children, to obey her husband in life and death even if he was devoid of qualities[65] such a woman is compared to *Lakśmī*.

A family is the smallest complete social unit. It has to undertake two types of duties for satisfying its basic needs: first, the procurement of the means of subsistence and second, preparing these for the enjoyment. The procurement of the means of subsistence will be the duty of the man whereas the means of subsistence for enjoyment as the duty of procreation and rearing of children can be easily adjusted with it. Even, the duties of the collection and expenditure of wealth, keeping everything clean and looking after the household duties are given to the woman.[66] The highest duty which has been prescribed for her is to serve her husband. It is stated that by the service of her husband a wife can attain heavenly bliss.[67] She is enjoined upon to follow her husband in every action.[68] She must know her husband's mind and should be polite and obedient to him.[69] "A faithful wife who wishes to attain heaven, the mansion of her husband, must do nothing unkind to him, be he living or dead."[70] In another verse of Manu we find that "while she, who slights not her lord, but keeps her mind, speech and body devoted to him, attains his heavenly mansion, and by good men is called *Sādhwī* or virtuous."[71] Thus the specific norms envisaged for women reinforcing a more or less consistent logical structure of gender relations.

In the *Smṛti* literature quite often we come across the word *vidhavā* which is used for a widow. Obviously certain question therefore arises as to what would be the status of a widow in the Indian society? Would she be allowed to survive her husband if so could she marry again? If she marry would she receive considerate treatment from the family and the society? Could she hold or inherit property so that she could lead an honourable and independent life after her husband's death? Or would she to be compelled to die with him to become *satī?*

It is true that in the great controversy that raged at the time of the legal prohibition of the *Satī* custom by Lord William Bentick, it had been argued by the then pandits that the custom had a Vedic sanction. To support Vedic pundits it was maintained that the funeral hymn in the Ṛgveda refers to widows ascending the funeral pyre of her husband. "The case, however plausible" as Prof. Altekar points out "that it is only by fraudulently changing the last word from '*agre*' into '*agneh*' ". The verse in question refers to women with their husband living, coming forward to anoint the corpse before it was consigned to flames, and contains no reference whatsoever to any widow immolating herself on her husband's funeral pyre."[72]

The *Atharvaveda*, however, shows that the funeral rituals of the *vedic* age preserved some formalities regarding the custom of *satī*. Such as it was customary for the widow to lie by the side of her husband's dead body on the funeral pyre. She was, however, asked to come down and prayer was offered that she should lead a prosperous life enjoying the bliss of children and wealth.[73] From this statement it is clear that the custom of sacrifice of the widow at the pyre of her husband was not prevalent in the Vedic period.

Other *Vedic-Saṁhitās*, the *Brāhmaṇas* and *Āraṇyakas* give evidence that the wife of the dead person is not to be immolated but to be brought to the world of the living. It is thus clear that the Vedic age expected the widow rather remarry than to immolate herself. The reason that led to dislike the custom of *satī* in the Vedic age can only be inferred. Probably the finer cultural outlook of the Vedic Aryans helped them to convince that the custom was a barbarous one. There are no traces of the *satī* custom down to 400 BC. The *Brāhmaṇa* literature (1500 BC to 700 BC) is silent about it. The *Gṛhyasūtras* dated c-600 to c-300 BC describe numerous rituals and *Saṁskāras* but the custom of *sati* does not figure among them. Even, the details of funeral rituals and procedures have been laid down in them. *Āśvalāyana Gṛhyasūtra* refers to that the widow was to be brought back from the funeral pyre either by her husband's brother or disciple or by an old trusted servant.[74] In the *Āpastamba Dharamasūtra* one can find that a widow is not to become a *satī* but live a hard life of penances and austerities. *Manusmṛti* and *Yājñavalkyasmṛti* have laid down detailed rules about the duties of women and widows but none of them even mention that it would be commendable for a widow to burn herself alive on the funeral pyre of her dead husband. They recommended that a widow should lead a chaste life. It is true that some *Smṛtis* and *Purāṇas* refer to the performance of the *satī* rite but they neither hold it as an ideal for the widow nor they regard it as a religious duty. As Bṛhaspati says that "a woman is declared devoted to her husband when she is his companion in his weal and woe and if she dies when he dies".[75] *Viṣṇusmṛti* thinks the custom to be not illogical; it advanced the view that in spite of diversity of karman, a widow can go the way of the departed soul by dying after him.[76] It seems that Viṣṇus did not put stress on it, he merely mentions it as we find that he is one of the earliest *Smṛti* writers who did recognize the widow as an heir to her husband; he also allows her to remarry.[77] Similarly, *Bṛhaddharma Purāṇa* says that a widow who follows her husband on the funeral pyre though she commits a great sin does good to the departed soul.[78] From these statements one can gather that these writers allow the custom only as a second alternative and regard ascetic life as preferable to it. Though the *Vasiṣṭha Smṛti* did not favour the burning of a widow with her dead husband, it did not allow her to live a happy and comfortable life. There were of course restrictions on her dress, her food and her enjoyment also.

Medhātithi admits that the custom has been mentioned by *Aṅgiras Smṛti,* but maintains that it has no authoritative value, for it is opposed to an express Vedic text which prohibits suicide to all.[79] Thus, the custom of *satī* has not been given much importance in *Smṛti* period. It is just mentioned to show its existence among a minority.

The age depicted in the great epics, the *Rāmāyaṇa* and *Mahābhārata*, is the age more or less corresponding to the age of *Dharmaśāstras* as well as the age of *Manusmṛti* but nowhere to be found the case of *satī* in the *Rāmāyaṇa*. None of the wives of Daśaratha or Ravana are represented in the epic as accompanying their husband in the funeral pyre. Only in the *Uttarakāṇḍa*[80] one can find that Vedavati's mother became *satī*. But the analysts of the *Rāmāyaṇa* hold view that this story is more a legendery than a historical one. A major portion of the *Mahābhārata* which had been composed in and around 5th century BC records only a few cases of *satī*. The first to be mentioned is the case of Mādri when the king Pāṇḍu died. It is to be noted that while Mādri was about to ascend to the funeral pyre of her husband, the assembled sages tried their best to dissuade her from her resolve. But Mādri was unmoved by their arguments by saying that she is determined to die with her husband. The reasons being given by her as that her desires were not as yet satisfied. Secondly, Pāṇḍu died without fulfiling his desire for her, so it was her duty as a wife to bring satisfaction to him in the next world. Thirdly, because she might find it difficult to treat evenly her sons and stepsons. No argument of any religious merit is assigned by her or by anybody else.[81]

The *'Strī-Parva'* is full of lamentation and funerals, but there is not a single case of *satī*. In the *Mausalā Parva* of the *Mahābhārata* it is to be found that after the death of Vāsudeva, his four wives – Devaki, Bhadra, Rohiṇī and Madirā ascended the funeral pyre of their husband[82] and as a result attain the region of felicity with Vāsudeva. The news of Kṛṣṇa 's demise made his five wives, Rukamiṇī, Gāndhārī, Sahaya, Haimavati and Jambovatī at Hastinapur to ascend the funeral pyre without their husband's body. Only Satyabhāmā retires to forest for practising penance.[83] Shakambari Jayal rightly points out that "at the time when these portions were composed the attractive rewards of being *satī* were hinted at to encourage the custom".[84]

Because as against these, we find in the *Mahābhārata* a references to widows who survived their husbands. For instance, the wives of Abhimanyu, Ghatotkocha and Droṇa did not become *satī*.

From the description of the epics it appears that the custom of *Satī* was though prevalent but by no means common. Before the 5th century AD there is probably no text in any of the *Śrūtis* and *Smṛtis* to show recommendation or approval of the custom of *satī*. But, in the later period, this was projected as the only way left for a widow since it was due to her sins that such a calamity had beallen her.

The advocacy of the later *Smṛtikāras* to the merit of joining the husband in heaven for eternal enjoyment which could devolve upon a *satī* had a great effect on the society. The theory of *Karma* was also modified to support the custom. It is well-known fact that the *karmas* of the two persons would lead them to different destination and a relation could not join dead person in the other world by dying after him.

But the *satī* was an exception, her self-sacrifice was enough to annihilate her husband's sin, so as to raise him to heaven to live in eternal union with his wife. Besides the practice of self-immolation was glorified by the ideal of *'Pātivratya'* (faithful and loyal to husband)

Verses attributed to Paithinasi recommended *satī* to women of castes other than the Brahmins. With this result the custom was gradually developing mainly among the warrior classes, i.e., the Kṣatriyas as well as among the Vaiśyas. From 8th century onwards there was struggle for supremacy among Pālas, Pratihārs and Raṣtrakūts. The political situation of the country resulted in constant wars and inevitably the increase of war-widows. The widows of the conquered could never feel secure under the protection of a conqueror. Thus, they preferred self-immolation. From 11th century onwards in Rajputana the custom of *satī* was an object of the highest veneration. To be praised and worshipped by the community or society was another cause of encouraging the custom. Kalhan's *'Rājtaraṅgiṇī'* refers to worship of *satī*.[85] Among the ruling Rājpūt families of North India, the custom became firmly established during the period between 1200 AD to 1400 AD. The reason behind was that to preserve honour by burning herself on an occasion of foreign invasion. It was a common practice for Rājpūt women to perform *Jauhar,* i.e., mass-immolation so that they would not be molested at the hands of the invaders. The average Rājpūt princess seem to have been the most willing to accompany their husbands remains to the funeral pyre. During the period between 800 AD to 1100 AD the custom of *satī* became more frequent in the northern India and quite common in Kashmir, particularly in the ruling families. The history of Kashmir deals with the cases of *satī* in the royal families. To them widowhood was a great calamity. So far the South India is concerned one cannot find references of *satī* from the well-known ruling families such as the Pallavas, the Cholas and the Pāṇḍya down to 900 AD. Though the custom was not unknown especially among the upper classes, but it was not common. Perhaps the reason was more political than social. The attacks of the invader always centred around North India. Consequently, when the menfolk died in the battlefield, the only way out to save their woman's honour was immolation. But in South India political condition was not so disturbed. Women were respected and were safe during this period.

It is to be noted that the custom of *satī* was prevalent among the castes other than the *Brāhmaṇas* and the *Śūdras.*

There was some ambiguity as regards Brāhmaṇ widow becoming *satī*. Surprisingly, the *Padma Purāṇa* extols the custom but prohibits it to Brāhamaṇa widow. It even declares that any person helping a Brāhmaṇa widow to the funeral pyre will be guilty of the dreadful and unatonable sin of the murder of a Brāhmaṇa *(Brahmahatyā)*.[86] The *Mitākśarā (Ācāra-V.86)* also recommends *satī* for all the castes except Brāhmaṇa widows or widow with infant children or expecting mother. As the commentator Mādhava on Pārāśara explains the view of the text, that it did not mean the prohibition of a Brāhmaṇa widow to become a *satī,* it only says that this action should not be taken under the emotional influence. It should be the result of full and mature deliberations.[87] Though the Brāhmaṇa a community took pride on their ascetic and self-denying code of life they began to feel that they should not be far behind of the Kaṣatriyas, so far the custom of *Satī* was concerned. The custom therefore began to be followed by a few Brāhmaṇa families. Over and above the *Vyāsa-smṛti* (dated 600-900 AD) for the first time recommended a Brāhmaṇa widow for becoming *satī.*[88] It was a very late development. The lawmakers of earlier centuries who were against Brāhmaṇa widows becoming *satī,* stated that it was a kind of suicide. The *Mitākśarā* quotes Aṅgīras (*Ācāra*-V-86) who says that this type of suicide neither takes the husband nor the wife to heaven. The later *Smṛti* writers however, barring few gave it a religious sanction for the *Brāhmaṇa* widows too.

But the *Śudra* widows were not allowed to become *satī*. Probably because being the lowest of all the castes, they could not be put at par with the higher castes.

At the same time, the authorities prohibit those wives who have not attained the age of puberty, or pregnant or have children very young, from becoming a *satī.*

Now, the question comes those who were surviving their husbands what would be their duties? What the lawgivers have prescribed for them? Under the rules of the *Purāṇas* and *Smṛtis* a widow had to lead an austere life. She should sleep on a Kuśa and was not allowed to use a cot. She took only one meal a day, she made oblations everyday in memory of her husband and listened to recitations of the *Purāṇas* . She was not allowed to wear coloured clothes. She should be free from laziness, anger and bad company. These are the duties to be performed by a widow remaining celibate, failing which as *Skanda-Purāṇa* says, she falls into a lower region.[89] It also advocates the tonsuring of widows, i.e., the shaving of the head which was absolutely unknown down to 300 BC. From the textual analysis, it is clear that she was debarred from taking part in religious rituals, social ceremonies and ceremonial festivities. They had to lead a life of enforced celibacy.

The widows either could pass their remaining life in widowhood or have some children by *niyoga* or remarry. Appointment of a wife or a widow to procreate a son from physical relation with an appointed male[90] is called *niyoga.* When the notion of achieving heaven was at its height, it was thought that only sons could lead their parents to heaven. To die without a son was regarded as a great spiritual calamity and in that case his wife could produce a son for her dead husband by the system of *niyoga*, not only to perpetuate her husband's lineage but to ensure a seat in heaven for him. For the purpose of *niyoga* practice, generally the appointed male had to be either her younger brother-in-law or any *Sapiṇḍa* relation or a person of the same *gotra* when a person was not able to produce progeny due to his inability or death. It naturally became the sacred duty of a brother to see that a son was raised on his sister-in-law for the spiritual benefit of the deceased or the incapable. The importance of child has been shown in *Mārkaṇḍīyasmṛti* which considers a childless widow as impure. When she meets in the way there is danger of fight, but a widow having a son is as good as bride.[91] Therefore, the practice of *niyoga* was the only method to have an issue. The brother-in-law of a woman regarded as the most eligible person for this duty. If it was made with a stranger it was apprehended that he might be a claimant to the family property and would exercise his influence over the son born from him and eventually manage to transfer the child's share in his name. To prevent this situation, the appointment of a widow for the purpose of *niyoga* should be primarily with her brother-in-law.

The practice of *niyoga* was not directly hinted in the *Vedas*. Perhaps the reason may be that as the Aryans were a virile race, they did not feel the need for such a custom and secondly there was a custom of widow remarriage.

The custom of *niyoga* for wife was not so much prevalent in the time of *Smṛti,* but for a widow it was allowed with a great favour. The *Gautamasmṛti* recommends a chaste life for a widow but if she wishes to have a son provided she does not have any issue from her first husband, she could have one son through the system of *niyoga.* The person preferably would be the younger brother-in-law.[92] Vasiṣṭha also approves of *niyoga* and recommended only one son through this system. The only provision was that she should not choose a stranger if a brother-in-law was available.[93] The system of *niyoga* is also advocated by Nārada and Yama. Yama states that "for a woman, the life of an ascetic has not been prescribed either in Śruti or in the Śāstras, begetting progeny, indeed from one of her own varṇa is her sole duty."[94] The *Yājñavalkyasmṛti* too lays down that a sonless widow could raise one son by *niyoga.* But Vijñāneśwara the most famous commentator on *Yājñvalkyasmṛti* forbids *niyoga* in general in the *Mitākśarā* and interprets the text mentioning it applicable to a girl who is only betrothed and not married.[95]

The *Mahābhārata* is replete with cases of *niyoga.* In the great epic Sudeśnā, Kuntī, Saradandayini, Madamayanti and Mādri practised *niyoga* in coverture,[96] while Ambikā, Ambālikā and the Kṣatriya ladies practised it in the state of widowhood. But those were rare cases.

The practice of *niyoga* was fairly common upto 300 BC, but after that it encountered considerable opposition because society felt that such temporary unions were undesirable from several points of view. The practice was discouraged by Āpastamba, Baudhāyana and Manu. Āpastamba argued that the son by *niyoga* would belong to the begetter and would be of no spiritual benefit to the women's husband. Baudhāyana concurred with him. Manu though in the beginning approves of *niyoga* for a sonless widow and allows her to have only one son through *niyoga* with the permission of the elders. But later on he condemns it as beastly and declares that it was no longer permissible to follow it specially in the case of *Brāhmaṇa.* He says that among *dwijātis* a widow should never be appointed to raise issue from another, for by doing so ancient *dharma* would be violated.[97]

Despite their vehement condemnation, they have laid down detailed rules about *niyoga* procedure. It indicates that their opposition remained ineffective for a long time. They succeeded at least in restricting its scope. They allowed only one son to be raised by *niyoga,* though the earlier practice had permitted three.

There are some conditions laid down for *niyoga* system.

The father or brother of the widow should assemble the *gurus* who taught the deceased and should appoint her for *niyoga.* The body of the appointed should be anointed with ghee or oil and he should approach the lady during *Ṛtu* period[98] (period for conceiving). Actually, the purpose of *niyoga* is to procreate a son only. There should be no sexual desire behind it.[99] The custom could have led to corruption in the society since the appointed male was to have relations with the female so long she did not conceive. This was later objected by the *Smṛtikārs.* Manu further says, "after the birth of a son they were to regard themselves as father-in-law and daughter-in-law. The physical relations with a widow were only allowed in *niyoga,* otherwise there was punishment for 100 *paṇas* for the person, elsewhere the punishment is of *Chandrāyaṇa Vrata".*[100]

Thus, a custom which could lead to corruption was prohibited for the *Brāhmaṇa* female. The *niyoga* was then meant mainly for *śūdras* as well as for the *Kṣatriyas* in case there was no heir to the throne.

During the 9th century AD Visvarupa allowd *niyoga* only to *śūdras* as a general rule and to *Kṣatriyas* in case of extinction of the line. But for *Brāhmaṇa* widow *niyoga* was forbidden.[101] It seems that as among the *śūdras* the question of chastity did not arise, therefore it was recommended for them. To a *Brāhmaṇa* widow, chastity meant something and probably for that reason *niyoga* was not approved for them.

From 6th century AD it appears that the custom was not freely allowed. It was just only to get a son. A sonless widow neither could possess any sort of property nor she could adopt a son as an adopted son was having lower status than a son got from *niyoga.*[102] So it was proper to beget a son from *Sapiṇḍa* or brother-in-law. The reason might have been that the son was considered of the family of the deceased person.

As to the child born of this union would be identical from this point of view of the blood relationship with the dead husband of the wife.

Regarding this system Prof. Kane draws attention that if the interpretation of Manu (IX 69-70) be accepted the word *'vidhavā'* would have to be taken in two different senses in Manu and other texts, e.g., in IX-60 where Manu speaks of *niyoga*, the word means a girl promised to a bridegroom who died before the marriage ceremony had gone through while in Manu (IX-64) *'vidhavā'* means a widow whose husband died after marriage was completed. To say the least, this contravenes the canon of *'Mīmāṁsā'* interpretation that the same word in the same passage or context should have only one meaning.[103] He further writes that "Bṛhaspati refers to the fact that the *'Manusmṛti'* first described the ancient niyoga and then forbade it and adds that in former ages men possessed *'tapas'* and knowledge and could strictly carry out the rules, while in *'dvāpara'* and *'kali'* ages there is great deterioration of power and so men of these times can not practice *niyoga"*.[104] Prof. Altekar holds the view that "those who opposed the custom of *niyoga,* no doubt stood for the ideal of purity and constancy in sex relations".[105]

If a widow get a son through *niyoga* that son is called *'Kśetraja'* as he was born of *'Kśetra'* or field i.e., wife and the husband is *'Kśetrikā'*. A wife is just like land belonging to her husband. So any person who sows seeds in the land with his permission or even after his death the begetter has no right to own the offspring. And that son had a legal status in the family. Though Manu condemned the ancient practice of *niyoga*, he had to make provisions for the *'Kśetraja'* sons regarding partition.[106] Because Manu recognized the fact that customs die hard.

Evidence of widow remarriage in early Indian society is conflicting. There are verses of permission as well as of prohibition. During the period when *niyoga* was allowed widow remarriage was also not unheard of, though it was not generally appreciated. The sacredness of the marriage tie renders widow remarriage impossible in India. The concept is that husband dies, but in real sense he is not dead.

Though the widow remarriage prevailed in the Vedic society, it was not a frequent one. A widow was allowed to remarry if she so desire, it is evident from the verse in *Ṛgveda* in which the widow who lay on the pyre by the side of her dead husband was asked to rise and come to the world of the living.[107] In one place, *Atharvaveda* refers to a woman marrying second time. A ritual is observed to secure the union of the new couple in heaven.[108] As there is no suggestion to the effect in this passage that the widow could remarry only with her brother-in-law, it is clear that she could marry a person who was outside the circle of her late husband's family. But the usual procedure for the widow as Prof. Altekar opines that it seems to have been to marry a younger brother-in-law who was very often unmarried at that time.[109]

References to regular remarriage of widows in Vedic literature are few, probably because *niyoga* was then more popular than remarriage.

The period between C 400 BC to C 100 AD notices that *Dharmasūtras* allow remarriage even when the death of the husband was not proved and was only presumed. *Vasiṣṭha Dharmasūtra* mentions that even a *Brāhmaṇa* woman having children should wait for five years only, if her husband gone out on a journey and does not return, if she is unwilling to go to him, she should marry a near relative; only she should not wed outside the family, if there is an eligible person within it.[110] It is significant to note that Vaśiṣṭha is not referring here *niyoga* but he extends permission to remarry even to a woman having children. Kauṭilya even reduces the period of waiting to a few months only and allows woman to marry her brother-in-law or kin. If a woman violets the rule by marrying an outsider, not only she even those who have given their consent to it shall all be liable to punishment.[111] A contradictory provision can be found in *Nāradasmṛti.* On the one hand, Nārada thinks that a girl should get married only once but on the other hand he allows a woman to remarry if her husband expired or entered into a monastery or gone out on a long journey.[112] According to Pārāśara, "on receiving no tidings of a husband, on his demise, on his turning an ascetic, on his being found impotent or on his degradation, under any one of these five calamities, it is canonical for women to take another husband. A *Brāhmaṇa* woman should wait eight years for her absent lord and four years only, if she be childless, then let her marry again. A *Kṣatriya* woman should wait six years, and in case she has no issue, three years only. A *Vaiśya* woman if she has borne a child, four years, otherwise only two. For a *Śūdra* woman no period is mentioned for which she is to wait for her husband if it be heard that he is living, the rule is that the aforesaid periods are to be doubled when tidings are not received, aforementioned periods are enjoined. Such is the opinion of Brahma, the lord of men. In such cases, therefore, there is no harm in women marrying again".[113] Thus, Mādhavācārya, the commentator, though antagonistic to the remarrying of women, has distinctly admitted that the text of Pārāśara authorizes such remarriage under the calamities aforesaid.[114] But Ramanika Jalali points out that "commentator Medhātithi on Manu (V. 163) gives a new interpretation of statements of Nārada and Pārāśara a by saying that this was just for her maintenance and not for securing a fresh contact".[115] It is clear that the injunction for remarriage as expressed in the text can by no means be applied to the case of a betrothed virgin. It is to be noted that Pārāśara in the same text also mentions that "women who on the deceased of her husband, observes the *Brahmacarya,* attains heaven after her death". He next says that "She who burns herself with her deceased husband, resides in heaven for as many *kālas* or thousands of year... ."[116] This shows that Pārāśara a was not very particular about *Satī* but he definitely preferred that a widow should lead a life of austerity.

Manu, the greatest jurists is totally against widow remarriage. He has nowhere mentioned a second husband for a virtuous wife.[117] According to him a widow should not even think of remarriage.[118] Manu's argument is that the *vedic mantras* used in *'Pāṇigrahaṇa Saṁskāra'* are meant only for maidens.[119] How can widow be married with *Saṁskāras* and without *Saṁskāras* the marriage was not a legal bond.

In fact it was thought that a person's life has no meaning without a son. For *mokśa* and for progeny a son could be a reason of remarriage of an issueless widow. But Manu declares that "a childless widow who is virtuous and chaste can go to heaven".[120] *Viṣṇusmṛti* also supports Manu by saying that "even a sonless widow remaining *Brahmacāriṇī* goes to heaven."[121]

Manu was resolute in his attitude towards the remarriage of widows or to beget children through *niyoga.* If woman did so on her own, neither was she respected nor were her children given the same social status as the children of a woman who is married for the first time. Such one is called the son of a *'Punarbhū'* which literally means re-wedded. There are certain controversies regarding the word *'Punarbhū'*.[122] *Vasiṣṭha Dharmasūtra* says that "a *'punarbhū'* is a woman who leaves her husband and lives with another person depending on his family only. Again if she leaves a husband who has deserted or a mad husband or her husband is dead and she remarries, she is called as *'Punarbhū'*". Manu interprets the word *'Punarbhū'* in this manner "that a woman who goes to another person but remarries the person with whom she had physical relations previously is called *'Punarbhū'* of that very person".[123] But both Yājñvalkya and *Viṣṇusmṛti* stated that whether a girl has physical relations or not when she marries second time, she becomes *'Punarbhū'*.[124]

A son born of this union come to be known as *'Paunarbhava'* whose status in the society has been defined by the *Smṛtikārs*. According to Manu, *'Paunarbhava'* son of a *'Punarbhū'* has no authority to inherit any property nor he was given a good status in the society.[125] Commentator Medhātithi states that a son begot from remarriage is authorized only for food and clothing, he has no right in the property. On the other hand, the adopted son has more rights as he can inherit it, if in the absence of a legitimate son.[126] *Vasiṣṭha Dharmasūtra* place *Paunarbhava* son in the fourth rank among the other sons.[127] Manu includes the *'paunarbhava'* among the *Brāhmaṇa* as that are not to be invited at *'Śrāddhas'*.[128] Thus, lowering the position of the *'Paunarbhava'* son the *Smṛtikārs* seem to be discouraging widow remarriage indirectly. Angiras clearly says "a woman once given to a man in marriage if again given to another is called *Punarbhū* and one should not eat at her place".[129] It appears from the two words *'Punarbha and Paunarbhava'* that the remarriage of a widow was in vogue in India from early times. It is known to Vaśiṣṭha, Kauṭilya whose *'Arthaśāstra'* is certainly older than that of the extent of *'Manusmṛti'*. It not only allows the widow to re-marry but also the wife whose husband has not been heard of for a long time.[130] Vātsyāyana who belong to the same epoch as Nārada and Pārāśara makes it very clear that the position of the re-married widow approaches nearer to that of a mistress than that of a wedded wife.[131]

Widow remarriage was never looked upon with favour by Indo-Aryan society and whatever vogue it may have had in early times, upto the early centuries of the Christian era, it gradually fell into disfavour with upper castes. The *śūdras* were always regarded as impure and no religious ceremonies could make them pure.[132] It was believed that chastity among them was limited. Whether a śūdra widow died with her husband or not she could not have achieved heaven. Therefore she did not require to die to prove her chastity.[133] This would explain for the absence of *Satī* among the sudras and prevalence of *niyoga* and widow remarriage among them.

However, a girl whose marriage rituals are performed but marriage is not consummated is regarded as a maiden by Vaśiṣṭha who pleaded for her marriage.[134] Laghu-Śātātapa even supports that such a girl is really a virgin, so she is allowed to marry again as a matter of course.[135] Baudhāyana also holds the same view.[136]

Significantly those who opposed widow remarriage were not against the re-marriage of a child widow. As the marriageable age gradually becoming lower, the problem of the child widow raised question. Probably the society looked upon the problem sympathetically. As we find in the later portions of the *Mahābhārata* which declares that no derogation would attach to a child widow if she married again; her sons will be fully entitled to other oblations.[137]

Almost all the *Smṛti* texts recommend eight types of marriage of which some are condemned while the rest are said to be virtuous. These are *Brāhma, Daiva, Ārṣa, Prajāpatya, Asura, Gandharva, Rākśasa and Paiśāca.*[138] The most important is that irrespective of the form, marriage was indissoluble. Here the term 'divorce' cannot be used in the modern sense but it generally denotes only dissolution or suspension of a marital relation.

Both in the *Ṛgveda* as well as in the *Atharvaveda* references are to be found that there can be no dissolution of the sacred bond of marriage.[139] According to *Āpastamba Dharmasutra,* both husband and wife proceeds towards hell by dissolving the marriage vow.[140] Manu declares that "let mutual fidelity continue to death" this in few words, may be considered as the supreme law between husband and wife. "Let a man and woman, united by marriage constantly, beware lest at any time disunited they violate their mutual fidelity."[141]

One can find from the *Dharmaśāstra* literature and *Smṛtis* that desertion of wife was permitted before the beginning of the Christian era under certain well-defined circumstances such as Manu says, "For a whole year let a husband bear with his wife, who treats him with aversion, but after a year, let him deprive her of her separate property and ceased to cohabit with her." He further says that "She who neglects her lord, though addicted to gambling fond of spirituous liquors, or diseased must be deserted for three months and deprived of her ornaments and household furniture".[142] Medhātithi the commentator on Manu, on the other hand, is not in favour of taking all the belongings away from her but it is just to set her right.[143] Kulluka's view in this case is that "only those things should be taken away which she has got from her husband and she should be provided with clothing and food".[144] But, on the other hand, "She who is averse from a mad husband, or a deadly sinner, or an eunuch, or one without manly strength, or one afflicted with such maladies as punish crimes, must neither be deserted nor stripped of her property".[145] Both P.V. Kane and R.M. Das are not ready to accept this separation as divorce. Their views are that even when the husband was allowed to abandon his wife for her faulty nature, she was in most cases entitled to at least starving maintenance.[146]

As one can leave his wife who gets aborted,[147] the wife also can abandons her husband under certain circumstances. Manu states that "a wife is not to blame, if she abandon a husband who is impotent, insane or suffering from a incurable or contagious disease".[148] Though Manu has allowed remarriage for an abandoned woman, it seems this has been allowed only in limited cases. For Manu has no passage advocating, supporting or conceding separation. To Manu marriage is indissoluble for life.

Kauṭilya's *Arthaśāstra* which conforms a great part of the *Smṛti* texts gives detailed rules of divorce intended for the couples who found it impossible to live with each other. They were however applicable only to four unapproved marriages, viz., *Gandharva, Rākśasa, Paiśāca* and *Asura*. These marriages were generally common among the lower section of the people, thus, it can be implied that the divorce is favoured among them and not among the higher castes. But it was not unknown to them. Kauṭilya lays down that "by mutual disaffection a divorce shall be granted. If a man apprehending danger from his wife, sued for divorce, he had to return to her whatever presents he may have received at the time of marriage. If it was the wife who was the complainant, she had to forfeit her proprietory rights in her husband's family. No divorce, however, was permitted, if the marriage was performed by any of the approved forms viz. *Brahma, Daiva, Prajāpatya and Ārṣa.*"[149] The divergent opinions about the issue of divorce indicate that two ideologies were prevailing one favouring partial divorce and other forbidding it.

Thus, the status of women as depicted in the *Dharmaśāstras* clearly shows that a woman as a girl child, as a married woman and as widow has to observe a set of prescribed duties and sacraments in their lives. Actually in the ideology of Manu and other *Smṛti* writers the home and the family constitute the bedrock of society and woman is that figure on whom the stability and sanctity of the home and household life depend. The lawgivers had also a conception of woman according to which they did not like woman to be exposed to the rough and an unprotected independent life; and it is in this spirit that Manu says "a woman shall always be taken care of by some one – she is not fit for freedom."[150] The lawgivers tried to prescribe whatever suited in a particular environment. Therefore strictures are imposed on woman by which *Vedic* education of girls was prohibited and marriage ceremony was regarded as *upanayana* for them. It also leads to early marriage of girls specially prepuberty marriage was preferred. As a mother of a son she gets the highest place but as a wife she has to worship her husband. Moral codes prescribed for a widow include self control, limited and simple diet and dress. These restrictions must have become the morals of that time which are very idealistic. But ideals are generally not fully successful in practical life and it is for that reason Nārada and Pārāśara allow widow remarriage. Manu of course was totally against it. But, the mention of *'Punarbhū'* by him confirms that widow remarriage was existing during that age. In some passages Manu records the existence of sons of widows[151] and marriages of girls who had secretly conceived,[152] at one place a girl whose proposed husband passes away before the actual marriage or one whose marriage has not been consummated is allowed further marriage.[153] The recognition of a variety of marriages and of different kinds of sons and provisions for them shows the practical and liberal attitude of Manu and his consideration for woman in general. But he maintains that for the virtuous widow there is no second marriage or raising of issue by another.[154] Strictures on women in Manu and other *Smṛtis* should not so prejudice us as the real intention of all the *Śāstrakāras* is to praise the greatness of chastity i.e. *'pātivaratya'*. In fact, Manu and other *smṛti* writers adopted two standpoints first conceding to some extent as a result of the vogue and the second stating their personal or ideal opinion.

Notes

1. *Manusmṛti*; Ed. by Ganga Nath Jha, Bhāṣya of Medhātithi, Vol. I & II, Asiatic Society of Bengal, Calcutta-1932 – II 10.
2. MM P.V. Kane; *History of the Dharmaśāstra*, 5 Vols., Poona, 1930-58, Vol I (1st edition) p. 304.
3. *Cultural Heritage of India*; Pub. The Rama Krishna Mission Institute of Culture, Calcutta, Vol. II, p. 335.
4. *Manusmṛti*–IX, 3.
5. Ibid.–IX, 4.
6. *Atharvaveda*; Ed. by Pt. Rama Sharma Acharya, Comment of Sayana, Barely (U.P.) 1965 – III, 23.33.3.
7. *Bṛhadāraṇyaka Upaniṣad*: Ed. & translated by Robert Earnest Hume, Oxford Univ. Press, 1954.
8. *Atharvaveda*–III. 23.2.
9. *Pārāśara Gṛhyasūtra*; Ed. by Gopal Sastri, Banaras, 1926 – I, 16-19.
10. Śaṁkha-Likhita, quoted in Vīramitrodaya Saṁskār Prakāśa, p. 140.
11. Medhātithi on Manusmṛti ; translated by G.N. Jha, Calcutta 1920-39 – II, 28.
12. *Āśvalāyan Gṛhyasūtra*; Ed. by F. Max Muller, *Sacred Books of the East*, Vol. 29 Pt. I Delhi, 1964, – I˜5.12, 16.6, 17.18.
13. *Vedavyāsa Smṛti Aṣṭādaś Smṛtiyān*; Ed. Khemraj Kishan Das, Bombay 1830–~ I˜.16.
14. *Atharva Veda*–~I˜X, 5, 18.
15. *Hārītasmṛti*; Ed. Vinayak Ganesh Apte, Anandhashram Sanskrit Granthavali, Vol.-48–~X˜XI, 20.
16. *Pārāśara Gṛhyasūtra*–24.
17. *Gobhila Gṛhyasūtra*; Ed. F. Max Muller, *Sacred Books of the East*, Vol. XXX, Pt-II, 1892, Pra.2, Kandika.
18. *Hārītasmṛti*; quoted in *Smṛti Candrikā*–I, 60-63.
19. *Śaunaka, Bṛhaddevatā*–~I˜I, 89-91.
20. *Bṛhadāraṇayaka Upaniṣad*–~I˜II, 6,8.
21. Ibid., II, 4.
22. Ibid., I, 4.3.
23. V.S. Aggarwal; *Pāṇini Kālīn Bhārat*, Banaras, 1955–pp. 281, 295.
24. *Gobhila Gṛhyasūtra*–~I˜, 3-15; II, 3; I .4, 13-19.
25. *Rāmāyaṇa of Vālmīki*; trans. H.P. Sastri, 3 Vols, London 1952-59–II, 20-15; II, 25.44; II 24.2.
26. Ibid., II, 103.30.
27. Ibid., II, 117-19.

28. A.S. Altekar; *Position of Women in Hindu Civilisation*, Banaras, 1956–p. 238.
29. *Hārīta Dharmasūtra*: Quoted in Vīrmitrodaya–p. 404.
30. *Manusmṛti*–III, 121.
31. Ibid., II, 66.
32. *Yājñavalkyasmṛti*: Ed. Hari Narayana Apte, Commentary of Aparaka, Ānanda Āśram Press, 1825–I, 13.
33. *Manusmṛti*–II, 67.
34. *Mahābhārata of Vyās*, Trans. by P.C. Roy, Vols18, Calcutta, 1893-96–XII, 12.12ff.
35. *Mahābhārata*–XII, 320.
36. B.S. Upadhyaya: *Women in Ṛgveda*. Banaras 1941, pp. 50-54.
37. *Āśvalāyana Gṛhyasūtra–I*, 8-10; *Āpastamba Dharmasūtra*, ed by A. Chinnaswami Shastri, Banaras, 1932–3.8.8.
38. *Ṛgveda*; with the Commentary of Sāyaṇa (Part I to IV) Ed. Pt. Ram Sharma Acharya–X 85. 46, Ed. by Pt. Ram Sharma Acharya with the commentary of Sayana Part I to IV.
39. Ibid., I, 126. 6-7.
40. *Baudhāyana Dharmasūtra*; Ed. by Umesh Chandra Pandey, Varanasi, 1972–IV 1.11.
41. *Vasiṣṭhasmṛti*; Ed. by Pt. Rama Sharma Acharya, Sanskrit Sansthana, Barely (U.P.) 1966–XV, VV. 24-25.
42. *Pārāśarasmṛti*; Ed. by Pt. Vamana Sastri, Vols I &II with the commentary of Mādhavācārya, Bombay Sanskrit Series, 1893-1911–VII, 7.
43. Ibid., VII-8.
44. Manu–IX. 90.
45. Ibid., IX. 93.
46. Ibid., IX. 94.
47. *Viṣṇusmṛti*; Ed. by Pt. V. Kṛṣṇamacharya, Vol I & II, Madras, 1964–XXIV, 40.
48. Manu–IX. 89.
49. Kulluka *on Manusmṛti*; Ed. by F. Max Muller, *Sacred Books of the East*. Vol 25, Oxford 1886–IX. 4.
50. *Yājñavalkyasmṛti*; op.cit (Ācāra), 13.
51. Samvartasmṛti: Dharmaśāstra Saṁgraha, Ed. by Jivananda Vidya Sagar, Bhattacharya, Calcutta, 1876–VV. 67-68- quoted in Chandesvara Grhastha Ratnakar, p. 46.
52. Kulluka on Manu–IX, 94.
53. Ibid., IX, 88.
54. *Bṛhad Yama Smṛti*: Ed. by Pt. Ram Sharma Acharya, Bees Smṛtiyan Series, Barely, 1966–III, 21-22.

55. A.S. Altekar; op.cit. p. 59.
56. Manu–I, 32.
57. Ibid., IX, 26.
58. Ibid., III, 56.
59. Ibid., IX, 26.
60. Ibid., IX, 27.
61. Ibid., IX, 28.
62. Ibid., IX, 17.
63. M.V. Patwardhan: (ed.) *Manusmṛti,* Motilal Banarasi Das, 1968, pp. 143-44.
64. *Manusmṛti*–V, 159.
65. Ibid., V, 151, 154.
66. Ibid., IX, 10.
67. *Viṣṇusmṛti*, op. cit., XXV, 15.
68. Ibid–XXV, 2.
69. *Dakśasmṛti: Dharmaśāstra Saṁgraha*; Ed. by Jivananda Vidhya Sagar Bhattacharya–IV, 7 Calcutta, 1876.
70. *Mānava Dharmaśāstra* or *The Institutes of Manu*; Ed. by Rev. P. Percival, New Delhi, 1982–V, 156.
71. Ibid. V, 165.
72. A.S. Altekar, op.cit., p. 117.
73. *Atharvaveda*–XVIII, 2-1.
74. *Āśavalāyana Gṛhyasūtra*, IV, 2.18.
75. *Bṛhaspati Smṛti*; Ed. by F. Max Muller, *Sacred Books of the East*, Vol. XXXIII, Delhi 1965.
76. *Viṣṇusmṛti*, 20, 36.
77. Ibid; 17,43.
78. *Vṛhaddharma Purāṇa;* Ed.by M.M. Harprasad Sastri, Varanasi, 1974.
79. Medhātithi on Manu–V, 157.
80. *Rāmāyaṇa*–II, 17.14.
81. *Mahābhārat*–I, 138, 71-72.
82. Ibid., XVI, 7.18.
83. Ibid., XVI, 7, 73-74.
84. Shakambari Jayal; *The Status of Women in the Epics*, Motilal Banarasi Das, 1966, p. 180.
85. *Kalhan; Rājtaraṅgiṇī*: Trans. by Ranjit Sitaram Pandit, N. Delhi 1977–II, VV. 56-57.
86. *Padma Purāṇa*; Ed. Anandaashram Sanskrit Series, Poona, Sristi Khanda, 49, 72-73.

87. *Mādhava on Pārāśara*; Ed. by Chandrakānta Tarkālankār, Calcutta 1973, ch. IV, 31.
88. *Vyās Smṛti*, ch. II, V.53 V. 53.
89. *Skanda Purāṇa* ; Ed. by Nag Sharan Singh, Delhi, 1982 Kasi Khanda-V̄, 71-84.
90. *Gautam Smṛti*: *Bees Smṛtiyān*, Ed. by Pt. Ram Sharma Acharya, Barely, 1966–XVIII, 4-8.
91. *Mārkaṇḍeya Smṛti*; Ed. by Pt. Ram Sharma Acharya, Barely 1966, 12, 11.
92. M. N. Dutt; (trans) *The Dharmaśāstra*, Calcutta 1906-1908, p. 699.
93. *Vasiṣṭha Smṛti*–XV, 19.
94. *Smṛti Candrikā of Devaṇṇbhaṭṭa*, trans. by J.R. Ghorepure, Bombay, 1948, p. 596.
95. *Mitākśara* on Yājñavalkya (Ācāra) 68-69.
96. Manu–IX 59-62, 64-68.
97. *Vasiṣṭha Dharmasūtra*–XVII, 56.
98. Yājñavalkya–I, 68.
99. Ibid. I-82.
100. Manu–II 234-237.
101. Viśvarūpa on Yājñavalkya (Ācāra), 69.
102. *Ṛgveda*–VII, 57.
103. P.V. Kane, op.cit, Vol II, Pt–I, p. 603.
104. Ibid.
105. A.S. Altekar; op.cit. p. 149.
106. Manu–IX 120-121.
107. *Ṛgveda*.
108. *Atharvaveda*–IX 5. 27-28.
109. A.S. Altekar; op.cit, p. 151.
110. *Vasiṣṭha Dharmasūtra*–XVII, 67.
111. *Kauṭilya Arthaśāstra*; Trans. by R. Shamasastry, (4th edition) Mysore, 1951–III, 4.
112. *Nārada Smṛti; Smṛti Sandharva*, Vol I & II, Calcutta, 1952–XII, 28, 97.
113. Pārāśara–IV, 28.
114. Mādhavācārya on Pārāśara .
115. Ramanika Jalali; op.cit, p. 180.
116. Pārāśara–IV, V. 159.
117. Manu–V, 162.
118. Ibid., V, 157.
119. Ibid., VIII, 226.

120. Ibid., V, 160.
121. *Viṣṇu Smṛti*–XXV, 17.
122. Vasiṣṭha–XVIII, 20.
123. Manu–IX, 176.
124. Yājñavalkya–I, 67.
125. Manu–IX, 160.
126. Medhātithi on Manu–IX, 160.
127. Vasiṣṭha Dharmasutra–XVII, 18.
128. Manu–III, 181.
129. *Aṅgiras Smṛti*; (ed.) Kṛṣṇa Aiyanger, Madras, 1953, 6.5.
130. Kauṭilya–III, 4.
131. P. Chakladar, *Social Life in Ancient India; Studies in Vatsāyan's Kāmasūtra*, Calcutta-1929 pp. 181-184.
132. Manu–II, 62.
133. *Vyās Smṛti*–I, 16.
134. Vasiṣṭha–XVII, 66.
135. *Laghu Śatātapa*; (ed.) Vinayaka Ganesh, Anandaashram Press, 1851–V.44.
136. Baudhāyana–II, 2,4,7.
137. *Mahābhārata*–XIII, 55.7.
138. Manu–III, 21.
139. *Ṛgveda*–X 85.2; Atharvaveda–XIV, 1.18.
140. *Āpastamba Dharmasūtra*; ed. A. Chinnaswami Sastri, Banaras, 1932–II, 10.27,6; I, 10, 28, 19.
141. Manu–IX, 45.
142. Ibid. IX, 77-78.
143. Medhātithi–IX, 77.
144. Kulluka on Manu–IX, 77.
145. Manu–IX, 79.
146. P.V. Kane, op.cit, Vol II, Pt. I, p. 620.
147. Pārāśara–IV, 20.
148. Manu–IV, 79.
149. Kauṭilya–III, 3.
150. Manu–X, 36, 39, 50, 51.
151. Ibid., III, 174; IX, 175.
152. Ibid., IX, 172-173.
153. Ibid., IX, 69, 176.
154. Ibid., V, 162.174.

V

Economic Status of Women in *Dharmaśāstras*

11

Gender Perspective of Law in Classical India

V.C. Srivastava

Let us now analyze the position of women in relation to rules and laws of the *Dharmaśāstras*. The attitude of the *Dharmaśāstrakāras* to women may present the background for the analysis of the position of women in the eyes of law in classical India and its ethical and moral contents.

Attitude to Women

By and large, the attitude of Indians in the Vedic period was egalitarian in the sense that women were equal partners in sacrifices and were equally educated and intellectually evolved and participated independently in public life. However, in some references, their intellectual inferiority and emotionalism have been pointed out. In spite of their exalted position, the women were discriminated and denied property rights. The Epics – the *Mahābhārata* and the *Rāmāyaṇa* had high praise and honour for the women and regarded them as goddess of prosperity for the family and a symbol of innumerable virtues and a model of idealism. Against this picture *(sādhvi)* the epics also refer to non-virtuous *(asādhvi)* woman.

Manu has given exalted status to women when he says that where women are honoured there the very gods dwell and are pleased. For the prosperity and welfare the women should be respected. Wife and husband should do *dharma* and *karma* together. In spite of this exalted status he does not allow them any freedom except in marriage when he says that she is subject of guardianship of the father during childhood, of her husband during her youth and of her sons after the death of her husband. Vātsyāyana who is quite liberal in respect of women does not permit unrestrained freedom to them. They were denied many *saṁskāras* like *upanayana* and denied the recitation of the Vedic *mantras.* Manu and other *Smṛtikāras* had very poor opinion about women and branded them as the 'temptress', had disallowed remarriage and prescribed for suppression if she be drinker, diseased, rebellious, mischievous, wasteful, barren etc. It is interesting to point out that Varahmihir regards women as the *gṛhalakśmī* to be treated with respect and extols her virtues. Women are superior in virtues. Hārīta informs us that there were two classes of women - the *Brahmavādini* and *Sadyovadhū* and they are not equal to *śudras* as men are born from them and they can recite Vedic *mantras.*

Duties of Husband and Wife

The *Dharmaśāstras* prescribe rules for duties of the husband and the wife. Without entering into details of these rules, one or two examples may be referred to here in order to show the ethical and moral as well as practical significance of such rules. Manu condemns a father who does not give his daughter in marriage at the proper time, a husband who does not approach his wife in due season, and a son who does not protect his mother after her husband has died. Supersession of wife is prescribed in case of justified causes. But the wife has no right to divorce an unworthy husband. This one-sided rule is not in conformity with equity, justice and morality. Nārada has referred to the rule that the potency and virility of a man has to be checked before marriage. This rule must have saved many women from impotent husbands. It is a very forward looking, ethical and just rule since divorce of husband was not allowed. Nārada refers to different types of wives – *Punarbhū* and *Svairiṇi* and this is an unjust custom. *Niyoga* has been declared by Manu but Bṛhaspati says that this cannot, be practised by mortal in the present age when the virtue have declined. Such cases of ethical laws and rules may be multiplied.

Property Rights of Women

The property rights of women in classical law may be analyzed with a view to demonstrating as to how much and how far they were based upon equity and justice or the ethical and moral values of the Indian tradition. It may be discussed under four heads:

1. Daughter's right of inheritance.
2. Widow's right of inheritance.
3. Other female relations' right of inheritance.
4. Women's right at partition.

Generally, the women were not entitled for a share in the inheritance. There is an old saying that a son, a wife and a slave can own no property independently of the father, the husband and the master. However, among the female heirs the brotherless daughter was the first to succeed in establishing her right of inheritance. This happened as early as the *Ṛgveda.*[1] The daughter in the Vedic age were well-educated and independently evolved. Moreover, the Vedic Aryans had a prejudice against the adoption. Hence, they agreed to allow inheritance to a brotherless-daughter after making an agreement with his son-in-law that he will send back his first son to him for the continuation of the family of his maternal grandfather. Such daughter was known as *'Putrikā'*. It continued even down to 400 BC. The *Therīgāthā* refers to a brotherless daughter - Sundarī as a full heir to her father's estate.[2]

By 200 BC (the time for the emergence of the *Smṛti* literature) the position of female declined as they had no or very little education, denied Vedic mantras and their marriage age was lowered down. Probably all these happened in view of foreign invasion and settlement in northern India - the Śakas, the Pallavas and the Kuṣāṇas. There is reluctance to allow even a brotherless daughter to inherit her father's estate. Āpastamba allows a brotherless daughter to inherit her father's property only if there is no *sapiṇḍa* or teacher or pupil to claim the property.[3] It was a very difficult rather impossible situation because the agnates include relations upto the 7th degree. There is a further limitation that he should prefer a public cause rather than the daughter. Manu[4], Vasiṣṭha[5] and Gautam[6] do not mention the daughter in the list of heirs.

The *Mahābhārata*[7] prefers to allow the daughter to be heir when there is a subsidiary son, though she would be entitled to half of the property. Kauṭilya's position in this respect is similar. Yājñavalkya[8] supports the cause of the daughter and lays down that she should be the next heir after the son and the widow. Bṛhaspati[9] and Nārada[10] support the cause of daughters because the daughters are born from one's own body like the son. Kātyāyana held the view that the brotherless daughter should be regarded as an heir only till she is married and well settled in life. However, this view was not accepted and Yājñvalkya, Bṛhaspati and

Nārada took the lead. From 500 AD the daughter's right to inherence was well-established. However, the estate thus inherited was a limited one as it was only life-estate. However, the Bombay custom allows absolute ownership of her patrimony since 13th century AD. The Kolhapur Inscription provides an example of it.[11]

The above review shows that in respect of brotherless daughter the classical law was by far fair, though the condition to transfer the son for continuation of her father's family was not justified on ethical and equity grounds. Similarly, the provision for life-estate only or limited share in presence of *sapiṇḍas* was also not ethically fair. The transfer or reversion of *Putrikā's* son to maternal grandfather's family was tried to be justified on the custom that the daughter's son can perform last rites of maternal grandfather and his soul will rest in peace in such circumstances.

The Vedic period did not give right of inheritance to a married daughter. However, an unmarried old maiden daughter may get a share in competition to her brother. By 500 BC one school championed the cause of a daughter who has brother. The basis is a passage in the *Nirukta* but A.S. Altekar has rightly called in question the authenticity of this evidence. Generally the *Dharmaśāstras* did not favour for a share to a daughter who has a brother in patrimony. Kauṭilya also stands by this position. However, Śukra prescribes a small share to a daughter in patrimony in competition with her brother. Viṣṇu and Nārada also share this position. Nārada expressly shared the view that the daughter's share was only for maintenance till her marriage. However, some fathers divided their property both among their sons and daughters. The Mysore epigraph of 1168 AD refers to such a case. However, the denial of a share in the patrimony to a daughter was tried to be compensated by the rule that the brother should spend for his sister's marriage an account equal to one-fourth of his share.[12] This may be interpreted differently but it need not detain us here. This rule shows that the classical law was concerned with the welfare of the daughter. Since the property was generally landed, a share to a daughter married to someone in distant village may not have been very practical. Even a brother has to spend from his self-acquired property for sister's marriage. It might have created in every family absentee landlordism. But many modernists would say that this rule of no-share in inheritance was dishonest and an unethical act on the part of patriarchal and male-dominated ancient Indian society.

As it has been discussed there was a general prejudice against permitting women to hold property. Even wife who was considered as the joint-owner of the family property along with her husband was not allowed to have right of inheritance in husband's property when she looses her husband. Widow's right to inherit her husband's property remained unrecognized for a very long time. Besides prejudice there may be another reason for this denial. *Niyoga* system was in vogue and there may have been very few widows. Widows may have got husband's property not directly – but indirectly as guardian of minor sons who were entitled to inherit the property. They used to marry also. In Altekar's opinion this denial was not cause of much actual hardship in society. However, it is a question of right and justice rather than a question of hardship. Upto 300 BC widow's right to inherit husband's property was not recognized. The Vedic texts deny this right. Baudhāyana rejects this claim. Āpastamba says that in the absence of the son it should devolve on nearest male *sapiṇḍa* upto seventh degree rather than the widow, and in absence of any eligible *sapiṇḍa,* to preceptor and disciple for charity. Manu has also evolved such a scheme of devolution in case of a sonless person to his father, then brother, then a *sapiṇḍa* and *sakulya,* then a preceptor, a disciple for charity and lastly to king but not a widow. Elsewhere he recognizes even a mother also as an heir but not a widow. Kulluka – the 15th century commentator of Manu says that in IX.185 he means widow but this has not been accepted.[13] Medhātithi, the 9th century commentator who is quite liberal does not approve the widow's right to inheritance.

By the beginning of the Christian era *'niyoga'* and widow remarriage became in disuse due to various historical circumstances, specialy the foreign influx in northern India and general degeneration in morality. Early *Dharmaśāstras* and Kauṭilya allowed only maintenance to widow from husband's estate. Gautam proposed that the widow should be regarded at least a co-heir with other *sapiṇḍas.* Viṣṇu at the beginning of the Christian era advocated that widow shall be the sole heir, not co-heir on the failure of the sons. Yājñvalkya also favoured this rule. During the period from AD 400-1000 AD jurists were divided into two schools. The orthodox school was led by Nārada, Kātyāyana and king Bhoja of Mālwā. Nārada prescribes the maintenance of the widow while the property in case of sonless person devolves on the state. Kātyāyana held identical view. Bhoja would allow widow to be heir only if she submitted to *Niyoga.* But in his time *Niyoga* was not acceptable by a widow. Then this right – if she agreed for *Niyoga* would have been short-lived because the birth of the son would have deprived that right independently. Many jurists felt the need for providing the right to inherit to a widow but the prevailing patriarchal male-dominated society did not give them courage to advocate this right. Some jurists proposed halfway measures. Three types of measures had been enunciated:

1. She should be allowed to inherit property worth 2000 or 3000 silver *paṇas* in addition to *Strīdhana.*
2. She is permitted to inherit the moveable only.
3. She may be a deferred heir; when brothers-in-law fail and her parents-in-law had no objection to the property devolving on her.

However, reformist school was progressive and was not ready to accept it. Bṛhaspati prescribed the widow's right to inherit full share on the ground that the *Vedas,* the *Smṛtis* and sages have unanimously declared that the husband and the wife are the joint-partners of family property and together constitute one personality. As such, so long the wife (widow) is alive no one else can have that property. In the opinion of Vṛddha Manu the widow can offer funeral oblations to her husband and as such she should be allowed to inherit his property. Prajāpati has removed all doubts when he says that the widow has a natural right to inherit all her husband's property including moveable, immovable, bullion, ornaments, stores etc. Her rights are not affective by the living of elderly relations. If any male relation obstructs her in enjoyment of her inherited property the king shall punish him as a thief. Jīmūtavāhana, the founder of the *Dāyabhāga* school has defended widow's right to inherit her husband's property after his death in a judicious and highly ethical and moral manner as follows:

1. The wife acquires ownership of husband's property at the marriage and it cannot be terminated at husband's death.
2. Similarly it is also wrong to say that she may utilize only that much which is necessary for her maintenance. Viṣṇu says that the property of a man after his death will first devolve upon the widow, then to the daughter, parents etc. Here property means whole, not partial. As such it cannot be restricted.
3. He explains that early references in the Vedic and *Dharmaśāstra* literature denying the widow's right of inheritance actually refer to concubines and unchaste women. This has been criticized by modern scholars as a lame justification as it is wrong interpretation. Even in modern Hindu law chastity is a condition at the opening of the issue.

In spite of able advocacy by Reformist School specially *Dāyabhāga* it took a few centuries to be accepted in South India. However Deccan was more advanced as it accepted it from quite early times. The *Nirukta* informs us that it is customary for the southerners to accept property rights of woman. Yājñvalkya who pleaded for widow's right of inherence was a southerner. Two inscriptions of South India - one from Karnataka and the other from Tanjore certify the practice of the law of the widow's right of inheritance of whole property of the deceased husband. In Northern India it was introduced still later. Kalidāsa informs us that the property of a man without a son used to be taken by the king. Similarly *Kumārpālapratibodha* informs us that till 12th century it was not practised in Gujarat. Most of the digest writers writing after AD 1200 have recognized widow's right of inheritance.

Thus, by AD 1300 widow's right of inheritance was recognized. The *Mitākśarā* of Vijñāneśwara recognized widow's right of inheritance only if her husband had separated from the joint family before his death. This interpretation is correct because Yājñavalkaya prescribes wife's right of inheritance only if the husband is not a member of the joint family at the time of death.[14] Yājñavalkya makes it more explicit when he says that in case of reunion after separation only surviving coparcener will succeed, not the wife.[15] Vijñāneśvara includes inherited property under *Strīdhana* and hence to avoid passing of family's property to outsider, he has made this condition of separation from joint family. Most of the digest writers agree with this view.

Jīmūtavāhana, the founder of the *Dāyabhāga* school liberalized this still further. He made the revolutionary prescription that the widow shall inherit her husband's property even if her husband was a member of the joint family at the time of his death. As such he did not include it into her *Strīdhana.* Jīmūtavāhana has relied upon Bṛhaspati. But he did not declare it as an absolute one but only a limited one. To him it is only a life-estate. Many other jurists regard widow as a limited heir. She was not given the power to dispose of this property specially landed property except small portion for religious gift till 1200 AD. To dispose of even for religious and spiritual purposes, the permission of reversioners and sometimes even the entire caste was essential for a widow as is evident from inscriptions of South India, for example, Mysore inscription of the 10th century AD. Thus widow's inherited estate was a limited estate. There are, however epigraphical evidences to the effect that no permission was sought from reversioners in case of gift obtained by widow for religious purposes. For example Trichinopoly Inscription (12th century AD), Kolar Inscription (13th century AD) and other inscriptions of 15th-17th Century AD are proofs of this rule. Probably customs deferred from caste to caste and village to village. Mitramiśra (17th century of DP) pleads for widow's right to dispose of her inherited landed property for certain purposes - religious, maintenance if falls short of absolute right. Hindu Woman's Right to Property Act, 1937 invests the widow with the right to inherit her dead husband's property whether a part or separated member. Hindu Succession Act, 1956 (Section 14) also provides for it with retrospective operation of that Act. She holds the property in her possession as full owner and not a limited owner. The above review shows that the classical law was not absolutely fair to widows and it was with great hesitation and in a long period gave them right and was a limited right. Independent India has done justice by making them full owner of property rather than limited owner of property as was ultimately granted to widows in the classical law of India. Besides daughter and widows other females were also made heir such as mother and grand-mother in case of issueless son and grandson respectively. The right to inheritance of mother and grandmother was recognized quite early as is evidenced by Manu and other jurists but the classical law was very hard to daughter-in-law. Only one jurist Nanda Paṇḍit (1573) recognized her as heir but other did not recognize her right.

Women and Partition

The discriminatory attitude of the classical law of India is also discernible in respect of women and partition. Theoretically, a wife, soon after marriage, used to become joint owner with her husband in his property. The natural corollary of this joint ownership of classical India should have given the right to the wife to demand a partition against her husband in case of separation but the classical law did not grant this right. Yājñvalkya[16] lays down that a wife should get a third share in her husband's property if she is unjustly superceded. No other jurist of classical India had accepted this right. Some scholars have tried to justify such a stand on the ground that joint family system was the norm in those days and it was very unbecoming for a son to demand a partition while the father was alive. As such, the wife was also a victim of such a trend in ancient India. But this is no valid excuse for denying the right of a wife to demand partition in her husband's property if she is forced to live separately due to unjust supercession which was quite fashionable in those days when polygamy was permitted by the lawgivers on very unethical grounds. Thus, denial must have compelled separated wife to lead a miserable life economically besides the socially depraved status.

Let us consider normal cases of partition and women's rights. There are a few references in the Vedic literature to the partition by the father during his life time but we do not have any indication in these or other references whether the wife used to receive a share in it or not.[17] Many *Dharmaśāstra* writers expressly include the mother, the wife and the daughter among the parties entitled to a moiety.

Daughter and Partition

The case of the daughter in this respect has been discussed in previous pages. In short *Śāstric* opinion was not in favour of giving a share to daughter and wherever some of the *Dharmaśāstratiars* like Nārada have approved a share for the daughter with brother(s), the right was only for maintenance till her marriage or for marriage expenses by the brother. It is only Śukra who lays down that if the person divides the property in his life-time he should assign one share to his wife and sons, half a share to his daughters and one fourth a share to his daughter's sons. If the division takes place after his death the sister was to get one eighth share of the brother. Viṣṇu and Nārada have also allowed a share to the daughter but here the provision is only for her maintenance till her marriage. However, Śukra was in a minority and the daughter was in hopeless status in partition. However, a Mysore Inscription of 1188 AD refers to such a practice when a Machi partitioned landed property both among his sons and daughters. However, a saving grace was the rule, which enjoined upon a brother to spend on his sister's marriage an amount equal to one-fourth share.[18]

Wife and Partition

Yājñavalkaya and Kātyāyana allow the wife a share if the partition is in her husband's lifetime. Widowed mother is entitled for a share equal to that of her son according to Yājñavalkaya. Śukra[19] allows her only a one-fourth share. However, others insist that the mother should receive one full share. Some writers interpret it to mean only that much which is essential for her maintenance. The *Mitākśarā* objects to it as it is unreasonable and allows her a full share.[20] Thus, the *Dharmaśāstras* were not very fair to women's rights at partition also as in the case of inheritance. This demonstrates the dominance of patriarchal form of society in classical India and the position and status of women in terms of property rights had been quite deplorable and discriminatory. The whole situation was against equity and justice; howsoever one may justify it on grounds of joint-family system and sanctity of family life etc. and landed and immoveable nature of property in the main. The position in classical India vis-a-vis law and legal rights will not be complete without a discussion of the *strīdhana.*

Women and *Strīdhana*

Probably to compensate for the denial of property rights to females, and for the fictional joint ownership of family property by husband and wife the classical jurists evolved a special category of movable property exclusively for the wife only – the *strīdhana.*[21] It is difficult to define it. It can be described as ancient lawgivers have done. It is a property over which the females have more or less absolute right in normal times. The *strīdhana* developed from the custom of brideprice *(śulka).* It used to be retained in full or fraction to the daughter by father and she has full control over it. The Vedic literature permits absolute right of a female on her *strīdhana.* The *Dharmaśāstras* recognize this right on *strīdhana.*

Manu includes six types of gifts in the *strīdhana:*

1-3. Gifts by parents and brothers at any time.

4. Gifts by husband subsequent to the marriage.

5. Presents by anybody at marriage or at the time of departure to her new home.

Manu denounces those who would deprive women of these presents at husband's death. Viṣṇu adds three more categories in this:

1. Gifts given by the son.
2. Gifts given by any other relation.
3. Compensation to wife for supercession.

In short, the *strīdhana* consists of all types of gifts by relations to women at marriage or subsequent to it, but gifts by non-relatives subsequent to the marriage and the wages earned by the wife are not included in it. From the 7th century AD the scope of the *strīdhana* came to be enlarged. Devala includes maintenance and accidental gifts in it. Vijñāneśwara taking advantage of the word *ādyam* includes in it properties by inheritance, purchase, partition, chance and adverse possession. The interpretation has been doubtful but this amplification of the scope of the *strīdhana* by Vijñāneśwara is his opinion in the changed environment and is good for women's rights and status. Hindu jurists of the medieval period are divided on this interpretation. Aparārka, Nanda Pandit, Mitra Miśra and Kamlākara concur with him while Viśvarūpa, Devaṇṇabhaṭṭa and Jīmūtavāhana have not accepted this interpretation.

The question of ownership of the *strīdhana* has been discussed by the *Dharmaśāstras.* Manu does not give the right to alienate her own property without her husband's permission. This prohibition was not equitable and hence not ethical and justified. To rectify the situation the *strīdhana* was divided into two categories:

1. *Saudāyika* – gifts by parents etc. over which the women had full control.
2. *Asaudāyika* – other property which she can use only during her life time.

Opinion of jurists of medieval times are divided on the question of the right of women in disposing of landed property included in the *strīdhana.* The general view was that she had no right to dispose of landed property. We need not enter into the complex question of inheritance of the *strīdhana* as it is not very relevant in the present context. Generally, the classical law gave the right of full control over the *strīdhana.*

Notes

1. *Ṛgveda* I.124.7.
2. *Therīgathā* No. 327.
3. *Āpastamba Dharmasūtra* 11-14-1-4.
4. *Manusmṛti* IX. 185.
5. *Vasiṣṭha Dharmasūtra* XV-7.
6. *Gautam Dharmasūtra* XVIII-21.
7. *Mahābhārata* XIII. 180-11.
8. *Yājñvalkyasmṛti* III-5.
9. Bṛhaspati XXV.35.
10. Nārada XIII.50.

11. *E.I.* III. p. 215.
12. Yāj-II.124.
13. Kulluka on Manu IX-185.
14. Yāj-II- 136.
15. Ibid., II, 138.
16. Yāj-I-76.
17. *Ṛ̣V*-I-70.6, T.S.III.1.9, 4-5.
18. Yaj. II-124, Manu-IX-158.
19. Śukra-IV 5-297.
20. Mit. On Yāj-II-136.

12

The Economic Position of Women in the *Dharmaśāstras*

Sati Chatterjee

In a societal system in which women had little direct participation in the production consumption-trading cycle and earning monetary remuneration/gain, inheritance was the main channel through which property, wealth, *vitta,* could come to the female members.

In the *Dharmaśāstras/Smṛtiśāstras* principles governing inheritance are codified in the *dayābhāga* section, *dāya* meaning what is given, to be given, to be shared/divided... *Manusmṛti, navama adhyāya* codifies principles of sharing out hereditary property in the *dāya-bhāga* section, *Yājñvalkyasmṛti* in the *dāya-vibhāga prakaraṇam* section of its *vyavahāra adhyāya* offers a neat formulation of the *Manu vacanam* with occasional exegetical commentaries of very interesting and important nature.[1] Other *Smṛtiśāstras* follow in line, frequently repeating/quoting Manu and Yājñavalkya as source reference. *Pārāśara Smṛti*, in a broken state, does not present the dicta in the voice of Pārāśara a himself, the *ṭīkākāra*, commentator Mādhavācārya with his enormous erudition quotes and endorses numerous utterances culled from *Śāstra* texts, Manu onward, various commentaries and manuals used in practice.

The laws of inheritance enunciated in these texts, with focus on the *Smṛtiśāstras,* may be studied in three major clusters:

1. Inheritance laws in general which cover the issue of women's share as wives, daughters and sisters, by the side of male successors,
2. Special laws of succession operative in the case of the *'Putrikā'*, where a daughter is formally chosen to perform in the role of a son, and
3. Separate laws governing the case of *'Strīdhanam'*.

I

Inheritance laws codified in these *Śāstras* have behind a male-dominated familial set-up in which, exceptions permitted, property descended down the male line of succession, and the concept of male custodianship determined the direction of thought, the attitudinal inflexion, in discourse related to hereditary laws.

In formulating general laws of inheritance priority was assigned to the eldest-born male child (we might recall Gāṅdhārī's sense of dismay when Kuntī had the eldest male child of the generation in Yudhiṣṭhira). The *'jyeṣṭa'*. the eldest son, is a father-figure, a junior patriarch, who, after the death of the father inherits the largest part of patrimony, and, in the role of a guardian, shoulders the responsibility of the entire family including the younger brother.[2]

"The eldest son can obtain the entire patrimony if he, like a father, provides for the younger ones."[3]

"As a father raises his children, so too the eldest brother must nurture the younger brothers."

After detailing the shares of paternal property among the sons, the Manu discourse glances at the women claimants, mostly in the position of dependants. Daughters, particularly unmarried daughters, certainly need resources to support them till marriage; and *Śāstras* say, they must be assured of this. All the brothers (sons of the deceased person), whatever their shares in order of seniority *(Jyeṣṭa-kaniṣṭha-paramparā)*, must assign one-fourth of it to the unmarried sisters, *Anurha Bhagnī(s)*. A brother, successor son, unwilling, or non-complying, would be declared patita, an outcast social ostracism then marking climactic point in penal dicta.[4]

As to the direct succession rights of the wife, Manu remains silent. *Yājñvalkyasmṛti,* however, makes an unqualified assertion that after the demise of the father, sons and the mother should have equal share of the property left behind.[5]

The *Mitākśarā* commentary qualifies the formulation adding that this refers to cases where the wife has no streedhanam, whereas, when the wife enjoys streedhanam the share should be half.

II

Daughters, dependent on parental support in their unmarried state, however, *Śāstrakāras* assure, would count as an equal, factor, or power in a special situation. This introduces the idea of 'empowerment' , startling in the modernity of the spirit it enshrines.

If a sonless father *(Aputraka Pitā)*, we are told, chooses a daughter to act as a son, she becomes perfectly entitled to all the inheritance claims, even as she is entrusted with all the responsibilities associated with a son. Ritual rites, very important in those days, too would vest in her hands. A formally enabled daughter, as in such cases, would be designated a *Putrikā.*

The *Śāstras* speak with charged eloquence, making the point that sons and daughters, both are one's own offspring, *Ātmajās,* and no differentiation should be made.[6]

The point is carried on to the next generation and Manu asserts that in the case of *Putrikās*, their sons would inherit this property, coming down from the maternal grandfather's side exactly as the sons's son would do. Emphatically the verdict is given that the son of a daughter is as much a grandson, a biological descendant, as a son's son, and that the practice of differential treatment, wherever it prevails, is most foolish and unacceptable.[7]

III

Yet another area of economic independence for women is her exclusive ownership of wealth falling into the category of *strīdhanam.*

Strīdhanam constitutes a special category altogether. In those days of abject dependence (Mary Wollstonecraft's phrasing) of women, this formed a secure corner of resources at her disposal over which no one else, not even the husband, had any control.

Manusmṛti defines six forms of *strīdhanam,* and these are mentioned in other *Smṛti* texts. According to Manu, the property or wealth given to a girl before the nuptial fire or at the time of marrige procession, as a token of love and affection, by her brothers, by her mother and by her father, constitute the *Strīdhana* of that person.[8]

In conditions which denied women direct access to productive economic activities, the sources of the treasure-trove naturally were (i) inheritance, and /or (ii) gifts.

(i) Inheritance from the parental side, acquired before or after marriage, is exclusively the women's asset;

(ii) So is what comes to her as gifts on the occasion of the wedding ceremony (the *adhyāgni* and the *adhyāvāhanik*), as gifts of love husband *(prītidatta)*, and as tokens of affection from the father, mother, brother after marriage (the *anvādheya*).

She is free in her lifetime to gift this property to any one; after her death it goes to her daughter /daughter's daughter. So definite is the female line of succession that would go to the daughter (and daughter's daughter) of her co-wives.

The husband, lord and master as he is, has no access to this possession of the wife; he can borrow from this in times of exceptional distress like serious illness, natural calamities like famine.

The *Mitākśarā* commentary on *strīdhanavibhāga* section in *Yājñvalkyasmṛti* cites supportive formulations from numerous Smṛti text, and this indicates the wide acceptance of the principle at that point of time.[9]

IV

Outside of these stipulations is the edict, the *anuśāsana,* that women are claimants to maintenance. Maintenance would come from the father in childhood, from husband in the prime of life, from the son(s) in old age. Denied independent economic engagements, women must be given adequate protection, they must be provided for.

Even when the husband deserts a wife and takes another, the earlier wedded woman must be given economic protection.[10]

When desertion is for no fault of the wife, the husband would have to assign one-third of his possession to her.[11]

In case the husband lacks resources, he must make subsistence provision for wife he deserts:

Women who have no sons, *aputraka,* must be provided for by the family – affirms Yājñvalkya.

V

The generosity, the compassion, the rational balancing of arguments evinced in the *Smṛti* text on the issue of women's claim to economic resources, all evolve out of the first premise that women form a secondary group, never entitled to independence.

How the descendents of women who composed *sūktas* of the *Ṛgveda,* women who equaled, even surpassed men in the field of highest intellectual enquiry and spiritual aspiration, came sliding down to such a state of dependency, is a bewildering puzzlement that awaits socio-historical explorations, both extensive and intensive.

Till then, we can only relate to the inner, and deeper, perception glimmering through these ancient texts, the perception that women have the adequacy potential, that given and even floor, a level field, they can perform, they can deliver. The unqualified reliance on the *Putrikā* is assuring. We do not know what compulsions clouded truth-perceptions that always come through the outmoded rhetoric of male domination in the Smṛti Śāstras.

Yet, engaging in an objective scrutiny of the ancient modality of experience, we can try to locate the grains of gold lost in heaps of chaff. And these, few though in number, could perhaps pay our passage to "modernity"- "modernity" which is Indian, and at the same time, and for the same reason, without borders.

Notes

1. The commentaries, of much later dates, often add orthodox emphasis relevant in the contemporary social ambience, e.g., Mitākśarā exegesis of Yājñvalkya, *Vyavahāra,* 124. Commentators indeed make interesting contributions to the discourse. Kulluka Bhatta explains the intended implications of this Manu injunction pointing out that 'sister' ***(bhagnī)*** here not only refers to one's own ***sahodara*** sisters, but step-sisters baimatrikas too; the Mitākṣarā, on the other hand, narrows it down to 'sisters, by mother of the same caste – Kulluka, the commentator, presumably of earlier time, opening up, the later one straitening the range of responsibility of brothers (sons), and the range of the rights of the sisters (daughters). ***Mitākśarā*** also introduces the qualifying clause that 'one-fourth' in the context need not apply to the case of each sons's share, but to the

total property left by the deceased person – irrespective of the number of claimant daughters. The intention here is to hold as much of the property as possible to the male line of succession.

2. ज्येष्ठ एव तु गृह्णीयात्पित्र्यं धनमशेषतः।
शेषास्तमुपजीवेयुर्यथैव पितरं तथा॥ Manusmṛti IX.105

3. पितेव पालयेत्पुत्राञ्ज्येष्ठो भ्रातृन्यवीयसः। पुत्रवच्चापि वर्तेरञ्ज्येष्ठे भ्रतरि धर्मतः॥[3]

ज्येष्ठो भ्राता विभागाभावेऽनुजान् भ्रातृन्भक्ताच्छादनादिभिः पितेव विभृयात्।
अनुजाश्च भ्रातरः पुत्रा इव ज्येष्ठे भ्रातरि धर्माय वर्तेरन् ॥ Ibid-108

4. Yāj-II- 123.

5. पितुरूर्ध्वं विभजतां मानाऽप्यंशं समं हरेत।। Mahabharat XIII.80.11

6. यथैवात्मा तथा पुत्रः पुत्रेण दुहिता समा।
तस्यामात्मनि तिष्ठन्त्यां कथमन्यो धनं हरेत् ।। Manu. IX.9.130

7. पौत्रदौहित्रयोर्लोके न विशेषोऽस्ति धर्मतः। तयोर्हि मातापितरौ संभूतौ तस्य देहतः।।
पौत्रदौहित्रयोर्लोके विशेषो नोपपद्यते। दौहित्रोऽपि ह्यमुत्रैनं संतारयति पौत्रवत् ।।Manu. IX.133-139

8. अध्यग्न्यध्यावाहनिकं दत्तं च प्रीतिकर्मणि।
भ्रातृमातृपितृप्राप्तं षड्विधं स्त्रीधनं स्मृतम् ।।
अन्वाधेयं च यद्दत्तं पत्या प्रीतेन चैव यत्।
पत्यौ जीवति वृत्तायाः प्रजायास्तद्धनं भवेत् ।। Manu. IX.194-195

9. *Mitākśarā* on Yāj-I.143.145

10. अधिविन्ना तु भर्तव्या महदेनोऽन्यथा भवेत् ।
यत्रानुकूल्यं दंपत्योस्त्रिवर्गस्तत्र वर्धत ।। Yaj. I.74

11. आज्ञासंपादिनीं दक्षां वीरसूं प्रियवादिनीम् ।
त्यजन्दाप्यस्तृतीयंशमद्रव्यो भरणं स्त्रियाः।। Yaj.I.76

13

Studying the Economic Position of Women in *Dharmaśāstras*: Perspectives in Occupation, *Strīdhana,* Property and Inheritance

Annapurna Chattopadhyaya

Studying women's history in the western as well as eastern countries has opened up a new chapter centering around women's identity, socio-economic position, status, occupation, livelihood, *strīdhana,* property rights, inheritance etc. A galaxy of renowned scholars and historians in the western and eastern zones concentrated their attention on women's study including their multifarious problems. Before throwing dim light on the economic position of women in ancient India, based specially on the *Dharmaśāstras*, I should recognize some valuable books and articles written by illustrious scholars.[1]

The economic position of women since the Vedic period up to the 19th and 20th centuries is undoubtedly a controversial subject matter. Much have been discussed about this topic. I have decided to focus on the *Dharmaśāstras* which include the *Dharmasūtras, Gṛhyasūtras, Smṛtis* and also *Arthaśāstra* of Kauṭilya.

Men and women, or males and females are/were to be grouped under different heads such as (i) aristocratic class (i.e., the nobility, rich and educated class), (ii) the middle class, (iii) the lower class (in criteria of castes or uneducated and economically poor), and (iv) tribes. It is noticeable that the socio-economic status of women should be judged in the background of that period. For example, it may be pointed out that the socio-economic status of women ranging from the Vedic period up to the 13th century AD could not be judged or considered in comparison with their status in the 20th century or 21st.

The economic position of women is closely related to their social position. So, it is very difficult to draw any border line between social and economic position of women. The terms position and status do not connote same meaning. The term status has a legal connotation and it means the power of women to enforce the legal rights and obligations. There were no uniform rules and customs pertaining to the privileges of sexes and as such the status of women varied in accordance with the region, tribe or social milieu to which they belonged. The status of women belonging to the upper classes was much lower than that of the lower sections where women enjoyed higher status and greater legal privileges. For example, the women section of the tribal class like the *Dombis, Cāṇḍālīs* and the *Savaris* serve as equal partners of the male section in religious affairs like *tāntric* rituals. Tantrism admitted both women and *śūdras* into its ranks and laid great stress on the use of magic rituals.[2] It should be noted that the *Dharmaśāstras* literature is largely concerned with the social pattern of the higher classes.

For determining the economic position of women on the basis of the *Dharmaśāstras,* it is essential to discuss their position from the Vedic period onwards. In the *Ṛgvedic* period women, obviously the elite class, enjoyed social equality and freedom. Gārgī and Maitreyī for example were recognised as *Brahmavādinīs* (enlightened women) whose erudition was supposed to have granted them equal powers as their male counterparts.[3] This is not the general picture of the society which was patrilineal and dominated by the male person in the *Ṛgvedic* period. The patriarchal system tended to keep the status of women at a low level and the emergence of the joint family with special property rights for the male members reinforced male domination. The society though patriarch in nature and structure during the early Vedic period women took an active part in economic production. Besides performing domestic chores, they were engaged in various economic pursuits as is indicated by the occurrence of the following terms. These are *vagitri*[4]*/siri*[5] (female weaver), *pesaskari*[6] (female embroiderer), *bidalakari*[7] (female splitter of bamboos), *ragyitṛ*[8] (female dyer), *upalapraksini*[9] (women corn grinder), etc. These indicate how women used to earn their livelihood by accepting a number of professions. The teaching profession was followed by women from the Vedic down to the *Sūtra* period. Mention may be made of Gārgī who took part in public debates.[9a] Apālā is stated to have cared for her father's fields.[10] Among women the name of Viṣpāla who lost a leg in battle may be mentioned.[11] Thus, it is evident that women could take part in wars which constituted an important economic activity in the Vedic tribal milieu.[12] The Buddhist and the Jaina texts also refer to the women of the *Bramavādinī* class, i.e., who remained unmarried to carry on their studies. Most of the Buddhist nuns whose songs have been preserved in the *Therīgāthā* were maidens born in well-to-do families. The Jain texts refer to Jayantī, daughter of the king of Kauśāmbi who remained unmarried in order to devote herself to religion and philosophy. She carried on discussions with Mahāvira himself on abstruse questions of philosophy and became a nun. Pāṇini (IV. 1.63) refers to women students of Vedic *śākhās*. *Kātyāyana* in his *Varttikā* (IV.1.48) refers to women teachers who were called *upadhyāya* or *upādhyāyi* as distinguished from *upādhyāyinis,* i.e., wives of teachers.[12a] The necessity of coining a new term shows that women teachers were large in numbers. Patañjali also refers to a special designation for the women scholars who made a special study of *Mīmāṁsā* philosophy.

Besides teaching and research on higher education, women generally received training in fine arts like music, dancing and painting. Some of them also chose military training. This is indirectly proved by the term *Sāktiti,* a female spear-bearer mentioned by Patañjali (IV. 1.15.6).

In the period of the later *Vedas* and *Dharmaśāstras,* women gradually withdrew from public life and economic production. They became dependent on male kinsmen. In the *Brāhmaṇa* literature specially in the *Aitareya Brāhmaṇa,* it is stated that daughter was the source of sorrow of her parents and on the other hand son was the protector of his parents. By the time of the *Smṛtis* and the *Purāṇas* women were reduced to complete subjugation of the male section and they were described along with property and *śūdras.*[13] Sukumari Bhattacharji supporting this view has pointed out that in the period before 1200 AD even upper caste women were equated with *śūdras.*[14] Uma Chakravarty in 'Whatever Happened to the *Vedic Dasi*?' has shown how in the 19th century a deliberate misconception of Brahmanical norms of womanhood was set in motion.[15]

In the Mauryan period from the *Arthaśāstra* it is known that women could earn their livelihood through spinning and weaving.[16] Kātyāyana, a lawmaker of the 6th century lays down that wealth obtained by women through mechanical arts such as spinning belonged to *strīdhana.*[17] Thus, it is evident that women could earn their livelihood by spinning.[18] Besides, the occupations like prostitution, joining the flower, perfume trade and participation in a traditional troupe were open for women.[19] Widows were also allowed to work. Young women who were cripple could also earn through weaving.[20] Women ascetics and nuns were not debarred from this activity. Besides, mothers of prostitutes, retired women servants of the king, retired temple prostitutes (*devadāsīs)* were all permitted to accept this occupation.[21] In the Mauryan period textile industry was very lucrative. Both men and women were employed in the textile industry though women were permitted to do the lighter work. The system of wage is also mentioned. Women were paid according to the amount of work completed and payment was to be made only on completion.[22] In this context, it is to be noted that from very ancient times cotton manufacture was of prime importance. Moreover, women were also employed as bodyguards like our present day's security guards. The female bodyguards of the king are mentioned in Kauṭilya's *Arthaśāstra* which informs us that the king getting up from his bed shall be received by troops of women armed with bows.[23] Besides, women were also employed as attendants and spies of the kings. "Of the women some are in chariots, some on horses, and some even on elephants, and they were equipped with weapons of every kind as if they are going on a campaign."[24] It is interesting to point out that the *Bhārhut* sculptures portray a woman riding a fully caparisoned horse and carrying a standard.[25] All personal services of the king were performed by women whose trustworthiness and efficiency had been tested and the procession of the royal hunt (*vihāra-yātrā* of the *Aśokan* inscription) was marked by elaborate disposition. Crowds of women generally used to surround the king and outside of this circle spearmen were ranged.[26]

Not only from the *Arthaśāstra* it is evident also from the *Kāmasūtra* that women belonging to the lower castes freely followed industrial and agricultural pursuits.[27] Kauṭilya refers to women earning their livelihood as tenant tilling for half the produce and *Vātsyāyana* refers to *Cārsani* women who were engaged in a variety of occupations.[28]

Concerning *gaṇikās* or public women and their role in the palace and in social life both Kauṭilya and Greek writers including Megasthenes,

Strabo, Arrian and others spoke in details.[29] In the age of *Vātsyāyana*, i.e., in the Gupta period, it is written that women who possessed special proficiency in the arts were respected for the value of their art and their company was sought for by all lovers of art. Such respected position was acquired by *gaṇikā* in the society.[30] A Mathura inscription has preserved the memory of a pious Jaina *gaṇikā*.[30a] In this context, it is to be noted that upper class courtesans were both well-read and accomplished musicians and dancers. In spite of feudal exploitations practised on them by the state they had an independent income. Some of them were very powerful even in political sphere. Both the Pāla and Sena rulers of Bengal patronised them and cities like *Rāmāvati,* the Pāla capital of Rāmapāla were proud of the beauties of their public women.[31]

It is also interesting to note that in the Buddhist period Āmrapāli (or Ambapāli) enjoyed a prestigious position in the society as is known from the *Vinayapitaka* of the *Mūlasarvāstivādis.*[32] Āmrapāli was a daughter of Mahānāma, a rich citizen of Vaiśālī. Āmrapāli was recognized by the Assembly as a *strī-ratna* (jewel of a woman). Āmrapāli was exceedingly charming and accomplished in all the sixty four arts.

Kauṭilya's *Arthaśāstra* also reveals the same state of things. A prostitute noted for her beauty, youth and accomplishments was to be appointed superintendent of prostitutes on a salary of 1000 paṇas (per annum). For regulating the profession, rules were to be framed and every month two days' earning had to be paid to the state. The prostitutes had to attend court and were regularly employed in the royal household on a big salary, they held the royal umbrella, golden pitcher and fan. Moreover, they attended the king seated on throne or a chariot. They were also employed in the storehouse, kitchen, bathroom and the harem of the king.[33] The life of the courtesans has been vividly described in the Tamil works of the *Saṅgam* age.

Slavery was a recognized institution of Indian society from the Vedic times. But ancient Indian society was not a slave society.[33a] The *Smṛtis* not only mention different classes of slaves but lay down various rules regarding their status. Obviously there were female slaves though in India they used to do all sorts of household service but they were not badly treated.[34] Men and women were used in production both agricultural and artisanal.[35]

Regarding *devadāsī* system a number of epigraphic records furnish the practice of *devadāsī*. In the Vaghli (Khandesh district) stone inscription dated *śaka* 991 (1069-1070 AD) there is a grant of Govindaraja making provision for dancing and singing by damsels (*Vilasini*).[36] In the inscription of the *Cahamāna* king Jojaladeva dated *samvat* 1147 (1090-91 AD) the courtesans of all temples are said to have been ordered to come in their best dress and celebrate a festival with music[37] and the king records an imprecation against all who might stop that practice. The Ittigi (20 miles east of Gadag) inscription dated 1112 AD records that a *Brāhmaṇa* named Mahādeva donated houses for the retinue of dancing girls.[38] This practice of *devadāsī* (minor girl) dedicated to the service of temples or *bhavins* (which term is known in the southern part of the Ratnagiri district) was held by the modern Indian courts to be immoral.[39] Besides, one record refers to a *devadāsī* (temple attendants).[40] During the early Buddhist times accomplished courtesans occupied a recognized position in the society.

It is also known that women carried on administrative work. According to Megasthenes, the Pandyan nation was governed by females. The *Sātavāhana* queen Nayanikā acted as regent during the minority of her son.[41] It is noticeable that women belonging to the higher class, i.e. the elite class were able to carry on the above mentioned types of jobs.

Thus, it is evident that women were engaged in different types of jobs as mentioned in the *Ṛgveda, Arthaśāstra, Kāmasūtra, Dharmaśāstras* and in epigraphic records. Manu has thrown a flood of light on diverse types of artisans and craftsmen like mechanics, weavers, carpenters, dyers, blacksmiths, jewellers, metal workers, basket-makers, chemists and druggists, etc.[41a] Besides, the Buddhist texts like the *Mahāvastu* and the *Milindapañho* and the Jain text *Pannavanna* have recorded a large number of artisanes and craftsmen. It is to be noted that Rajesh Prasad Singh in his treatise entitled '*Artisans in Manu*' has vividly described various types of artisanal jobs.[41b] But the role of women in those various occupations was absent. On the other hand, it is learned from the *Charyyapādas* that women of the tribal society like the *Śavaras, Niṣādas, Pulindas,* etc. were engaged in different sorts of artisanal jobs like basket-making, etc.[41c] Lastly, an important factor should be considered how feudal society was responisble for occupation and position of women in the society. It is recognized that both feudal and pre-feudal ideas emphasize contempt for manual work, domination of man over woman. In the feudal set up, agriculture is considered to be the most important, trade to be middling in value.[41d]

In the feudal phase, there is a tendency to degrade the position of women more and more and consider them as an item of property. Thus, strong male domination appears to be a characteristic of the feudal phase and absolute male superiority leads to the imposition of all kinds of disabilities on women.[42] However, we find that with the developments in material culture, i.e. from c.300 AD to c. 700 AD a large number of women folk participated in agriculture and other economic activities. It was due to freedom of marriage among members of the low orders. We find different marriage provisions in the *Dharmaśāstras* for higher and lower varṇas. The *vaiśyas* and *śūdras* were free to practise the unapproved forms of marriage which were open to the *brāhmaṇas* and the *Kāyasthas.*[43]

However, according to the earliest lawgivers, the women folk of the two lower *varṇas* were engaged in agriculture and service work. But gender bias was strong in the higher *varṇas* who preferred son to daughter. A list of mixed castes has been enumerated in details by Manu. The large-scale accession of the tribal people with their matriarchal traditions and family customs led to the insertion of new provisions in the marriage laws of the *Dharmaśāstras.* These marriage laws and multiplication of castes determined the socio-economic position of women.[44] These changes in the position of women seem to have been the result of the influx of tribal people into the Brahmanical system. Moreover, R.S. Sharma has pointed out how gross materialism of the industrial society weakened the family ties in the West and this also brought certain changes in the position of women in the East as well as in India.[45]

The economic position of women is closely connected with their property rights and *strīdhana* The economic position of women as per their occupation and livelihood has been discussed in a nutshell. The term *strīdhana* literally means woman's property. In etymological sense *strīdhana* means all kinds of property possessed by a woman. But in the ancient *Smṛti* works the word *strīdhana* was restricted to special kinds of property given to a woman on certain occassions or at different stages of her life. Manu, Kātyāyana, Viṣṇu, Nārada, Gautama, Yājñavalkya, Devala have given their definitions regarding *strīdhana* By the time of *Kātyāyana,* it included all property whether movable or immovable obtained by women either as a maiden or at marriage or after marriage.[46] The *Arthaśāstra* is of the opinion that ornaments and jewellery constitute *Strīdhana.*[47] *Strīdhana* as well as women's right to inheritance of property is elaborately discussed by Yājñavalkya, Kātyāyana, Viṣṇu, Devala, Vasiṣṭha, Baudhāyana, Gautama, Āpastamba and other *Smṛti* writers.[48]

In the Vedic period society though patriarchal in nature and structure accepted women's ownership in certain types of movable property mostly jewellery and gifts related to marriage. There are casual references to women's separate property. Landed estates were controlled jointly by the family. It was treated as part of patrilineal inheritance in which individual right to ownership and alienation of property was generally disregarded.[49] However, the right of complete ownership exercised by the individual over movable items of property led to the recognition of women's right to own some categories of property known as *strīdhana.* In domestic life the joint family system prevailed in the Maurya period. If the members of the family desired, the joint family could be dissolved.[50] A married woman had property of her own in the form of bride gift (*strīdhana)* and jewels and this was to some extent at her disposal in the case of widowhood.[51] If she married a relative of her deceased husband with her father-in-law's consent she retained properties given by her father-in law of her first husband. In the absence of male issue a man was free to marry another wife without paying compensation to his first wife. Thus, from the *śloka 'putrarthe kriyate bhāryā'* it is clear that wife is purchased only for son. Thus, it is also evident that son was desired and daughters at the same time were neglected and dishououred.[51a] It should be remembered that since the Vedic period onwards a woman was considered to be the responsibility of her father in childhood, her husband in youth and her son in old age. She was expected only to run an orderly household.[52] This ancient doctrine of perpetual dependence of woman on male is repeatedly amplified by Manu and Yājñavalkya.[53] In the *Arthaśāstra,* it is repeatedly stated that ornaments and jewellery constitute *strīdhana.* It is also mentioned that maximum amount of subsistence is fixed at 2000 *paṇas* and there is no limit of giving *abadhya,* i.e., ornaments,[54] etc.

During the period of the *Dharmaśāstras* the sphere of *strīdhana* expanded. For instance, the scope of *strīdhana* was considerably widened by Yājñavalkya. According to Manu, *strīdhana* comprises six types of gifts. These are: (i) before the nuptial fire *(adhyāgni),* (ii) in the bridal procession *(adhyāvahanika),* (iii) given in token of love *(dattam ca prītikarmaṇi)* (by her father-in law and mother-in-law), (iv) received from her brother, (v) mother, or (vi) father *(bhratṛmatṛ-pitṛpraptam).*[55] At the same time, Manu states that *strīdhana* excludes not only all inherited property but also gifts received from any relatives other than her close kinsmen. Besides, Manu has stated six categories of property which is acquired by inheritance, purchase, partition, seizure or finding. By excluding all inherited property from *strīdhana* Manu has laid emphasis on the property acquired by her own labour which must not be treated as *strīdhana.* From this statement it is evident that at least some women in Manu's time had earned wealth through the pursuit of mechanical arts like spinning.

Regarding *strīdhana,* besides six-fold gifts enumerated by Manu, Yājñavalkya includes other kinds of wealth such as (i) gifts subsequent to her marriage *(anvādheya)* from her cognate, (ii) cognate relations *(bandhudatta),* (iii) obtained as price *(śulka)* of household utensils of beasts of burden of milch cattle, ornaments and slaves, and (iv) was presented on her husband marrying another woman (*adhivedanika).*[56] The same is the opinion of *Kātyāyana.* In the *Āpastamba Dharmasūtra* we find that in a partition wife could claim her ornaments and wealth given to her by her relatives.[57] Vasiṣṭha similarly prescribes such view.[58] Baudhayāna acknowledges the daughter's right to own her mother's ornaments.[59] In the Vedic literature there are no specific references to woman's right to inherit property. In the period of *Sūtras* and *Mīmāṁsa* property ownership was discussed. The Brahmanical theorists denied woman's right to inherit their husband's or father's property except the right to own movable property in the form of *strīdhana.*[60] Some hold that daughters do not inherit.[61]

However, from the discussions based on the *Dharmaśāstras,* it is obvious that a woman could own property which she had received as gifts from her relatives at the time of marriage or inherited from her mother. Second point is that she had no share in family property. Property signified land, cattle, slave, variety of goods and objects including metal currency. Manu states that women may be owners but they cannot dispose of the property independently.

It is interesting to point out that according to Manu and Yājñavalkya women are entitled to own and bequeath their special property or *strīdhana.*[62] Not only queens and princess made donations but ordinary women also are found to grant donations of various kinds out of their own property for pious purposes. The votive inscriptions commemorate donations not only by Buddhist and Jaina female lay worshippers but also by a housewife, the wives of cloth dyer, a merchant, a caravan leader and the like.[63] Property of women consisted of ornaments, costly dress and household articles and gifts acquired at the time of marriage. Manu is of the opinion that woman was the subject to the control of the husband as regards her *strīdhana.*[64] According to Manu, the property of wives, faithful widows as well as barren and deceased women is to be specially protected by the king and its misappropriation by their relatives is to be punished like theft by the king.[65] Regarding property right Gautama, Baudhāyana, Vasiṣṭha have expressed their individual opinion.[66] In the *Dāyabhāga* of Jīmūtavāhana, it is expressed that *strīdhana* and inheritance to it were very complicated matters. Jīmūtavāhana the expounder of the Bengal school who perhaps in the last quarter of the 11th century by introducing laws has improved proprietory condition of woman. He implicitly states that women possessed power over her property which might be sold according to her will. According to him, her husband do not have control over his wife's property. *Dāyabhāga* enumerates that wealth is *strīdhana* which is given to a woman by the house-builder or goldsmith, etc.[67] Viṣṇu adds that what obtained from sons also belonged to *strīdhana.*[68] Devala includes the profits of money lending to the list of *strīdhana.*

Concerning succession or inheritance to *strīdhana* several schools of Hindu lawgivers differ from each other perhaps more widely on inheritance of *strīdhana* than any other subject matter. All schools agree that as regards succession to *strīdhana* daughters are preferred to sons.[69] The succession to *strīdhana* varies as the women is unmarried or married and at the same whether marriage was approved or unapproved. Unmarried daughter is preferred for inheriting *strīdhana,* Pārāśara holds the same view as enumerated by Kātyāyana.[70] Kauṭilya prescribes that if a woman dies during her husband's life time, her sons and daughters divide her *strīdhana.*[71] If she has no sons, her daughters divide it. Kātyāyana is of the opinion that sisters whose husbands are living should share *strīdhana* with their brothers.[72] This is the rule of law about *strīdhana* and partition among brothers and sisters. In the absence of sisters or in failure of taking her share the wealth should be occupied by brothers.

However, as regards inheritance to *strīdhana,* one simple and straightforward rule should be laid down that the woman's sons and daughters should succeed together taking equal shares. Another suggestion would be that when there are no descendants of the woman herself, then the husband should be the next heir.[73] When the *strīdhana* is that of a maiden, the heirs in order should be her brothers and sisters, then her mother, then her father and after the father the latter's nearest heir.[74] Again, according to the injunction of the *Dharmaśāstras,* this is evident that a widow could be a coparcener with her sons in the property of her deceased husband only if she did not already own sufficient amount of *strīdhana.* In this context it is significant to note the arguments made by some scholars that the development of productive forces in the early centuries of the Christian era initiated social process leading to the break up of large family communities into small nuclear families and this necessitated a change in the *Dharmaśāstra* law allowing the sons to have the right to partition the ancestral land even if the father was unwilling.[75]

Thus, the above mentioned analysis on the position of women in the sphere of economy, specially occupation, property and inheritance based on the *Dharmaśāstras,* has thrown light on contradictory views and statements. Sometimes it seems that women's right to inheritance has been categorically denied in the *Dharmaśāstra.* But, from the 2nd century BC onwards, there seems to have been a reversal in the unfavourable attitude of the Brahmanical lawgivers for women's right to property.[76] This is evident from the contemporary *Pāli* texts and epigraphic records which mention a large number of women as donars.[77]

However, two facts are thus highlighted. First, is the deterioration in the social status of women. Second, in a patrilineal society women were granted right to inherit immovable property mainly to save it from falling escheat to the state in the absence of complete ownership over inherited property. It is also revealed how woman's right to property was retained. A widow could only inherit a portion of her husband's property if she led a chaste and religious life. Woman's chastity, religious and sexual morality were demands of the society. The question arises what are the criteria of determining chastity of character? One thing is clear. This is how the position of women was degraded. The *Smṛti* writers like Manu piled up restrictions on the day to day life of woman married or unmarried or widow.

This is the picture of the position of women from the Vedic period onwards specially on the laws enumerated by the *Dharmaśāstras.* Even in Sarat Chandra Chattopadhyaya's novel *'Devdāsa'* (in Bengali) Devdāsa is telling Pārvatī: Pāru, you have come to me at midnight, you will be treated by the society as immoral and unchaste woman. I am male person, so the society will forget my unchaste character but not yours. Herein lies the difference between man and woman, male and female even in the 19th-20th centuries.

However, women had to travel a long but thorny way from the Vedic period up to the present era. Gradually, a good number of laws were passed to strengthen the economic position of women. In this context, the Hindu Succession Act, 1956 needs a specific mention. Under the provisions of this act, a daughter was equal sharer of her paternal property and absolute owner of *strīdhana.*[78] But, the publication of *'Towards Equality'* has clearly revealed that whatever might have been granted to Indian women in the Constitution they had gained very little in real life.[79]

Yet, in spite of many drawbacks, lacunae and limitations in determining the position of women in India as well as in the West at present in the days of globalization we expect the ideas and views of the westerners and easterners will be exchanged and be united in the ocean of humanity at *Bhāratavarṣa* for the upliftment of liberty, freedom, identity, existence and individuality, etc. of women. The words of Rabindranath Tagore may be quoted here:

> "*dive or nive, milave, milive yave na phire,*
> *ai Bharater Mahamanaver sagara tire.*"[80]

They will give and they will take, they will unite and be united. And will never go away from the ocean shore of the great humanity of *Bhārata.*

Rabindranath Tagore has expressed his views, visions and thoughts in many of his poems and *nāṭakas* regarding ideal position of women. According to his view, there is no question of domination or subordination, feminism or antifeminism. Both men and women are co-partners in every sphere of life. This is exquisitely revealed in his *'Citrāngadā gītināṭya'* in which the expression of *Citrangada* is very significant: *'yadi parsve rakho more samkate sampade ... pave tave tumi chinite more'*[81] (i.e., if you keep me with you either at the time of adversity or at prosperity, you can understand my real entity). In another poem it is stated: *amra dujana purush-o-nari'* i.e. we are two-male and female. Both man and woman jointly will do their duties in the family, in the society, in political affairs, in economic spheres and everywhere. Both will serve the nation and the human-being of the whole world. Again Kabiguru has expressed thought in one of his poems: Women are the gifts of the absolute being and she has come to this world to strengthen, to enlighten fame and prestige of man. When these ideas will be realized there will be no question of oppression and equal rights will be established for both man and woman.

Notes

1. Ratnabali Chatterjee, *Veiled and Unveiled Women in Medieval Bengal,* Sectional President's Address, section II, 62 session, 2001, *Proceedings of Indian History Congress,* pp. 160-176; A.S. Altekar, *The Position of Women in Hindu Civilization,* revised and enlarged in 1956, Delhi, reprint 1962, 1973; B.S. Upadhyaya, *Women in Ṛgveda,* 3rd ed., revised, New Delhi, 1972; S.K. Das, *Economic History of Ancient India,* Calcutta, 1922; R.M. Dass, *Women in Manu and his Seven Commentators,* Varanasi; Bhupendra Nath Datta, *Hindu Law of Inheritance* (An Antheropological Study), Calcutta, 1987; Parbhati Mukherjee, *Hindu Women's Right of Property,* Delhi, 1978.
2. Annapurna Chattopadhyaya, *The People and Culture of Bengal, A Study in Origins,* Kolkata, 2002, Vol. 1, Part I, pp. 319-323, 334-343, 354-358; R.S. Sharma, *India's Ancient Past,* Oxford, New Delhi, 2005, p. 295; Sashibhusan Dasgupta, *Bauddha Dharma –O-Charyyagiti,* Kalikata, 1376 B.S., pp. 96-131. (Occupation, religious life, life patterns and culture of the tribal women are widely described in the Charyyapadas).
3. Sukumari Bhattacharji, *Prachin Bharate Nari* in Ratnabali Chatterjee and Gautam Neogy(ed.), *Bhārat Itihāsa Nāri* (in Bengali), Calcutta, 1989, pp. 3-5.
4. Ṛgveda, X, 71, 9.
5. Ibid.
6. *Vājasaneyī Saṁhitā,* XXX, 9; *Taittiriya Saṁhitā,* III, 4, 5, 1.
7. *Vājasaneyī Saṁhitā,* XXX, 8.
8. Ibid., XXX, 12.
9. *Ṛgveda,* IX, 112. 3.

9a. *Ṛgveda,* X, 85, 26; Bhim Sain Narang, *Concept of Strīdhana in Ancient India,* Delhi, 1990, p. 3.

10. Ibid., VIII, 80.
11. Ibid., I.112.10; I. 116.5.
12. R.S. Sharma, *Conflict, Distribution and Differentiation in Ṛgvedic Society,* Proceedings of Indian History Congress, 38th Session, Bhuvaneshwar, 1977, p. 179.

12a. (ed.) R.C. Majumdar, Pusalkar and others, *History and Culture of the Indian People, (The Age of the Imperial Unity),* Vol. II, Bombay, 1953, p. 563.

13. *Agnipurāṇa, 253, 63-64; R. S. Sharma, Perspective in Social and Economic History of Early India,* New Delhi, 1983, pp. 39-40.
14. Sukumari Bhattacharji, *Prācīn Bhārtīya Nārī, op. cit.* pp. 3-5.
15. Uma Chakravarty, Whatever Happened in Vedic Dasi ? Orientalism, Nationalism, a Script for the Past in Kumkum Sangari and Swadesh Vaid (ed.), *Recasting Women, Essays in Colonial History,* New Delhi, 1989, pp. 27-28.
16. Romila Thapar, *Cultural Pasts, Essays in Early Indian History,* Oxford pub, paperback, New Delhi, 2003, p. 412.

17. P.V. Kane, *History of Dharmaśāstra,* Vol. III., Poona, 1946, (2nd edn., Poona. 1968-77), p. 776; R.S. Sharma *India's Ancient Past,* 2005, p. 242 (*strīdhana* is discussed in details).
18. Ibid.
19. Romila Thapar, op.cit., p. 412.
20. Ibid.
21. Ibid., p. 413.
22. Ibid., p. 414.
23. R. Shamasastry (trans), *Kauṭilya's Arthaśāstra,* Mysore, 1961, Book I., chap. XXI, 42, p. 41.
24. McCrindle's Megasthenes, Stabo, XV, 1, 53; (ed) K. A. Nikantha Sastri, *A Comprehensive History of India, The Mauryas and Sātavāhanas,* 325 BC - BC. 300 pub. by the Indian History Congress, New Delhi, reprint, 1957. p. 55.
25. (ed.) R.C. Majumdar, Pusalkar and others, *History and Culture of the Indian People (The Age of the Imperial Unity),* Vol. II, Bombay, 1953, p. 564.
26. (ed.) A.K. Nilkantha Sastri, *A Comprehensive History of India,* Vol. II, p. 55.
27. *Kāmasūtra of Vātsyāyana,* Benaras (ed.), p. 300; H.C. Chakladar, *Social Life in Ancient India, Studies in Vātsyāyana's Kāmasūtra,* reprint, New Delhi, 1990, p. 103.
28. H.C. Chakladar, op. cit., pp. 103-104; R. Shamasastry, *Kauṭilya's Arthaśāstra;* Jaimal Rai, *A Factorial Study of the Status Determinants of Women in Ancient India,* Proceedings of Indian History Congress 1989-90, pp. 139-140.
29. (ed.) A.K. Nilkantha Sastri, *A Comprehensive History of India,* Vol. II, p. 69.
30. Ibid., p. 480; H.C. Chakladar, *Social Life in Ancient India: Studies in Vātsyāyana's Kāmasūtra,* New Delhi, 1990, p. 201.

30a. *Luder's List,* No. 102.

31. Sukumari Bhattacharji, *Prostitution in Ancient India,* op.cit., pp. 201, 209.
32. B.C. Law, *Buddhist Studies* Vol. I, Calcutta, 1931, p. 137; (ed.) R.C. Majumdar, Pusalkar and others, *The History and Culture of the Indian People,* Vol. II, p. 568; R. Shamasastry, *Kauṭilya's Arthaśāstra,* Mysore, 1961, Bk., II., chap. XXVII, p. 136.
33. (ed.) R.C. Majumdar, Kusalkar and others, *The History and Culture of the Indian People,* Vol. II., p. 569.

33a. R.S. Sharma *India's Ancient Past,* p. 180.

34. Rhys Davids, *Buddhist India,* London, 1903, p. 55; Romila Thapar, *Cultural Pasts,* p. 511.
35. Romila Thapar, *Cultural Pasts,* p. 511; P.V. Kane, *History of Dharmaśāstra,* Vol. III.
36. *Epigraphia Indica,* Vol. II, p. 227.

37. Ibid. Vol. XI, 26 & 27.

38. Ibid. Vol. XII, p. 58.

39. P. V. Kane *History of Dharmaśāstra,* Vol. II, part II, Poona 1946, pp. 903-904.

40. *Luder's List,* No. 921.

41. A.S. Altekar, *The Position of Women in Hindu Civilization,* reprint, Delhi, 1973, p. 220.

41a. R.S. Sharma, *Light on Early Indian Society and Economy,* p. 74; *Manusaṁhitā,* Chap. III-XI; III. 64; IV, 219; V, 116, 129; VII, 75, 138; VIII, 65, 102; IX, 239, 265; X, 99, 100, 129; XI, 219.

41b. *Indian History Congress jubilee,* Vol. II, pp. 95-110.

41c. Sashibhusan Dasgupta, *Bauddhadharma-O-Charyyagiti* (in Bengali), Calcutta, 1376 B.S., pp. 103, 118, 120, 122 (*vahirer dombi tant vikray kare ar kare chamgadivikri).*

41d. R.S. Sharma, *Early Medieval Indian Society: A Study in Feudalism,* Longman, Delhi, 2001, p. 271.

42. Ibid., pp. 271-272.

43. Ibid., pp. 295-296.

44. Ibid., p. 242.

45. R.S. Sharma, *Historiography of the Ancient Indian Social Orders: Light on Early Society and Economy,* Bombay, 1966, pp. 12-15.

46. P.V. Kane, *History of Dharmaśāstra,* Vol. III, 1946, pp. 774-775.

47. (Trans.) R. Shamasastry, *Kauṭilya's Arthaśāstra,* Mysore, 1961, Bk., III, chap. II. 152., p. 172.

48. P.V. Kane, *History of Dharmaśāstra,* Vol III., pp. 770-802.

49. Ibid., Vol. III, p. 593 ff.

50. (ed.) A.K. Nilkantha Shastri, *A Comprehensive History of India,* Vol. II, p. 681.

51. Ibid.

51a. Ibid., p. 68.

52. N.N. Bhattacharya, *Proprietory Rights of Women in Ancient India* in Kumkum Roy (ed.) *Women in Early Indian Societies,* (B.D. Chattopadhyaya General ed.), New Delhi, 1999, pp. 120 – 121; (ed.) Panchanan Tarkaratna, *Manusaṁhitā,* Calcutta, 1397 B.S., Chap, IX., slokas 2-3, p. 248 (*Pitā rakṣati kaumare, bhartā rakṣati yauvane, rakṣanti stavire putra na strī svatantryamaharti)*

53. (ed.) Panchanan Tarkaratna, *Manusaṁhitā,* chap. IX., 2-3; Yājñavalkya, I, 85-86.

54. (Trans) R. Shamasastry, *Kauṭilya's Arthaśāstra,* Mysore, 1961, Bk., III, chap. II., 152, pp. 172-173; Priyadarshini, Women and Patrilineal Inheritance during the Gupta Period, *Proceedings of Indian History Congress*, 2001, p. 73.

55. (ed) Panchanan Tarkaratna, *Manusaṁhitā,* Chap IX, 194-195, p. 272. (*adhyagnadhya, vayanikam dattancha pritikarmani bhatrmatrpitapraptam,*

shadvidham strīdhana in smrtam anvadheyancha yaddattam patya pritena chaiva yat).

56. Ibid., (ed.) Panchanan Tarkaratna, *Manusaṁhitā,* Chap. VIII, 416, p. 246. (*Bharyya putrascha dasascha traya eva dhana h smrtah yat te samadhigachchhanti yasya tattasya taddhanan).*

57. *Yājñavalkyasmṛti,* ii, 147; P.V. Kane, *History of Dharmaśāstra,* Vol. III, p. 774.

58. *Āpastamba Dharmasūtra*, II, 6. 14. 9.

59. *Vasiṣṭha Dharmasūtra,* XVII, 46.

60. *Baudhāyana Dharmasūtra,* II, 2.3.43.

61. Ibid., ii, 2. 3. 46; *Priyadarshini,* Women and Patrilinal Inheritance during the Gupta Period, *Proceedings of Indian History Congress*, 62nd session, 2001, p. 72.

62. Priyadarshini, Ibid., D.N. Mitter, *Position of Women in Hindu Law,* Calcutta, 1913, p. 450.

63. (Ed.) Panchanan Tarkaratna, *Manusaṁhitā,* Chap. IX, 194-198, p. 273; *Yājñavalkya,* II.

64. *Luder's List,* Index of Misc, *Cambridge Economic History of India,* Vol. II, p. 478.

65. P.V. Kane, *History of Dharmaśāstra,* Vol. III, p. 771.

66. Panchanan Tarkaratna (ed.), *Manusaṁhitā,* chap. VIII, 28-29, p. 200.

67. *Vaśiṣṭha Dharmasūtra,* ii, 6.14.9; *Baudhāyana Dharmasūtra,* ii, 2.8.43; *Gautama Dharmasūtra,* 18, 20-23.

68. *Dāyabhāga of* Jīmūtavāhana, IV, 319-320,

69. *Viṣṇusmṛti,* XVIII, 18.

70. P.V. Kane, *History of Dharmaśāstra,* Vol. III, chap. xxx, p. 788.

71. Ibid., p. 791.

72. Ibid., Vol. III, p. 791; R. Shamasastry, op.cit., Mysore, 1961, Bk. III., chap. II, 153, pp. 174-175.

73. P.V. Kane, *History of Dharmaśāstra,* p. 791.

74. Ibid., p. 802.

75. Ibid.

76. R.S. Sharma, *Indian Feudalism,* 1st ed., Calcutta, 1965, reprint, 1987, Chap. III, pp. 114-117, 124; B.N.S. Yadava, *Society and Culture in Northern India,* Allahabad, 1973, p. 140; Subira Jaiswal, Women in Early India: Problems and Perspective, *Proceedings of Indian History Congress*, 42nd session, 1981, pp. 58-59.

77. Priyadarshini, Women and Patrilineal Inheritance during the Gupta Period, *Proceedings of Indian History Congress*, 62nd session, 2001, p. 71.

78. Vijaynath, *Dana, Gift System in Ancient India: A Socio Economic Perspective,* Delhi, 1987, pp. 66-67.

79. Sir Gooroodas Banerjee, *Hindu Law of Marriage and Strīdhana,* Calcutta, 1923, p. 319 (for exhaustive treatment of *strīdhana,* Dr. Jolly's *On Adoption, Inheritance and Partition,* 1885, pp. 226-270.

80. *Towards Equality, A Report of the Committee on the Status of Woman in India,* Government of India, Ministry of Education and Social Welfare, Nw Delhi, December, 1974.

81. Rabindranath Tagore, *Sanchayita,* poem, *Bhārat-tirtha* (Visvabharati, 1969), pp. 506-507.

Rabindranath Tagore, *Gitavitan,* trtiya khanda (3rd part), 1398 BS., Calcutta, Visvabharati, *Chitrangada,* p. 705.

14

Property Rights of Daughter in Ancient India with Special Reference to *Dharmaśāstras*

Anita Singh

Right from the earliest times, longing for a make child has been a common feature of almost all human societies. Nevertheless, we find frequent references in the Vedic literature to daughters being fondly caressed and affectionately brought up by parents. Ordinarily girls were no doubt less welcome than boys but we must add that there were also some parents in the society who would perform special religious rituals for the good luck of getting learned and capable daughters.[1] In early Hindu society the female sex used to get their identity recognized only after they got married in the role of 'wives', so any notion of daughters being recognized was a remote possibility.

The major factor which affected women's economic status was their property rights. The evolution of women's property rights was a gradual process. Initially a woman herself was regarded property and could be gifted or sold. The question of property right emerges from the private ownership of the land as a property. Landed property could be owned only by one who had the power to defend it against actual or potential rivals. Women were obviously unable to do this and so could hold no property in Vedic age. Since the daughter was expected to get married and leave her father's family, she did not have any right over her father's property. *Ṛgveda* clearly orders that *'auras* sons' should not give any paternal property to their sisters.[2] Āpastamba regarded the daughter to be the last inheritor in the list of the successors. He would rather prefer the property to be given for a public cause than to a daughter.[3] Vasiṣṭha,[4] Gautama[5], Manu[6] do not mention the daughter in the list of their heirs. According to Baudhāyana, a daughter had no right to inheritance even if she was the only issue of her father. She could only inherit the ornaments of her mother.[7]

Still later on, we notice *Dharmasūtrakāras* recognizing the daughters' right in property in limited respect. Though we do not find a daughter inheriting the whole of ancestral property in her own right but we get frequent references to a daughter's share in the property and her special separate share in the form of dowry. Daughters were classified legally as – Brotherless daughters (as *Putrikā, Putrikāputra*) and Daughters with brother.

Brotherless Daughter : Amongst women a brotherless daughter was the first to get her right of inheritance recognized and amongst the brotherless daughters *Putrikā* or the appointed daughter got precedence over the others. *Putrikā* or *Putrikāputra* was of two kinds : one when a sonless man appointed his daughter as his son, then she was called *putrikā* and treated like a son, the second when the son of the *putrikā* was considered as the son of his maternal grandfather. Addressing his son-in-law, he might say "the male child born of her shall perform my funeral rites".[8] Between a son's son and a son of an appointed daughter, there was regarded no difference neither with respect to worldly matters, nor to sacred duties for their father and mother sprang from the body of the same man.[9] Gautama had assigned full right of inheritance to *putrika* through a ritual but Baudhāyana recognized the Putrikā's son as the inhenitor of the property because he alone is entitled to offer funeral cakes to his maternal grandfather.[10] Kauṭilya recognized a brotherless daughter as inhertor without any restrictions.

This custom of appointing *putrikā* through a ritual gradually died out as any brotherless daughter was considered to be a *putrikā.* Still an appointed brotherless daughter had a superior claim as compared with a son by adoption or purchase.[11] Kauṭilya lays down that on the death of the mother, her property shall be divided among her sons and daughters. In the absence of son he justifies the appointment of the daughter by saying, "A son is even as onself, a daughter is equal to a son; how can another heir take the estate while such daughter is there."[12] But if after a daughter has been appointed, a son be born to her father, the division is to be equal, for there is no rights of primogeniture for a woman.[13] For even if a putrikā died before giving birth to a son, her husband was entitled to inherit the property of his father-in-law.[14] Thus, it is clear that daughters whether married, unmarried or appointed had some rights of succession in ancient India.

The daughters were considered same as sons were considered to be, both were considered the representatives of their parents. Hence even having the patriarchal society next to sons, the daughters had all rights to inherit the property of their father. Ancient Indian lawgivers were considerate in giving some share directly or indirectly to the daughter, Yājñvalkya has recognized the claim of the daughter to inherit the property of her father who died without a son, just after the widow.[15] Viṣṇu had also given her the same place in order of succession. Nārada allows her the second place, i.e., just after the son. He mentions that it is justified because the daughter continues the line of the father just like a son.[16] How then can her right of inheritance be defeated in the absence of the latter?

The *Mahābhārata* in one place maintains that it would be manifestly unfair and inequitable to allow a subsidiary son to get an inheritance, when there was a daughter to claim it.[17] She must at least get half the property, if not the whole.[18] Like Yājñvalkya, Bṛhaspati also says, "the wife is declared to succeed her husbands property, and in her default the daughter."[19] He points out that the daughter springs from one's own body just like the son, how then can anyone inherit the property when she is still alive?

But this right extended to daughters by the Hindu jurists, had limited disposition, a brotherless daughter was regarded as an heir only till she was married and well-settled in life. Kātyāyana was its chief exponent and says, "let the widow succeed to her husband's wealth, provided she be chaste and in default of her, let her daughter inherit, if unmarried."[20] Although Nārada has given the daughter a share in her father's property, she was not entitled to take her share after her marriage. The Mitākśarā has followed Kātyāyana in preferring the unmarried daughter to the married one as an heir. The Mitākśarā states that among the married daughters one who is not well-to-do is to be preferred to one who is well placed.[21] Yājñavalkya declares the *'Putrikā'* or the son of *'Putrikā'* to be equal to that of an *'aurasa* son', *putrikā* was herself considered son (*Putrikā eva sutan*).[22]

It may be noted that in this period the practice of *putrikā* was getting obsolete, although mention of the practice continued. Viṣṇu, therefore, takes a contradictory position. On the one hand, he writes that the daughter will inherit after the mother and on the other hand, he observes that whether she is made a *putrikā* or not she is as good as a *Putrikā,* who according to the custom gets precedence over the mother. Pārāśara a says "If a man dies sonless his maiden daughter shall receive his property, if there is no maiden daughter then the married daughter."[23] Viśvarūpa held that Yājñvalkya recommends only the *Putrikā* as successor to a sonless person and employs the plural in order to convey that several daughters may be appointed as sons.[24] Devaṇṇabhaṭṭa, agreeing with Vasiṣṭha, said that putrikā is the third of the different kinds of sons. Thus being in the category of secondary sons, she takes property like the *kśetraja* son even when the widow is still alive.[25] Jīmūtavāhana says again, "A daughter's rights of succession to the property of her father is founded on her offering funeral oblation by means of her son."[26] And he adds "the daughter is heiress of her father's wealth in rights of the funeral oblation which is to be presented by the daughter's son".[27] Based on the above conjunction of religious or spiritual, unmarried daughter is first entitled to inherit, but if there be no maiden daughter the succession devolves on her who has or is likely to have male issue.

Daughter With Brothers: A general opinion of Hindu society was that sisters should get no share in the patrimony, if they had brothers. Ancient *Dharmasūtrakāras* were conscious about the concern of the daughters, their marriage, dowry, maintenance. Kauṭilya has clearly said that if there were 'unmarried daughters' (*Kanyā*), they were to 'be paid adequate dowry' for their marriage (*Pradanika*) from the paternal property. He also mentions that unmarried daughters shall be paid sufficient dowry (*pradahikam*) on their marriage.[28] She is entitled only to being property looked after and maintained till she is married. Though Manu[29] does not give the daughter any right of partition in the paternal property even after the death of her parents, he entrusts brothers with the duty to give one-fourth share to their unmarried sisters.[30] If there were many brothers and sisters, then the brothers had to give portions to their sisters each out of his share, one-fourth part.[31] Some scholars claimed that both the married and unmarried daughters should get some share in their father's property. Buddhism was more liberal towards daughters, a daughter was recognized as a legal entity she was fully entitled to a share in the patrimony in addition to what she received as mother's legacy. Sometimes she even got all the property of father in preference to mother and brothers. Nārada also assigns a share to the daughter along with the brother in her father's property.[32] According to him, "To the eldest son a larger share shall be allotted, and a lesser share be assigned to the youngest son. The rest shall take equal shares and so shall an unmarried sister". Viṣṇu[33] declares, "Mothers are entitled to a share proportionate to their son's share and so are the unmarried daughter." But their intention does not appear to have been to allow the daughter to take away her share after her marriage. Nārada expressly declares that the daughter's share in the patrimony was intended only for her maintenance till her marriage.[34]

Thus, we find that all the jurists of the period assign to the daughter (who has brothers) one-fourth share out of the father's property. This share no doubt, was for her maintenance till her marriage and also for making adequate provision for her marriage. However, in no case was she allowed to take away her share after her marriage.[35] A general rule, however has been laid down that a brother should spend for his sister's marriage an amount equal to a one-fourth share.[36]

Commenting on Yājñavalkya, Viśvarūpa remarks that the brothers should perform the marriage ceremony of their sisters and for that purpose if there was no money set apart by the father then only they should be given one-fourth part of their share.[37] Hindu jurists, however declare that their intention is not so much to assign a one-fourth share to the daughter as to make adequate provision for her marriage.[38] To get his sister married, was the sacred duty of the brother, and if her one-fourth share was insufficient for the purpose, the brother was required to spend an amount even equal to his own share.[39] From 200 AD we find a general deterioration in the daughters' share in the patrimony. The provision of ˇshare made by Manu and Yājñavalkaya led to varied interpretations by later jurists. Since marriages had become obligatory for girls, it was naturally laid down that reasonable expenses in connection with them should be a charge on the family property. Later jurists' prime concern was to make adequate provision for sisters' marriage, if the family property was extensive and the reasonable expenses of a suitable marriage did not amount to the legal one-fourth share, the sister was not to take away with her balance unspent.[40] Jīmūtavāhana held the opinion that if the ancestral wealth was small the provision for the marriage of the unmarried daughter should be made by giving her a one-fourth share but if wealth was ample then she should get only as much as was necessary for her marriage.[41] If the father had no son and if he died without performing his daughter's marriage, the widow was bound to spend one-fourth part of the husband's property on the marriage expenses of her unmarried daughters.[42]

With regard to precedence amongst daughters Smṛticandrikā lays down the following rule, "where there is competition between a daughter unprovided and one unmarried, both being of the same class with their father and possess the other qualifications mentioned in the text, the unmarried alone first takes, the maintenance of such daughters out of the wealth of the father being indispensable. On failure of such a daughter, the unprovided takes, such a daughter being destitute of the means of subsistence owing to the inability of the husband to maintain her, although he is bound to do so. In default of unprovided daughters, the daughter provided or enriched and possessing the qualifications of equality of class etc., takes such a daughter, though provided, being competent to inherit".[43]

Daughter's Share in Strīdhana: The position of a daughter was further protected in case of the death of her mother by providing her exclusive right over *strīdhana*. The *dharmaśāstrakāras* from early times lay down that *strīdhana* should devolve upon daughters. Yājñavalkya provides that after the death of the mother, the sons should pay the debt of mother and the rest of the *strīdhana* should be taken by the daughters and on their failure it goes to the sons.

As regard to the preference of daughters to the succession of *strīdhana* the *Mitākśarā* holds that it is due to the daughters having more particles of the mothers body in her, than the son.[44] According to Viṣṇu,[45] if she (mother) dies leaving children, her wealth goes in every case to her daughter. Nārada also supports that the *strīdhana* of a woman should be inherited by her daughters, and in their absence by the daughter's children. Bṛhaspati and Pārāśara prefer the unmarried daughter to inherit her mothers property.

In an agricultural society where the joint family was the unit, the threat of segmenting the cultivable land owned by the family was very real. The motive of patriarchal family system was to keep the immovable property intact and in such a patriarchal society where the marriage was obligatory and the daughter was to leave the father's family and as she was not allowed to offer funeral oblations to his father the *Dharmaśāstrakāras* made as best legal provision as was possible in such a social backdrop.

Notes

1. *Ṛgveda.* VII. 15.
2. Ibid., III. 31.2.
3. *Āpastamba Dharmasūtra* II. 14.23.4.
4. Vasiṣṭha XV. 7.
5. Gautama XXVIII. 21.
6. Manu. IX. 185.
7. Baudhāyana. II. 3.44.
8. Manu. IX. 127.
9. Ibid., IX. 133.
10. *Baudhāyana Dharmasūtra* II 3.15.
11. K.C. Jain. *Baudha Aur Jain Agamon Mein Nārī,* Amritsar, 1967, p. 250.
12. Manu. IX. 130.
13. Ibid., IX. 134.
14. Manu. IX. 135.
15. *Yājñvalkyasmṛti* II. 127.
16. Nārada. XIII. 50.
17. *Mahābhārata* II-80.
18. Ibid., XIII. 88-22.
19. Bṛhaspatī XXV. 55.
20. *Mitākśarā*, chap. II. Sec. 2, p. 2.
21. Manjushree, *The Position of Women in the Yājñvalkyasmṛti* Delhi, 1997, p. 130.
22. *Yājñvalkyasmṛti* II. 128
23. Pārāśara a quoted in *Smṛtitattva,* p. 191.
24. Viśarūpa on Yājñvalkya II. 136, 137.
25. Savita Vishnoi, *Economic Status of Women in Ancient India,* Meerut, 1987, p. 149.
26. *Dayābhāga*, ch. XI, Sec. II 2.3.
27. Ibid.
28. Savita Vishnoi, op. cit., p. 53
29. Manu. IX. 104
30. Ibid., IX 118
31. Prof. Indra. *The Status of Women in Ancient India,* Lahore 1940, p. 191.
32. Nārada, XIII. 13.

33. Viṣṇu. XVIII. 34-35.
34. Nārada, XIII. 27.
35. Savita Vishnoi, op. cit., p. 89.
36. *Yājñvalkyasmṛti* II 124.
37. Viśvarūpa on Yājñvalkya, II. 124.
38. Devala in *Smṛticandrikā* (Vyava), p. 625.
39. *Vyavahāra Mayūkha*, p. 582.
40. *Smṛticandṛkā*, p. 265.
41. *Dayābhāga*, III 2.36-39.
42. Ibid., XL 1.66.
43. *Smṛticandṛkā*, ch. XI. Sec. II. 28.
44. *Yājñvalkyasmṛti* II. 117.
45. Viṣṇu, XVII. 21.

VI

Dharmaśāstras in the Light of Colonial and Post-Colonial Interpretations

15

Revisiting *Dharmaśāstras* during the Colonial Period

Binda Paranjape

Colonial period brought about a significant change in the socio-political life of the Indians. In some respect the early phase of the colonial rule is considered as a period of Indian renaissance. This is primarily in the context of social reform movement and their success in changing the societal outlook of Indian intelligentsia. Social reforms vis-á-vis the lives of Indian women especially the lives of upper caste Hindu women are highly noteworthy. However, while evaluating the effects of the social reforms one needs to pay serious attention to the political backdrop with which these reforms were inter-linked.[1] Present paper is an attempt in highlighting the political dimension of the reform movements related to women resulting into passing of certain legislation for the first time in India.

Sources for the study of this topic are heterogeneous. Going by the usual classification followed by the historians, the sources can be grouped as the tangible sources such as sculptures, paintings etc. and the non-tangible literary sources by way of contemporary writings. The images of women in various contexts reflecting the stereo-typical identity of women from various classes can be seen in contemporary paintings, caricatures etc. The context in which they occur defines their position from the point of view of the creators of these visuals and the audience for which they were meant. This study involves the understanding of arts and aesthetics along with the awareness of the socio-political and at times even the religious conditions of the contemporary times. For example, using the figure of *Bhārat Mātā* as a source of understating the changing perception regarding women during the colonial period needs to go deep into the cultural imperatives of the people who created it and of the people for whom it was created. This kind of study is primarily a study of symbols and signs (semiotics) and their cultural context.[2] For present paper these sources are not used. Here the focus is on the literary sources.

The literary sources for the study of the social reforms of the colonial period are mainly in the form of journalistic writings produced by the reformist and their opponents, the records of the arguments and the judgment pronounced in the legislative assembly and the law courts, the records of the resolutions passed in various social forums, the biographical narratives of women as protagonist and the life sketches of the reformers. In addition to these direct sources there are literary works in the form of fictions, dramas, lyrical narratives etc. produced during this period. The literary sources of this period are in English and in different Indian languages. In recent times there have been a good number of works undertaken which throw light on the potential of the literary texts as sources for reconstruction of the position of women during the colonial period.

One of the major problems faced by the historians while using the literary sources is regarding the language itself. Any historical text always has the possibility that it may walk out of its historical context and reproduce itself in the contemporary times. In other words the texts that are written by women in the historical period may not be really the representation of the contemporary women as one might think of that being so. These could be the works of women who were conditioned to think and express in a certain way.[3] Besides, if valued in terms of volume then majority of the texts are works of 'men' regarding 'women'.[4]

I

During the nineteenth and twentieth century laws were passed to make the position of women in India legally stronger than ever before. However, passing of acts like that of abolition of *satī*, widow remarriage, age of consent, etc. are not just the legal reforms. These were closely linked with the national movement and the identity formation of different religious communities in India.[5] The law giving certain rights and dignity to women was a net result of certain issue-based debates. The history of such debates however, does not end at that point. In fact, it serves as a mid point of the history in retrospect and history after the passing of these laws. The retrospect of the reforms shows that the discussion on the issues regarding women was oscillating between the national priorities set by two different groups of political leaders. One of them insisted on achieving more and more political autonomy, while the other felt that the reforms should be on the top priority. In fact, majority of the reformists were of the opinion that the reforms are the best possible under the British rule and are needed without delay. The famous Tilak-Agarakar controversy in the Western India can be seen as an example here. Agarakar and others, who were called as '*sudhāraks*' in Marathi, were considered as the worst opponents of the national cause by the other camp. On the issues regarding the reforms especially related to women Tilak often ridiculed Agarakar in his Marathi newspaper *Kesari*. The '*non-sudhāraks*' failed to see the urgency of the social reforms vis-á-vis women as can be seen in Tilak's supposed statement "let *Swarāj* be there I will host marriages of a thousand widows".[6] Major arguments of the opponents of the reforms were that the British should not be allowed to interfere into the sacred laws of the religious communities in India and there was no concept of secular laws in pre-British India).[7] In case of Hindus the problem was complicated further because of its caste dimension. Once again to cite example from western India, one can see the positions taken be Jyotiba Phule and M.G. Ranade. Phule, searching for the ultimate reality through his social philosophy of "Stayashodhak Samaj" openly criticized the Brahmins for being directly responsible for the degraded position of the women and the lower caste people among the Hindus.[8] Phule was a member of the lower caste and Ranade was a Brahmin. Ranade, was the follower of the ideal of "Prarthana Samaj" and he did not take much radical stand. In fact, due to some of the decisions taken in his private life Ranade became a controversial person in the debates regarding widow marriage and age of consent. The principle and practice dichotomy existed in Bengal as well. Examples from the lives of Ishwar Chandra Vidya Sagar and Raja Rammohan Roy can be cited here.

The reformists were also divided as being radical and moderate. Some of the reformists were extremely critical about the *śāstras* and the customs and advocated the cause of secular laws under the influence of the Western liberalism while the few others within the same group suggested religious conversion as a reform. The moderates were not so iconoclastic. They either avoided being critical about the *śāstras* or used their knowledge of Sanskrit to find support of the *śāstras* to the cause of reforms. Gopal Hari Deshmukh alias '*Lokhitwadi*' an ardent supporter of widow marriage wrote in Marathi journal "whether the shastras support it or not, it is better to leave the *śāstras* aside and bring about this change".[9] In this context two prize wining essays published in 'Oriental Christian Spectator' in the year 1888, one can have the glimpse of different views of moderates and extremists on the issues related to women's right to education.[10] Hari Kesavji one of the authors of the above said texts took the position that the *śāstras* need to be reinterpreted in modern times, however, he does not dismiss them. Whereas the other author, Tirumal Rao wrote more in praise of the missionaries and avoided talking about the *śāstras*. The reformist who suggested conversion to Christianity opined that the *śāstras* are not unanimous on any social issue and the Hindu traditionalist would always find ground to oppose the social reforms. The austere commitment of the Christian missionaries towards giving relief to the worst sufferers of social order and their work towards the promotion of the formal education of women impressed some of the reformers. Their frank praise of the missionary became the ground for the contestation of the reformist and traditionalist. The reformists were condemned as anti-nationals because the missionaries were viewed as the facilitators of the British rule in India.

The traditionalist sharpened their tools against the reformists regarding the issues for which there was a strong support of the *dharmaśāstras*. This was possible because the colonial masters introduced a new administrative system where the spaces reserved for localized negotiations between the various contesting groups were occupied by the impersonalized social legislations passed at various stages. The British, while establishing the constitution of the personal law, used the Islamic and Brahmincial scriptures as the law books of Indians. A fact that the scriptures, at least the Hindu scriptures were rarely used as the sources of law during the pre-British period was not given enough consideration. Manu was declared as 'the parent of Hindu jurisprudence'. Pandits were invited to interpret the *Śrutis, Smṛtis* and other texts. Thus, during the colonial period the scriptures, more than any other period of Indian history became the sources of law.[11]

II

First instance of invoking the *Dharmaśāstras* was the debate regarding the custom of *Satī*. Abolition of Satī Act was passed in 1829. Passing of this act started the process of demanding many more of such governmental interventions in bringing about a change in the position of women in India. Even the otherwise critics of the British rule also acknowledged the role of the government in promoting the cause of women. As early as in 1843, the government was reminded of its responsibility towards opening schools for girls in the Marathi press.[12] The issue of formal education given to girls put the traditionalists at a disadvantageous position vis-á-vis the *Dharmaśāstras.* There they took a stand very much in consonance with the dominant patriarchal ideology. Giving education to women could not be opposed on the basis of scriptures because deleting the examples of the women intellectuals (the category of the Vedic women seers) from the discourse would have made the claim of the Indian cultural superiority weak. Hence, at this point it was thought wise to speak of the evils of the modern western civilization and express the fear that if the Indian women were educated in the school the moral foundation of Indian social life would start deteriorating. However, the moderate reformists did talk of Gārgī and Maitreyī, the women intellectuals of the Vedic period who were held in high esteem by all the caste Hindus of the time. Thus, the *Dharmaśāstras* came to be handy to the reformist also and it worked on the minds of the majority of the Indians creating the favourable opinion towards the reforms. The argument of the traditionalists in the ultimate analysis did not sustain. This can be best seen in case of the discussions regarding The Child Marriage Restraint Act of 1929 or popularly known as Sharada Act. It would be very interesting to note that the traditionalists who were in favour of the age of marriage of a girl to be raised to 14 went for a convenient compromise i.e. taking the help of the expiation rules led down by the *Dharmaśāstras* to ward off the evil effects of the act of marrying the daughter after she attains puberty.[13] Another feature of this debate is that the traditionalists were not unanimous on the opposition to the bill of the age of consent. Bipin Candra Pal who had a lot in common with Tilak did not oppose the bill even while Tilak vigorously campaigned against the said bill.

One of the logical corollaries of the Abolition of Satī Act of 1827 was the beginning of the discussions on the possibility of the marriage of a widow. It emerged as purely indigenous movement. Here the reformers had to fight on two levels. One was that there is no direct evidence in favour of the widow marriage in the *Dharmaśāstras* and secondly the traditionalists would not agree on the point that the widows were in a pitiable condition in India. The sexual deprivation as a notion was considered absurd in Indian context and more so it was considered as a Western unhealthy thought which was trying to corrupt the minds of the Indians. The only deprivation which was considered somewhat recognizable was that the widows were given food only once a day.[14] Besides, accepting that the widows are ill-treated in the Hindu upper castes would have created a problem in the consolidation of the Hindu identity. Hence it was thought wise to summarily deny the cruel treatment given to the upper caste Hindu women saying that the Hindus were mild and merciful by nature and they cannot indulge in such an act.[15] The major problem in this respect was of the superstition attached to the widowhood.[16] The ultimate credit of a married woman was seen in her death before her husband. Thus, a widow was considered indirectly responsible for the death of her husband. It was a lapse on part of the woman who could not acquire enough merit to die with all the insignia of a married woman. The fear of a man was of his survival if a widow was really an evil soul who would also cause his death as she did of her earlier husband. This kind of superstition was really difficult to fight even on the grounds of the scriptures. The kind of arguments brought forth by the traditionalists while opposing the Widow Marriage Act of 1856 clearly show this fear psychosis. One of the arguments states that a marriage is a sacrament for the Hindus and it is sanctified by the recitations of the sacred chants. Since these chants are presupposing the status of the bride as a virgin the marriage of a widow cannot be sanctified with these chants. Hence, the marriage of a widow would only mean a sanction given to the illicit relation between a man and a woman. The moderate reformers brought forth the arguments of *niyoga*[17] quoting from the sacred books. The caste dimension of this whole debate is very interesting. The problem of widow-marriage was more acute in case of the higher castes viz. the Brahmins, for, the custom of a widow-marriage was very much prevalent in the lower castes. Getting the legal sanction to the marriage of a widow was more a need of the upper castes for one more reason. Marrying a girl child preferably at the age of eight or definitely before puberty was a compulsion on an upper caste father. One of the arguments in favour of the child marriage was that the raising the age of marriage of a girl would mean forcing the girl's father into a sinful act. However, the other side of the argument was that the age difference between the groom and the bride would be so much that at times if the groom was marrying for the second time, the daughters of his first marriage would be older than the second wife. Also such an imbalance in the age of the groom and the bride was creating more and more number of the child widows. Between the superstition and the paternal feeling towards the child widows the second was more powerful and the Widow Remarriage Act was passed. It is said that Ishwar Chandra Vidyasagar was moved by the plea of his mother to find support for the widow-marriage in the Śāstras. The reformer used all his skills of Śāstric knowledge and not only supported the cause by favourable arguments but accepted a widow as his daughter-in-law.

The Arya Samajis accepted the widow marriage in principle; however the practice probably remained restricted to the virgin widows. Some sections of the Arya Samajis prescribed a system similar to the ancient *niyoga* i. e. a widower and a widow can live together by mutual consent up till the birth of two or at the most four children to be divided among them.[18] The passing of the Widow Remarriage Act, however, opened a new issue i.e. the issue of the inheritance to the remarried widow. Here the act proved to be a problem creator for the women of such castes where the customary sanction was already there for widow-marriage and accordingly there were customary rules regarding the property inheritance. The new Act and the subsequent provisions made in accordance to that suited to the upper castes but put the lower caste women in trouble.[19]

Certain debates did not result into the passing of the legislations but they were discussed very fiercely due to certain specific incidences. In 1934-35 there was a 'Test case' in the Solapur court where a widow whose head was not tonsured (as was a practice among the Maharashtrian Brahmins and the woman belonged to that caste) sought entry into a temple to worship the god in the same manner as was done by the other people. She was denied that permission by the temple priests on the basis of the customary restriction on the widows. Hence she challenged the priests and the case came before the said court. The basis on which the then sub-judge Mr. Bagali gave his decision in favour of the widow brings forth many arguments from the *Dharmaśāstras*.[20] First and foremost was the misreading of the texts e.g. the word *charmashirah* cited by the priests as support of their acceptance of the practice of the tonsure of a widow was found to be the name of a Vedic teacher and not a synonym of a widow, as was taken it to be. Secondly if the tonsure was to be taken in the context of the funerary rites then it would mean that it was to be done only once i.e. at the time of those rites. The true spirit of the tonsure was the asceticism and that cannot be forced by a custom. Here, the most important thing brought forth by the judge was that the customs may have sanction of some stray texts written by individuals to satisfy interests of certain social groups but they cannot be forced on the individuals who become the victims of such customs. The importance of the decision given by Mr. Bagali can further be seen in the light of certain peculiar incidences e.g. when a *non-tonsured* Brahmin widow died in an accident there arose a problem of her funeral. The Brahmins would not perform it because she was not eligible for a funeral according to the Śāstric tradition and the barber would not tonsure the head of a dead body. Ultimately an untouchable was called to burn the body without any ritual.[21] One can imagine how the widows, who even otherwise were considered as inauspicious, must be shuddering at the thought of their fate after death. The *non-tonsured* widows were treated worst than the untouchables. The dilemma of the women whose husbands were alive in the matters related to the issue of a tonsure of widows was whether to support it because their men wish it so or oppose it because they themselves are women. The role of Śāstras also is significant in this matter. It was said the food prepared by the *non-tonsured* widows will not be taken by the Brahmins who perform rituals. Not only that the families where they allow the widows to have hair intact almost would be treated as excommunicated. The Brahmins will not perform religious rites for them and in absence of such rituals the social acceptability of the family would be endangered. In this situation certain Śāstris took it on them to show that there is no scriptural legitimacy to such a practice and they would partake food in the house of such Brahmins who have the *non-tonsured* widow inmates. This strong injunction by certain Brahmins helped the reformers and the practice of the widow tonsure was abolished without any legislation.[22]

In the matter of the tonsure of the Brahmin widows the attempt made by Jyotiba Phule, a person from the non-Brahmin community is worth noting. He appealed the barbers not to give their services to the Brahmin widows. This definitely must have had a great impact. As has been stated above the custom of the widow's tonsure slowly died out and there was no need for bringing about legislation to that effect. In that sense this can be taken as a true triumph of the reformers.

Many more local issues were raised as regards the women during the colonial period. British Government slowly withdrew from the matters which they considered sensitive to the minds of the Indian elite class however, the reforms continued and so did the discussions on the *Dharmaśāstras.* Today, while looking at the history of the struggle for the rights of the women during colonial period one can but feel overwhelmed by the complex situations faced by the reformers. As were their difficulties innumerable so were the diverse sources from where the support to the cause came. The study would remain incomplete if one does not talk about the foreigners who supported the reform movements in India and created conditions favourable in many ways. The prime amongst them were Annie Besant and sister Nivedita. It would be interesting to see what kind of ideal was set before the Indian women by these sympathizer of Indian culture. They advocated the cause of education and overall growth of the Indian women but wanted the Indian women not to get influenced by the Western abusive practices. The new woman was to be well-educated, self-sufficient and at the same time an epitome of the virtues led down in the scriptures. Her ultimate goal was not expected to be radically different than the one for which there was a sanction of the scriptures and of tradition which was primarily male dominated.

The discussion on the reforms vis-á-vis women during the colonial period in the context of the *Dharmaśāstras* can be summed up in the words of Lata Mani, "Tradition was thus not the ground on which the status of woman was being contested. Rather the reverse was true: woman in fact became the site on which tradition was debated and reformed".[23]

Notes

1. Madhu Limaye, *Indian National Movement: Its Ideological and Socioeconomic Dimensions.* 1989, pp. 328-344.
2. Garaldine Forbes, *Women In Modern India* 1998. See the illustrations in this book.
3. Dr. P. Sudhir, "Reconstructing Women's History; Problems and Paradigms", in *Women's Studies'*, A. Suryakumari (ed.)1993.
4. Kumkum Roy *The Challenges Of Women's History*, in A. Suryakumari (ed.) ibid. p.74.
5. Maitryi Chaudhuri, *Indian Women's Movement,* 1993. pp. 74-86.
6. Popularly attributed to Tilak. What is important is that it is quoted in support of the argument regarding the issue of the reform for women need not get the priority. D.V. Tahmankar, Lokamanya Tilak , (1965) pp. 48-49.
7. Maitreyi Chaudhuri, op. cit., pp. 71-72.
8. Maitreyi Chaudhuri, Ibid., pp. 38-40.
9. Lokahitwadi wrote his *Shatapatre* during the mid-19th century.
10. P. Nilesh, "Reflections on Two Prize Winning Essays on Female Education in Western India in the Early Nineteenth Century" in the *Proceedings of the Indian History Congress.* Aligarh, 2000. pp. 485-494.
11. Maitreyi Chaudhuri, op. cit., pp. 35-36.
12. Preeta Nilesh, op. cit., p. 489.
13. Kamalabai Deshpande, *'Striyanchya Kayadyachi Vatchal'* (1960). p. 258.
14. P.N. Bose, *A History Of Hindu Civilisation During British Rule* (1982), pp. 40-41.

15. Ibid., pp. 41-42.

16. Ibid., p. 39.

17. *Niyoga* was an ancient practice by which a women could get a child from a relative or such legitimate man after the death of the husband or if husband was alive then with his consent. The heroes of *Mahābhārat* were supposed to have been born by *Niyoga*.

18. P.N. Bose, op. cit., p. 45.

19. See the 1896 case of Vithu vs, Govind belonging to Dudra caste. The question of the property of the deceased husband held by succession by a window after marriage was a customary law in the caste of that woman. However after the Hindu window's remarriage Act of 1856 such a right was forfeited. For the details of the case see Maitryi Chaudhuri, *Indian Women's Movement,* pp. 36-37.

20. For the details of the case see Kamalabai Deshpande, ibid., pp. 273-285.

21. Ibid., p. 262.

22. Ibid., p. 268.

23. Lata Mani, "Contentious Traditions: The debate on Satī in colonial India," in *Recasting Women: Essays in Colonial History,* ed. Kumkum Sangari and Sudes Vaid (1989), pp. 117-118.

16

The Nineteenth Century Construct of *Dharmaśāstras*: A Historiographical Enquiry

Priyamvada

In this paper an attempt has been made to understanding of the study of nineteenth century discourses on India's glorious past. The Widow Remarriage Act, Female Infanticide Act – there was a sudden spurt in the legislation related to women's issues in the nineteenth century.[1] As a corollary, there were sections of societies, Indian and British, which were split into two broad halves in the ensuing debate. What followed was an intense reemergence of the ancient scriptural facts instrumental in the pro- and anti-reformist constructions of women. I will make a brief study of the various historiographical schools of thought and the different interpretation rendered to the ancient scriptures during this period. I intend to speculate on the possible motives behind the undertaking of such studies. Was it a colonial attempt to 'recast' women as scholars like Kumkum Sangari, Uma Chakravarty, Lata Mani, Susie Tharu, Sumant Banarji would have us believe?[2] Or was there a 'hidden agenda' of using women as currency in the complex set of exchanges that the struggle for hegemony between the Indian Western-educated pro-British and the paternalistic civilizing British bureaucracy presumed?

Nineteenth century was the age of 'women'. A reawakening the glorious past of India, induced by the coalition of various facts was witnessed even at the beginning of this century. The study of women in *Dharmaśāstras* was taken up in different school of thoughts with motives that were entirely unlike each other. Uma Chakravarty in *Whatever Happened to the Vedic Dāsī* has very clearly demarcated different ideological groups that studied India's past during this period and the logic of their study.[3] The Imperialist school represented the Orientalist strand whose reconstruction of the glory of Indian civilization in the ancient past was taken over lock, stock and barrel by 19th century Indian writers to build a picture of Indian civilization, not just for a particular region like Bengal but for the whole of India. The other stand was the Utilitarian and Evangelical attack on contemporary Indian society, especially on the visibly low status of women. These two schools of thoughts, coalesced in the work of early nationalist writers where most enduring and successful construction of the image of womanhood in the works as a counter to the real existence of women in the humiliating present.

William Jones and H.T. Colebrooke contributed most substantially to the notion of a 'golden age', which has existed in a remote and unchartered period of Indian History.[4] The women's question notably was not one of the themes foregrounded in the earliest work of the Asiatic society. Jones for example did not pay any attention to *'Satī'* and made only a passing remark on Gārgī, whom he described as 'eminent for piety and learning'. One of Colebrooke's first piece of research was 'On the duties of faithful Hindu widow' wherein he presented the textual position on *Sati*.[5] The essay reflects all the characteristic features of the historiography of the women question; the reference to a variety of ancient texts, the special authority given to texts over custom, the research for the authentic position as contained in the older and more authoritative texts and the confusion in reconciling contradictory evidence. However, it is significant that there is nothing in Colebrooke's essay to suggest that the *Vedas* were recognized either the oldest or the most authentic as the past was as yet unstratified and was perceived as one homogeneous whole. His account of *Satī* highlighted an 'awesome' aspect of Indian womanhood, carrying both the association of a barbaric society and if the mystique of the Hindu women, who voluntarily and cheerfully mounted on the pyre of her husband.

Colebrooke's essay on the *Vedas* was the first piece of work moving attention to the texts as a major achievement of the ancient Aryans. Of interest are the reference on Gārgī and Maitreyī, two of the most quoted example of the glory of the ancient Indian womanhood. It is significant that Colebrooke attributes no particular importance to the account of the conversation between Maitreyī and Yājñvalkya. Gārgī too appears merely as one of the contenders, neither less nor more important than the other participants in the debate with Yājñvalkya.

Jones, Colebrooke and a whole range of the students at the Fort William College, who form the earliest group of the Orientalists – themselves as engaged in reintroducing the Hindu elite to the 'impenetrable mystery' of its ancient lose. In short, the Europeans, who had successfully constituted there, own 'true' history were now engaged in giving to Indians the greatest gift of all a history.[6] The indigenous intelligentsia was not functioning within a political and a social vacuum. The natives were no passive recipients of the perception of the past then in process of being reconstituted.

The reconstruction of the past thereafter assumed practical and utilitarian function. The question was no longer one for the discovery and fragments of texts, or translated them, but as the movement for *satī* abolition gained momentum, satisfying the texts to establish authenticity became crucial. All this meant that apart from the general increase in the historical consciousness, the past was beginning to be classified and analyzed more rigorously to argue the debate of the present. Ram Mohan Roy epitomized this dominant trend among the indigenous intelligentsia in the first quarter of the 19th century and is best known for his crusade against *satī,* although his writing spanned a whole gamut of issues related to Hinduism.

The case against *satī* had been argued forcefully before Ram Mohan Roy by Mrituanjay Vidyalankar.[7] Together, Ram Mohan and Mritunjay introduced into *satī* a highly intellectual argument, one that evoked the highest goal of religion, which had never been evoked before in the case of women, expert in the dissident traditions as exemplified by Buddhism. The goal for women as spelt out by the ancient Hindu legislators was *Pātivratādharma.* But Mrityunjay and then Ram Mohan repeatedly asserted the opinion that the ultimate goal of all Hindus was selfless absorption in divine essence, a union that could not flow from the action like Satī. It was in this context in response to the social exigencies of the time that Ram Mohan imaginatively used the Maitreyī Yājñvalkya episode to argue against the subjection of women. Roy thus provided a concrete example from the earliest antiquity to reinforce Mritunjay's position that women had persuaded the highest goal of Hindu religion and in his view it were the wicked Pundits who have distorted the *Śāstras* in subsequent time.

While Chakravarti had explored the various schools of thoughts during the 19th century on women's study, Lata Mani attempts a more focused discussion on the Satī debate and at places even questions the attempts of Ram Mohan. He had used Manu as evidence. Manu in plain term enjoins a widow to continue till death forgiving all injuries, performing austere duties, avoiding every sensual pleasure, and cheerfully practising the incomparable rules of virtue which have been followed by such women as were devoted to only one husband.[8]

Rammohan produced similar proof from Yājñvalkya of the widow's right to live with her natal or marital family on the death of her husband. Rammohan deliberated which option, sati or an ascetic life was more meritorious.

This, most 'pointed and decisive' statement counters in his view the claims of advocates of *Satī* who also referred to the *Vedas,* but to a passage that Ram Mohan found abstract and open to multiple interpretations on. The sentence was: "O fire let these women, with bodies anointed with clarified butter, eyes colored with collyrium and void of tears enter thee the parent of water, that they may not be separated from their husbands, themselves sinless and jewels among women." Raja Ram Mohan pointed that this passage nowhere enjoins women to commit *satī* and offers a reading of it as an allegory of the constellation of the moon's path. In this interpretation the butter signified the 'milky path', collyriam, the unoccupied space between one star and another, husbands the more splendid of the heavenly bodies. Finally, allusion to ascending and entering the fire and understood as the rise of the constellations through the south-east horizon, considered as the abode of fire.

Lata Mani while refraining from questioning the genuineness of Raja Ram Mohan's concern on the *Satī* issue, does, however highlight the ambivalence in his statements where he expressly says that the *satī* issue should be decided as per the willingness of the women in question. It is however quite difficult to completely agree with Mani on this point. The aspect of willingness of the women may have been introduced by Ram Mohan as an attempt to conciliate the negative opinion on the issue and reading his words beyond such an explanation may lead to misinterpretation of what was a serious genuine attempt in the field of reform for women.

In seeking a psychological advantage over their subjects colonial ideology felt compelled to assert the moral superiority of the rulers in many subtle and not so subtle ways. One of the not so subtle ways was in the area of gender relations. The higher morality of the imperial masters could be effectively established by highlighting the low status of women among the subject population as it was an issue by which the moral inferiority of the subject population could simultaneously be demonstrated. The women's question thus became a crucial tool in the colonial ideology. History in turn came to occupy a lay position in the cultural conflict between the ruling power and the colonial subjects.[9] This was the obsessive concern with cultural questions in the reconstruction of the past.

The bulk of colonial writing in India focused on demonstrating the peculiarities of Hindu civilization, and the barbaric practice pertaining to women. The circulation of this negative perception was much wider than the Orientalist scholarship and probably preceded and outlasted the work of the Orientalist in revealing India's lost glory.

As Uma Chakravarti has pointed out, Swami Dayanand Saraswati differed from most exponents of the golden age theory in that while they wished to awaken their fellow subjects to pride in there past, he wished to venerate that past in colonial India. It appears that he began to think about the position of women while he was in Calcutta, and that he was especially influenced here by Vidyasagar.[10]

According to Saraswati, practices such as polygamy, child marriage and the seclusion of women did not exist in Aryan India, morever men and women had equal rights. In his *Satyārtha Prakāśa,* he stressed as the *Tattvabodhini Sabha* had done, the parity between men and women in Vedic India saying that girls were entitled to wear the sacred thread and undergo the initiatory ceremony of *Yajñopavit;* both girls and boys should observe *brahmacarya* for some years ; the minimum age of marriage for girls should be 16 and boys 25. The writing of historical literature of the period after the 1860s was permeated by an extension of British Orientalism through the work of Friedrich Max Müller (1823-1900) who more than any other Orientalist focused upon achievements of the 'Aryans' as containd in their ancient texts of *Vedas.* In the core of Max Müller which he himself valued most was his collection and publication of the full texts of *Vedas*.

Like the earlier Orientalists Max Müllar saw the recovery of the *Vedas* as bringing Hindus, the truth of the[11] ancient traditions. Though there are some references to women, it is significant that at no point in his writing Müller dwelt at length upon them. In fact there appears to be an implicit assumption that the Aryans patriarchal system did not itself pay much attention to women and certainly did not regard them as equal. Like all writer on that he too narrated the Maitreyī Yājñvalkya episode but concluded the passage with the remark that although women participated in the ritual they were not associated and therefore less were they admitted to the highest knowledge of the Atman or Brāhmaṇa. Cases like Maitreyī, according to him were the exception and not the rule.

He used Strabo's quotation on women in India in support of his view "Indians did not communicate their metaphysical doctrines to women thinking that if their wives understood these doctrines, learned to be indifferent to pleasure and pain, and to consider life and death are the same they would no longer continue to be slaves of others; or if they failed to understand them they would be talkative and communicate him the knowledge to those who have no right to do it".[12]

Max Müller goes on to say that this statement by the Greek writer was fully born out by the later Sanskrit literature; he quotes from the *Śrauta* and *Gṛhya Sūtras* where it is stated that the women were not allowed to learn the secret songs of the *Vedas*. There is thus nothing in his writing to suggest that he considered women to be spiritual or learned, in the Vedic period.

The fact that becomes clearly evident after this brief survey of sources is that women become critical matter for public discourse in the nineteenth century. The genuineness or even the presence of any form of concern for women is highly dubitable in the notion of women and scripture as repositories of tradition was common among the reforms and even those against reform movement. The core issue here was more of a concern to confront and negotiate moral challenge of colonial rule. Women were either viewed as weak creature that had to be protected through legislation and education, or the valiant keeper of tradition who must be protected.

Notes

1. This is what the historians and political scientists often refer to as the period of paternalistic colonialism.

2. See articles in Kumkum Sangari and Sudes Vaid (ed), *Recasting Women:Essays in Colonial History,* Kali for Women, 1989, New Delhi.

3. Ibid., pp. 27-88.

4. William Jones, *On the Chronology of the Hindus,*in Lord Teignmouth, ed. The Works of William Jones (London:John Stockade,Picadily, and John Walkes, 1807). IV, p. 64; H.T. Colbrooke, *On the Vedas, or Sacred Writings of The Hindus,* Asiatic Researches, 8 (1805), pp. 377-498.

5. H.T. Colebrooke, *On the Duties of A Faithful Hindu Widow,* Asiatic Researches, 4 (1895), pp. 205-15.

6. Jones, op. cit., Colebrooke, op. cit.

7. David Kopf, *British Orientalism and the Bengal Renaissance,* Calcutta: Firma K.L. Mukhopadhyay, 1969, p. 149.

8. See *The English Works of Raja Rammohan Roy*, Vol. 2, ed. J.C. Ghosh, New Delhi: Cosmo, 1982.

9. David Kopf, *British Orientalism and the Bengal Renaissance,* Calcutta: Firma K.L. Mukhopadhyay, 1969, p. 149.

10. Uma Chakravarti,*Whatever Happened to the Vedic Dasi* in Sangari and Vaid, op. cit, p. 43.

11. R.C.Dutt, A *History of Civilisation in Ancient India* 1888: reprinted Vishal, Delhi, 1972, p. viii.

12. Max Müller, *A History of Sanskrit Literature,* London, Longman Green, 1859, p. 9.

Contributors

Vinita Chandra, Former Research Officer, Institute of Development Studies, Jaipur.

Anjali Chatterjee retired from Department of History, Kamala Nehru College, University of Delhi.

Annapurna Chattopadhyaya former Head, Department of History, N.L. Khan Women's College, West Midnapur, Vidyasagar University.

Pranati Ghoshal, Senior Research Assistant, Indira Gandhi National Centre for the Arts, Varanasi.

Kapil Kapoor, Professor of English and Concurrent Professor, Centre for Sanskrit Studies, JNU, New Delhi.

Chandrakala Padia, Head & Professor of Political Science & former Director, Centre for Women's Studies and Development, BHU, Varanasi.

Binda Paranjape, Reader, Department of History, BHU, Varanasi.

Devopriya Roy, Master Student, Department of English, Jawaharlal Nehru University, New Delhi

Shalini Shah, Reader, Department of the History, Indraprastha College, University of Delhi, New Delhi.

Kavita A. Sharma, Principal, Hindu College, Delhi University, New Delhi.

Anita Singh teaches History at C.H.G.S., Kamachha, Banaras Hindu University, Varanasi.

Preeti Singh, Lecturer, Department of Political Science, Vasanta College for Women, Rajghat, BHU, Varanasi.

V. C. Srivastava, Former Director, Indian Institute of Advanced Studies, Shimla.

Priyamvada, Lecturer, Department of History, Mahila Mahavidyalaya, BHU, Varanasi.

Pushpa Tiwari, Department of Ancient Indian History, Culture and Archaeology, University of Allahabad, Allahabad.

Index